Living in

PARIS

JOSÉ ALVAREZ

Photographs by Christian Sarramon
and Nicolas Bruant

Translated from the French
by Deke Dusinberre

Flammarion

Artistic Director:
Marc Walter – Bela Vista
Editorial Director:
Ghislaine Bavoillot

Edited by John P. Apruzzese
Visitor's Guide translated by John P. Apruzzese
Typesetting by Octavo Editions, Paris
Color Separation by Colourscan France

Distributed in North America by Rizzoli International
Publications, Inc.
200 Park Avenue South
Suite 1406
New York, NY 10003

Originally published in French as *L'Art de Vivre à Paris*
© 1996 Flammarion

www.editions.flammarion.com

08 09 10 4 3 2
FC0423-06-III
ISBN-10: 2-0803-0423-2
ISBN-13: 9782080304232
Dépôt légal: 03/2008

Printed in Turin by Canale

CONTENTS

What makes Paris so charming, so seductive? Why does it arouse such admiration? What is the mysterious potion that gives it such sway over tastes and attitudes? Many of the world's great cities are older, or quainter, or bigger, more diverse, more modern, more energetic, more unpredictable, more concerned with their image. Yet on closer inspection, all of them soon exhibit some kind of anomaly, creating an uneasiness or imbalance which makes total commitment impossible.

Paris, on the other hand, nourishes Parisians and tourists in a sure, balanced, wholesome way. Everything here expresses a certain art of fine living, a way of grasping the essence of things with the ease of people whose natural grace draws attention, without flaunting their presence. Perhaps it is simply that Paris is the most feminine capital in the world. Her beauty, vitality, and mystery are crowned with that touch of femininity immanent in her tireless delight in being seductive and her insatiable pride at never being caught unawares.

It may seem risky to align the various features of the "eternal woman" and then apply them to such a mythic city, but it would be impossible to describe Paris without deciding to fathom its secrets and discover its private side. Such an analogy is not accidental, for it corresponds more closely to the truth than might initially be apparent. If false designs were attributed to Paris, its natural harmony would be spoiled.

When a woman is described as a "Parisienne," it means she displays a certain number of qualities rarely encountered in women who, obviously, are not from Paris.

Introduction

Preceding pages: It is impossible to conceive of Paris without its bistros and restaurants. Three spots incarnate this myth—La Palette in Saint-Germain-des-Prés, La Closerie des Lilas in Montparnasse, and Le Square Trousseau in the newly fashionable Bastille neighborhood.
Above: An upward glance toward Paris facades reveals the abundance of sculptural figures called atlantes and caryatids. At number 16 Rue d'Abbeville, for instance, four voluptuous women flank the windows of the main floor, or *piano nobile*.
Right: At the National Horticulture Society on Rue de Grenelle, opulent female figures and little *putti* bedeck the entrance with garlands of fruit and flowers, in honor of agricultural virtues.

The distinction is both physical and psychological. A Parisienne displays grace and chic of a different nature from those exhibited by women in Milan, New York or, indeed, Bordeaux.

A bona fide Parisienne is endowed with an elegance based on tact and harmony, style, and wit. In a friendly trade, the city has also acquired these qualities for itself. No din or discord ruffles the allure of a Parisienne. She displays an ease, a manner all her own when generating harmony without ostentation, or leavening conversation with humor (sometimes in the form of an ironic barb, because it is skepticism that once again underpins her self-assurance). She has a rebellious mind, but her revolutions remain dainty. With this heady swirl of qualities, it is hard to know whether Paris was created for women or women created for Paris. Moderation is the measure of its excesses; the passing of time, its fountain of youth; good humor, its fortress.

It is these "Parisienne" qualities that will insure the survival of Paris, more certainly than its history or daily reality. Its history is a series of tales which foreigners can never completely understand because, in truth, the stories pretend they have nothing to say. Although their message is always of the essence, even the finest love poem will never surpass love itself.

It is hard to tell whether Paris owes more to Parisiennes or vice versa, given a liaison in which infidelity takes the form of conversation—the surest way to be heard, and to repeatedly hear that one is loved.

The typical Parisiennes of bygone years have vanished, including the type quaintly named the Opera model (as though she

Above: The setting sun shines splendidly against Parisian facades and rooftops.

Right: The Eiffel Tower—a diva who requires constant attention—lets her lacy shadow fall to the ground. Viewed from the tower, Paris seems vaster and more luminous, constantly shifting in scale. As French writer and critic Roland Barthes wrote, "Visiting the tower is like stepping onto a balcony in order so see, comprehend, and savor the essence of Paris. . . ."

Below: Whatever the period, whatever the style, Paris always adds a feminine touch, as seen in this stone sphinx with her almost mocking smile, spewing water into the fountain at Place du Châtelet, unperturbed by the urban swirl around her.

were some souvenir of Paris designed for tourists), which referred to aristocratic ladies with a perfectly diaphanous silhouette. They faded into the darkness of the past when the last chandeliers illuminating balls attended by the likes of the young Marcel Proust were extinguished.

Paris has not found itself at a loss, however. New times, new methods, but same old habits: Parisiennes are mysterious in their mischievous, scheming ingenuity. They are constantly developing new ways to adapt to business and social life in the capital in order to appreciate every one of its delights, which after all are its raison d'être, its capital legitimacy. Pleasure is a type of inflation that does not dilute values because it tirelessly creates new needs.

Another of the city's cardinal virtues is its ability to come to terms with every epoch, taking every period in stride without abandoning a single one of its prerogatives as a capital of good taste and savoir-faire. Paris flatters itself that everything is still discovered, launched, and developed here—where it also dies faster than anywhere else.

While Parisiennes may occasionally let themselves be seduced by a foreign import, it will be treated like a curiosity, an exotic item that, like coffee, should be downed quickly. Paris is a welcoming, open city, and is therefore able to look abroad, allowing alien taste to reinvigorate its own without feeling a sense of abdication. Too proud to stoop to vanity, Paris has always known how to call on outside talent to revitalize its own tradition, which is above all composite and empirical.

True Parisians often come from afar, truly afar. They have a special air about them, a certain detail that changes everything. This "indescribable something" that the French call *je-ne-sais-quoi* is also something impossible to declare openly—for love is not something to be confessed or admitted. Paris retains the right to contradict itself; in short, it needs to embrace life fully—all of life.

Paris is never boring. A good antidote to depression is simply a short stroll—down a well-known avenue, or along some secret path, or even via an imaginary route (by mentally reviewing various locations, sensations, and attachments without ever leaving the room). Paris exists with such intensity that one must constantly reconstruct it for one's own private pleasure, during endless days and luminous nights. Similar to a child's deluded dreams of houses stuffed with goodies, an emotional map of enchanting sensations soon takes shape.

The city's special feeling of security undoubtedly stems from its architectural demeanor and from the harmony with which it has developed throughout its history—avoiding clashes and tragedies that end in ridicule, dodging disasters that culminate in stormy celebrations, nurturing proof of its successive splendors, accepting modernity by only half acknowledging it (insofar as aberrations such as the Eiffel Tower are perceived as strokes of genius). Though often present, mediocrity usually remains bearable, like a spoiled child who is better ignored; once again, time will ultimately do its work, as will the child.

Strolling up and down Parisian streets engenders a feeling of headiness that sharpens lucidity and vanquishes despair, at least for a while, until sleep—the big sleep—comes.

Below: Hector Guimard, the great Art Nouveau architect, left examples of his work scattered throughout Paris, notably in the form of Metro entrances (nicknamed "dragonflies" by certain locals). Like some of its companions, this entrance on Avenue Foch has survived the ravages of changing fashion. Such examples are all too rare, however, and further spur nostalgia for the days when pretty ladies of uncertain virtue and elegant gentlemen paraded down the avenue in magnificent carriages.

Right: It almost seems a miracle that a diaphanous glass wall can support such a massive clock. This metalwork masterpiece still ticks away, reminding Musée d'Orsay visitors that the museum was once a train station, and the sun still plays a constantly changing symphony of colors in the main hall.

The age-old city of Paris largely dates from the second half of the nineteenth century and the dawn of the twentieth. According to those who knew it in its youth, this century began with much promise. But then it succumbed to war-torn, bloody tomfoolery and to an obsessive negation of existence which, even in Paris, finally bequeathed a few architectural—and other—disasters.

One of the paradoxes of Paris is that it feeds on what it lacks, what it has been denied, what it has never possessed—and which it therefore appropriates for itself. Late at night when the city is most revealing—during perhaps a wonderful detour down an unfamiliar street, or in the dull hubbub of a still-open café—there emerges the distant sound of a story told over ond over, a story without end. A love story.

Just over a century ago, in their determination to modernize it, the authorities wanted to bring Paris up to date, which meant making it radically dateless. The Paris of today is a utopia built on its historical layers, which it reveals as much as it masks. It rose on a famous, almost mythic site, and although the ideal city was never completed, subsequent development faithfully followed that initial vision. Its final form is beholden to an imperious determination to make Paris a wonder of the world, a triumph of modern physical and moral science, an epicenter of taste and intellect. The gamble paid off.

The capital imagined by Napoleon III (1808–1873) and Baron Georges Eugène Haussmann—who were not exactly native Parisians—was to be a kind of Universal Exposition of perfection, simultaneously tradition-bound and forward-looking. Henceforth, everything had to converge on Paris.

The Second Empire (1852–1870) and three subsequent Republics fulfilled the ancient ambition of a monarchy that never managed to overcome the resentment created by scuffles with its turbulent capital city. This turbulence was perhaps just an indirect way of asking for yet another declaration of love—Paris, after all, was said to be two hours by horse from Versailles, when in fact it was Versailles that was two hours from Paris. In the days when distances were measured by the body, suburban ghettos had not yet formed. The gap between rulers and real life has long been discreetly occupied by many Parisians who "matter," and who have come from the provinces, indeed from abroad.

In addition to its standards of beauty, Paris represents intellectual consecration. It then turns into clever Paris, the focus of humanist Europe, a cultivated society that converges on the capital throughout the year. Paris is not only the heart of a nation, it is also the center of thinking and creative Europe. There was a time when all of educated Europe spoke French as its native tongue—two centuries later, Paris still aspires to be a haven for a certain freedom of thought. The genius of France resides in its language; that of Paris resides in its undramatic yet indomitable spirit of freedom.

Left Bank, Right Bank

The Seine draws Paris together,
even as it divides the city.
The villages through which it passes,
whether chic or modest,
truly make the capital what it is.

The Seine

The Seine flows inexorably through Paris, as do the centuries, caressing its banks rich in history and emotion. Without its river, the capital would lack its particularly special aura and elegance. The river banks, formerly wild despite their domestication, are now crowned with stone parapets that not only shield the river from the traffic on the quays but also carve the gentle curve of the river more distinctly, sketching a Cocteau-like profile across the urban map. The first rays of sun still entice idlers to flock to the river just as they did in the seventeenth century when lords, ladies, and the bourgeoisie would mingle there during the first fine days of spring, among modest fishermen and laundry maids. People swam in the nude, which led to debauchery that the police had to quell. "Everyone knows," wrote French moralist Jean de La Bruyère, "the long lane bordering the Seine where it enters Paris just after being joined by the Marne River. Men wade and bathe there during the heat of the dog days; they can be seen close up, jumping into the water, they can be seen getting out. It is a recreation: before the season has arrived, women from town do not yet stroll there, and once the season is over, they no longer stroll there."

Modestly majestic, the Seine is indispensable to the harmony of Paris. Depending on the season, it flows hurriedly (and muddy) or peacefully (and translucent). On certain days its waters resemble a canvas by Albert Marquet—yellow and heavy below a mercurial sky—while on other days it looks like a Monet—a fine mass of luminous blue

Preceding pages: The proud facades along Quai d'Orléans on the Ile Saint-Louis are a perfect example of seventeenth-century Paris. They have not forgotten their days of glory, and now apparel themselves in every shade of pink and mauve offered by the city's ever-gentle light.

Above: A more mysterious and more theatrical lighting bathes the towers of the Conciergerie (where Marie-Antoinette, among others, was imprisoned)—the light of Paris has the modesty to understate the capital's more tragic moments.

Right: At dawn, heavy barges from the north plow through the thick waters of the Seine. Seemingly motionless, they sometimes appear to be houses with backyards of coal or gravel, occupied by a dog with sea-legs or a few contemplative cats.

water, shimmering and metallic, reflecting the sky from which it almost seems to issue.

From time immemorial, the Seine has served as the axis of a city that it divides as much as it unites. Parisians like to define their turf, and perpetuate age-old disputes which seem incomprehensible to outsiders. Certain Left Bank families haughtily ignore the tribe camping on the other bank, such as those venerable families in the Saint-Germain neighborhood who thought a profitable transatlantic marriage was less compromising than a union with someone from the reaches of Monceau, Auteuil or Passy (suspected of dubious extraction and overly mercantile wealth). Even today, such unions are rare. Although people go to the opposite bank to work, they are relieved to return—whether office employee, artisan, or self-employed—to "the right side" of the river, everyone having his or her own. And the twain shall never meet, for only "shopkeepers" live and work on the same premises.

In its indolent progress, the Seine takes its time to approach and finally enter Paris, defining certain territories that are not really part of either bank. Paris is like an island in the heart of France, an island itself composed of twin yet radically distinct islands.

When Clovis I (466?–511), Frankish king and traditional founder of the French monarchy, established his residence there in the year A.D. 506, Paris already had a long history and was ready for a glorious destiny. It was not until A.D. 987, however, that King Hugues Capet (960?–996) would make Paris a "capital city."

The palace built on Ile de la Cité, the islet in the middle of the river, served as residence to four dynasties until Charles VII

Above: Almost a thousand years old, Notre Dame Cathedral presents its flying buttresses to the soft light of dawn. As the inspiration for numerous novels and legends, the cathedral recalls the days when Paris was a big village that sprawled at its feet, forming an inextricable web of narrow streets that were swept away by nineteenth-century urban developers.

Right: Down river, the quays provide a fringe of foliage for the facades of the Louvre, underscoring the varied beauty of a building that has been constantly rebuilt and modified throughout the centuries, thereby etching the story of the kings of France in stone.

(1403–1461) handed it over to the *parlement* in 1431. Four towers remain from that period (including the square and rather elegant Clock Tower), as well as the guards' room, the gendarmes' hall, and the kitchens.

The monarchy, which left Ile de la Cité for a sprawling residence known as the hôtel Saint-Pol, moved afterwards to the Louvre Palace and ultimately left Paris for Versailles, unaware that the divorce would be permanent. Subsequent attempts at reconciliation merely provided an occasion for violent disturbances of an almost marital nature. As far as Paris was concerned, the Revolution seems to have been largely a way of asserting its rights in the face of this slight, quite apart from any political issue.

The palace of the kings of France, largely erected in the thirteenth century by Louis IX (1214–1270), stood on the spot now massively occupied by the Palais de Justice (or main courthouse) and the Conciergerie. Although one might regret that eighteenth-century architects outrageously masked the Sainte-Chapelle when building the main body of the Palais de Justice, it was not fashionable at the time to take interest in vestiges of the past. The preservation of the chapel was therefore a singular homage to Saint Louis—the only Capetian king so canonized.

Across a narrow straight lies the Ile Saint-Louis, which for a long time was just a meadowy island where livestock grazed in the shade of poplars. Starting in the late seventeenth-century, however, people began building the magnificent town houses known as *hôtels particuliers*, each of which had an underground staircase leading to a water gate where an elegant boat was moored. The fashion for water travel meant that, on certain summer evenings, the Seine took on the allure of the Grand Canal in Venice.

Even today, Ile Saint-Louis remains a village within the city. Whereas the rest of Paris lives with the roar of cars and the squeal of tires, this island quietly lives a provincial life, away from it all. Its residents and shopkeepers even seem different, more welcoming than elsewhere. Despite the storefronts, the houses along the fishbone-arranged streets have retained their ancestral austerity as well as an impeccable alignment, which is not even disrupted by the church of Saint-Louis-en-l'Ile whose nave is strangely parallel to the street. Nothing distinguishes the church from the surrounding buildings, apart from its unusual openwork bell tower. There is a distinct taste for privacy here, a bourgeois charm which makes no pretence of being aristocratic. Land is strictly apportioned, so no rural dreams are entertained; from time immemorial, the island's inhabitants have always been extremely proud to be true Parisians. Today, an open window may offer a glimpse of high ceilings with occasionally polychrome beams, while behind the large carriage gates decorated with mascarons (or grimacing heads) rise monumental staircases with decorative balustrades.

Whereas the south-facing Quai d'Orléans and Quai Béthune are more joyous and more open to the city, Quai de Bourbon and Quai d'Anjou have retained their serene if somewhat glum grandeur. A curtain of trees shields them from prying eyes, from the crowd and noise. They brought out Balzac's pessimistic side, that undercurrent of his nostalgia for the aristocracy: "When walking through the streets of Ile Saint-Louis, the nervous melancholy that grips you is due to

nothing other than the solitude, the glum air of the deserted houses and grand residences. This island, the carcass of royal tax collectors, is like the Venice of Paris."

If the numerous plaques do indeed recount the truth, every residence on the island is of historical interest. One of the most famous, at number 17 Quai d'Anjou, is the hôtel de Lauzun, which belonged to the dashing duc de Lauzun—who spent ten years in the fort in Pinerolo, where Louis XIV (1638–1715) incarcerated him in an attempt to forestall his marriage to the king's niece. Renamed the hôtel de Pimodan in the late seventeenth century, the residence declined, in its own special way, into a miraculous haven for the finest minds of the day, housing in rather meager fashion the likes of poets Théophile Gautier and Charles Baudelaire (who rented a third-floor apartment for 350 francs per year.)

Further upstream, nestled in a curve of the quai at the head of the island, stands one of the finest seventeenth-century residences in Paris—hôtel Lambert. A brief visit is a must, if only to appreciate the irreproachable dignity with which the majestic residence has withstood the years, as well as its charming location on the Seine.

No other city can match Paris's enthusiasm for building bridges across its river. Paris boasts thirty-eight bridges, from every period, in every style, of every material. Two, in fact, are foot-bridges, while others are viaducts for the Metro (as the subway is called)—notably the Bir-Hakeim bridge, which thumbs its nose at the Eiffel Tower before tunneling into the hill of Chaillot.

The Pont-Neuf, or "new bridge," is in fact the oldest and certainly the finest in Paris; it was the first houseless bridge, providing Parisians with a totally new promenade that became enormously popular. Soon after its construction, new arrivals in town asked to see the bridge immediately, for it was where one could learn of the capital's latest caprices, where they could eat and drink while watching traveling showmen and listening to boasting merchants. Even today, the Pont-Neuf exercises intense fascination—in 1985 the American artist Christo transformed it into a canvas-draped sculpture, and in 1994 the Japanese fashion designer Kenzo completely blanketed it in flowers, composing a paean to spring.

Architect Androuet du Cerceau originally designed the Pont-Neuf, Henri III (1551–1589) laid the first stone, and Henri IV (1553–1610) inaugurated it in 1603. The statue of Henri IV can still be seen there—the

Left: Autumn deploys its rich palette around Quai de Bourbon on the Ile Saint-Louis—the sun caresses the bronzed facades of a series of mansions whose names recall the grand families of France and their magnificent past. At number 19 is the hôtel de Jassaud, the quai's finest residence and former studio of sculptress Camille Claudel.

Below: Quai Voltaire, opposite the Louvre, famous for its excellent antique dealers, also boasts the narrowest facade in Paris (at number 13), which in fact is the entrance of a house set back from the street, where painters such as Eugène Delacroix, Horace Vernet and Jean-Baptiste Corot lived.

Despite the raging traffic, Parisians still like to amble along the quays of the Seine in search of a book, old newspapers, or just a droll postcard. Booksellers' stalls (*extreme left, top*) are no longer exciting caverns of rare publishing treasures, but attentive strollers still unearth surprising companions for several hours of literary adventure. The Seine has always inspired artistic urges (*center left, top*); this round canvas, called a tondo, is like a magnifying mirror of the bridge. The game of *pétanque* (*far left, bottom*), a form of bowls played in the south of France, has now become a very Parisian pastime. Conducive to conversation, it is played in every neighborhood where a square or lane has escaped the domination of asphalt, as here on Place Dauphine, in front of the stone lions of the Palais de Justice. Another village pastime now cultivated by Parisians is gardening (*left and below*). There are ever-increasing numbers of talented florists who spur this enthusiasm. At the flower market pictured here, on Ile de la Cité, every floral whim is lavishly fulfilled.

raised hoof of his steed reportedly contains gold louis, while his right arm contains a small statue of Napoleon allegedly placed there by a fervent admirer of the emperor when the statue was re-cast by order of Louis XVIII (1755–1824). Henri IV's horse seems to be heading for the two Louis XIII pavilions flanking the entry to Place Dauphine, which André Breton mischievously described as the city's female pubis: "It would seem hard to believe that I am the first to be struck, on wandering into Place Dauphine via the Pont-Neuf, by its triangular form—slightly curved, for that matter— and the slit that opens it into two bisected spaces. It is impossible not to see [Place Dauphine] as the sex of Paris hiding beneath its leafy shade. Its fleece still burns several times a year from the torture inflicted on the Knights Templar on March 13, 1313, which some people assert had much to do with the city's revolutionary fate. . . . In this respect, I think it is absolutely significant that the base of the triangle, on Rue Harlay, coincides

Top left: The proud facade of La Samaritaine department store, glittering above the Seine at the foot of Pont-Neuf, has a rooftop terrace with one of the most spectacular views of the capital.
Bottom left: On the other side of Pont-Neuf is a statue of good King Henri IV, pointing toward the entrance to Place Dauphine, flanked by its red-brick facades (pictured right).

Right: Behind Henri's back is a spit of land called Square du Vert-Galant, where Parisians come to relax and flirt.

Top: The cast-iron sculptures of the Bir-Hakeim bridge reflect the colors of the Seine.

Above: Barges tied to the banks become waterside houses evoking the days when Paris was a busy port. Many of these vestiges of riverside lifestyle are inhabited year-round, and some have recently been converted into floating bars and cabarets.

Right: The metallic bridge in the foreground, known as Pont des Arts, elegantly spans the Seine in counterpoint to the vertical steeple of La Sainte-Chapelle, the bell towers of Notre Dame, and the tower of the Palais de Justice. The river underneath seems to pause dreamily for a moment before continuing its peaceful, winding route.

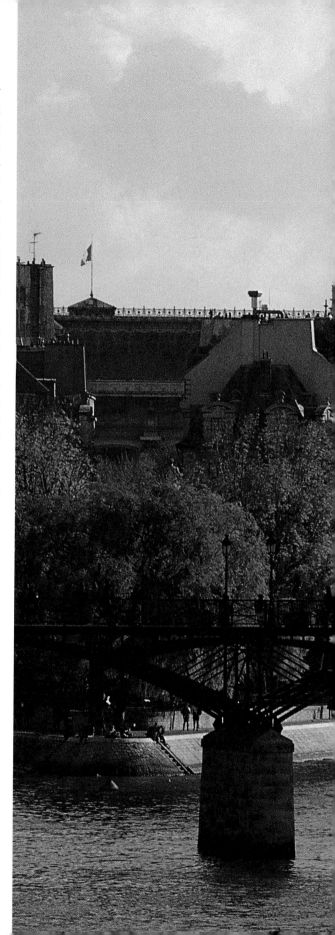

with the back of the Palais de Justice and its curving double staircase which, everyone should know, is guarded by stone lions. The proximity of this place of chastisement—which, moreover, surrounds that precious atonement device, the Sainte-Chapelle—underscores the taboo associated with Place Dauphine and designates it as a holy site in terms of everything related to Paris." One wonders what Simone Signoret and Yves Montand, who long lived on Place Dauphine, would have made of that story.

On the Right Bank of Pont-Neuf, the beveled glass of the proud department store, La Samaritaine, reflects the scintillating Seine. On the Left Bank is a pleasant skein of streets gathered by two low brick buildings forming a semi-circle, making it clear that, on this side of the river, any concessions to modern urban development are made with a great deal of reticence.

Down river, the Pont des Arts is a pedestrian bridge which provides the most wonderful view of the Seine, embracing countless memorable sites. The eye is treated to the most seductive spectacle Paris has to offer. Many like to be photographed on the Pont des Arts, where a promenade is likely to come to a temporary halt, to allow for daydreaming on a bench. Some years ago, a clumsy river barge destroyed one of the bridge's piers, but the footbridge was rebuilt in a way more authentic to its original spirit. The bridge, which is slightly higher than the quay, leads down to an Italian-inspired cityscape for, on the site where the former hôtel de Nesle once stood (the legendary residence of the duc de Berry), there now stands the Institut de France, home of the five national academies. Originally designed to

house the Collège des Quatre-Nations, the building features a gilded dome that sparkles like a magnificent reliquary. It was built at the behest of Louis XIV's (1638–1715) political mentor, Cardinal Mazarin, who had assembled an unequalled collection of art works at a time when plunder and corruption apparently did not tarnish political esteem. Mazarin died expressing only one regret—a somewhat mystical one, at that—namely, that he would have to leave his fabulous treasure behind. He soothed his conscience by leaving an appreciable part of the loot to the monarch, bequeathing the rest to the college that he founded there. Nearby is the royal mint, or Hôtel de la Monnaie, which almost seems to crouch below the quay. The haughty, rectilinear nudity of its architecture makes it appear somewhat solitary among its surroundings. Its stylistic rigor is as intriguing as the magical activity that takes place inside.

A quick half-turn, at dusk, provides a glimpse of the sun sinking behind the Arc de Triomphe after having briefly ignited the glass roof of the Grand Palais. Here, at dawn, a mist often rises from the river, drowning the overloaded barges advancing so slowly along the ribbon of water that they appear motionless. It is an optical illusion, however, for they soon pass beneath Pont de la Concorde.

Left: The Pont des Arts links two architectural masterpieces. Seen here, on the Left Bank, is the Institut de France, a pure gem of seventeenth-century architecture, while across the river is the Square Court of the Louvre, an example of Renaissance splendor.
Right: The sun inflames the rooftop spire of the Grand Palais as it sinks below the horizon, leaving behind an ashen cityscape.

Above: The Left Bank of Paris is full of small shops, both famous and anonymous. In the 7th Arrondissement, for instance, the Poujauran bakery maintained the excellence of traditional breads, while Deyrolle, on Rue du Bac, has elevated taxidermy to the status of art.
Near right: Paris abounds with decorative details like this ornate door-knocker.
Far right: Left Bank architecture and courtyards (*clockwise from top left*): an elegant seventeenth-century balcony; the monogrammed gate to the premises of a former coffee merchant

behind the Panthéon; Place Furstenberg, sheltered by mauve-flowered paulownia trees; a courtyard off Rue Monsieur-le-Prince that combines all the charms of these secret spots; guard-stones indicate that the Rohan courtyard is to be entered only on foot or on horseback.

The Left Bank

Starting from the Seine (which Blaise Pascal called a "road on the move"), an interesting itinerary weaves through a few of the modern capital's eighty quarters, some of which still bear their original village names, and many of which secretly cling to their own special identity. This tour of the southern hemisphere—that is to say, the Left Bank—begins via Rue de Lille (originally Rue de Bourbon), which was laid down in 1640 in a field belonging to the nearby Abbaye de Saint-Germain, as was Rue de Verneuil. These two streets, along with Rue de l'Université, Rue des Saints-Pères, Rue de Beaune, and Rue du Bac, bounded by Quai Voltaire and Boulevard Saint-Germain, now constitute the grid of an exceptional quarter noted for its prestigious antique dealers, its quiet, charming restaurants, and its upscale shops. The neighborhood displays rare architectural integrity and its atmosphere has barely changed in recent decades.

This village by the Seine embodies the Paris inhabited by the upper bourgeoisie and lesser aristocracy. Life is staid, and though outsiders are respected they always remain outsiders, especially if they come from another quarter. One glance suffices to determine if someone comes from somewhere else—that is to say from nowhere, as far as the locals are concerned. A village lifestyle has survived. It is absurd to claim, as some do, that in this neighborhood it is easier to buy a Louis XV commode than a baguette or pack of cigarettes. Everything is done with discretion—a sign of class, of people who have no need to stress their superiority. The most refined French is spoken here. Children

tend to own fewer electronic games than elsewhere. This little kingdom is nevertheless a democracy, and all the children attend the local municipal school—so much more chic than any private school—which is the mark of truly belonging to this tribe with its somewhat outdated manners. Future marriages are arranged here, from an early age. This part of Paris assumes the air of a provincial town, quiet and staid, sure of itself without being arrogant.

Nearby is the Faubourg Saint-Germain, a neighborhood passionately depicted by French writers Honoré de Balzac and, later, Marcel Proust. This "faubourg" (which initially meant an inner suburb), steeped in tradition, is dotted with a series of impressive residences, the most striking of which is the hôtel de Luynes, magnificent more for its size than its elegance. It was built in 1650 for the duchesse de Chevreuse, eldest daughter of Hercule de Rohan.

Place Saint-Germain-des-Prés was where Jean-Paul Sartre and Simone de Beauvoir used to stroll, right to the end of their lives. From their windows they could see the sole remaining tower of the original abbey church which, though it suffered so many fires and tragedies throughout the centuries, symbolizes the most literary of Parisian quarters.

The Abbaye de Saint-Germain-des-Prés once ran down to the edge of the flowing Seine, and rose free amid the reeds, extending as far as Rue du Four (where the abbey oven was located). It also boasted the largest library of its time. In addition to its own impressive collection of books and manuscripts, catalogued in the seventeenth century by Jean Mabillon (the father of French

history), the abbey library was regularly enriched by successive gifts and donations.

The boulevard is somewhat downcast up to Rue des Saints-Pères (which clearly marks the end of Faubourg Saint-Germain), lulling the stroller into an almost provincial melancholy. The street then suddenly comes alive with bookstores, restaurants (including the famous Brasserie Lipp, where the attribution of tables was long a barometer of political careers), and cafés (notably the intellectual, Paris-centered Café Flore, plus the more cosmopolitan Deux Magots), not to mention the movie theaters and boutiques that become less and less elegant near the Latin Quarter.

Saint-Germain-des-Prés, the cradle of French intellect and culture, cannot be compared to any other quarter. Certain streets near the church of Saint-Sulpice, for instance, would hardly be out of place in the provinces, while others, in complete contrast, seem subject to chronic insomnia. This neighborhood, in fact, has always led a double life: measured and studious, capricious and fashion-crazed—the one getting along quite well with the other.

Heading toward Rue des Ecoles, one enters the eternally famous Latin Quarter. Long devoted to learning, this is still where the city's major secondary schools and universities are located. Since its founding in 1530, the Collège de France has been home to some of France's finest minds, from humanist Petrus Ramus to scholar Guillaume Budé, and from historian Jules Michelet to writer and critic Roland Barthes. The institution cannot be compared to any other, for no diplomas are required to attend courses, or even to give them—professors are simply coopted. This means that during troubled times the Collège de France has remained a haven of open-mindedness and rebellion against entrenched establishment values.

Few Parisians truly know Paris. Judging by the calm that reigns around the Panthéon, this neighborhood seems rarely visited by anyone other than local residents—despite its truly special charm. A surprisingly dense cluster of very beautiful and varied buildings

Far left: Although Paris is invaded by cars, the harmonious layout of the city's major thoroughfares makes it possible to overlook the din. Here Rue Saint-Jacques, even though its facades are imperfectly aligned, presents a surprising image of harmony, crowned by the Sorbonne's observatory.
Left: This clock with its sculpted figures times the promenades of strollers enjoying the sun around the decorative pond in the Luxembourg Gardens.

Below: A rumbling foreground to the intriguing facade of the church of Saint-Sulpice is provided by the Fontaine des Quatre-Evêques, a fountain honoring four bishops. Every year this Italianate square hosts an antiques fair where quality books and curiosities are sure to be found.

surrounds the Panthéon, crammed together as though trying to give the monument some breathing space. The bold yet harmonious architectural juxtapositions in the Place du Panthéon evoke certain quarters of Rome where various layers of history have been perfectly wedded over time.

A marble plaque on Rue d'Ulm indicates the spot where, in an apartment transformed into a laboratory, Louis Pasteur began his research.

Nearby, Rue Lhomond (less famous than its neighbor, Rue Mouffetard) beckons visitors to push open the door of number 27. After crossing a vaulted porch, the rear of the private courtyard presents a magical weave of flowers and stone. This pure eighteenth-century gem boasts one of the most outstanding balconies imaginable. The future comtesse du Barry lived in the adjoining convent school of Sainte-Aure in her early youth, as a pupil named Jeanne Bécu.

The evening casts its gentle shadow over this scene, with the imposing, purplish silhouette of the Panthéon in the distance; the pink clouds of sunset passing overhead extend to the Luxembourg Gardens, with a

Although they do not always admit it, Parisians maintain a certain nostalgia for rural life, which they try to recreate in the city.

Top right: Thus the market on Rue Mouffetard is the same as it always was—noisy, colorful, good-humored.

Bottom right: A surprising stretch of green on Rue des Ecoles, recently landscaped, leads to the former Ecole Polytechnique.

Far right: At the end of a private lane off Rue du Cardinal-Lemoine, the hôtel des Grandes Ecoles occupies an oasis of luxuriant foliage, testifying to the Parisian taste for village life.

palace that looks like a piece of Italy imported to Paris. It was in 1605 that Marie de' Medici bought the residence of the duc de Piney-Luxembourg, set in the middle of a vast garden (formerly a disreputable wasteland called Vau Vert, which was the origin the French expression *aller au diable vauvert*, meaning "head out to the wilds"). Nostalgic for her youth spent in the Palazzo Pitti in Florence, the queen commissioned Salomon de Brosse in 1612 to build a new palace based on her ancestral home in Italy.

Not far from the academic Latin Quarter is the Montparnasse neighborhood, known for its artistic dynamism. Montparnasse can be reached via the unusual Jardin de l'Observatoire, a long floral lane which runs south from the Luxembourg Gardens and ends in a fountain sculpted by Jean-Baptiste Carpeaux, representing the four corners of the earth. The lane is then transected by Boulevard du Montparnasse, which serves as the backbone for a series of animated sidestreets which share its liveliness. The atmosphere has not changed since the golden age of Montparnasse. Grand cafés, a few restaurants, bar-and-dance halls, theaters, numerous movie theaters, and bookstores all draw today's substitutes for yesterday's artists. There are few antique dealers, however, and paradoxically even fewer art galleries.

Montparnasse represents a rare example of literary and artistic reconciliation between the intelligentsia and the common folk, from Lenin to Cocteau, and is still considered by Parisians and foreigners as a temple of extravagant, artistic, and cultivated Paris.

One evening in December 1927, a restaurateur from the south of France opened La Coupole, a brasserie and bar with a dance floor in the basement. Competition was soon fierce between this new restaurant and its neighbors on the boulevard, Le Dôme and La Rotonde. Tourists streamed through, in the hopes of catching a glimpse of painters such as Pablo Picasso, Kees van Dongen, and Foujita sitting on the terrace, just as their children, after the Second World War, would traipse through Saint-Germain-des-Prés in search of writers Jean-Paul Sartre and Albert Camus (indeed, the "Montparnasse Trinity" of restaurants also prefigured Saint-Germain's holy triangle of Brasserie Lipp, Les Deux Magots, and Café Flore).

Among foreign arrivals drawn to the red imitation-leather booths and neon lights were writers James Joyce, Ernest Hemingway, and Henry Miller. They were joined by Louis Aragon, who was never enthusiastic about the haunt on Place Blanche adopted by his fellow surrealists.

To the south, not far from Parc Montsouris, another proudly independent neighborhood clings to the hillside known as Butte-aux-Cailles. It boasts no outstanding building, but instead offers a coherent, quiet collection of small buhrstone houses. Butte-aux-Cailles has deliberately allowed time to pass it by, and its outdated feel represents a rejection of brutal "renovation." Such villages remain invisible to people in a hurry, yet they can be a source of unexpected discoveries. Thus the Bièvre River, now buried beneath the streets, once ran through a small valley dotted with greenery. In winter, when its waters froze, Parisians would come to ice-skate on the flooded meadows, which is distantly echoed in the otherwise enigmatic name of a street and a Metro station: Glacière.

Left-hand page: Whereas tourists used to traipse through Montparnasse in hopes of glimpsing Pablo Picasso, Foujita, James Joyce, or Ernest Hemingway on the terrace of a café, these days they admire the extraordinary variety of architecture that has retained its original cachet. The semi-circular pediments over the windows of this apartment block on Boulevard Raspail (*top*) are adorned with colored tiles, whereas the famous building by architect Henri Sauvage on Rue Vavin is covered in white "Metro" tiles highlighted with touches of color (*main photo*). In Passage du Maine, meanwhile, at the foot of the modern Montparnasse Tower, Lieu-dit Florists (*bottom*), miraculously spared the disastrous renovation of the neighborhood, creates outstanding floral compositions.
Above: Here a flower in mosaic blossoms on a house on Square Montsouris.

The Right Bank

In his *Treatise on the Sublime*, the seventeenth-century Spanish writer Baltasar Gracián noted that "the world is perhaps conquered more surely by taste than by arms." Paris understood this message, since its sense of tasteful balance operates everywhere, and is particularly evident on the Right Bank, where gardens, neighborhoods, monuments, and vistas are all coordinated in harmonious ensembles. Place de la Concorde, for example, is a sea of air and light, one of the most beautiful urban squares in the world—if not *the* most beautiful—even though it has lost the moats that once encircled it. It has also lost its original logic, namely to provide a superb western entry to the capital, opening onto the Tuileries Gardens and the Louvre. Yet this square still miraculously creates a sense of unity from highly composite elements—every epoch has left a mark, from ancient Egypt to the nineteenth century. It exudes an unmistakable impression of rigor, underscored by the eighteenth-century facades of the former Hôtel du Garde-Meuble, designed by Jacques-Ange Gabriel.

Extending beyond its strict confines, Place de la Concorde is visually bounded by the portico of the Palais-Bourbon across the river to the south, and harmoniously counter-balanced to the north by the vista up Rue Royale to the portico of the church of La Madeleine (so unreligious in its architecture that Napoleon considered transforming it into the headquarters of either the Paris stock exchange or the Bank of France). Meanwhile to the west, opposite the famous rearing horses sculpted by Guillaume Coustou, begins the legendary Avenue des Champs-Elysées, conceived according to a perspective laid out by architect André Le Nôtre through wooded grounds. To the east, finally, the Tuileries Gardens function as a varied arrangement of vast outdoor salons.

The successive stages of Paris become apparent once the previous contours of the capital become legible. Little by little, fortress walls burst open, only to be rebuilt further out. By the mid-seventeenth century, boulevards were laid out along the leveled ruins of the former ramparts, yet the Champs-Elysées was still designated *terra incognita*, a virgin continent, until the early nineteenth century. Under Louis XVI (1754–1793), the area was covered with woods and fields hosting a few refreshment pavilions and modest cafés (such as Ledoyen.) Once again, it was the Second Empire that truly "made" the Avenue des Champs-Elysées. Enormous luxury residences, lavish rather than elegant, were built there by the likes of the Rothschilds, the duc de Morny, and baron Roger, followed by the queen of Spain and the duchesse d'Uzès.

Moving up the Champs-Elysées (people generally go "up" rather than "down" the Champs-Elysées, except when military parades march down it), the lower end is flanked by landscape gardens. These gardens still feature a few of the graceful, early-nineteenth-century buildings which lent luster and renown to the avenue, namely the Ledoyen restaurant (where duelists used to mingle cheerfully) and the neoclassical Laurent Pavilion and Gabriel Pavilion. Many of these features were the work of architect Jakob Hittorff, a promoter of the use of cast

Left and below: The former Louvre Palace has now become the most beautiful, and perhaps the largest, museum in the world. Parisians hesitate between boasting openly about it and quietly adopting a natural reserve. Yet Paris has a duty to display good taste, elegance, and cultivation: the Corinthian columns and hieratic statues of the Louvre facade are set aflame by the sinking sun, while the grandiose new entrance, with a glass pyramid by architect I. M. Pei, sparkles like a thousand-faceted diamond.

Above: The bar of Fouquet's Restaurant on the Champs-Elysées is one of the places where chic Parisians meet and greet. Its wood-paneled walls are covered with photographs of the famous actors who have occupied the comfortable leather armchairs. *Below*: Reflections on a silver platter engraved with the Fouquet's name. *Far right*: Three views of Le Travellers Club, one of the most elegant clubs in Paris, located just off the Champs-Elysées in the former residence of the marquise de la Païva, a famous nineteenth-century adventuress. The bathroom displays oriental influence in its tiling and use of marble, onyx, malachite, and other semi-precious stones. The round bas-relief in alabaster, meanwhile, shows Venus riding a dolphin, while the elegant staircase in the hallway spirals above a floor inlaid with marble.

iron who designed the Gare du Nord train station as well as the gas lamps that now symbolize Paris.

Beyond the first traffic circle, bordered on its left by the austere iron fence of the former hôtel Lehon, is the hôtel de la Païva, named after Esther Lackmann, a demi-monde figure who married her way into the marquisat de la Païva, and who was known for her eclectic taste and activities (such as spying for Bismarck, to whom she was related through her second husband). It has now become the headquarters of the chic Travellers' Club, but still boasts the magnificent decoration in marble, malachite, and onyx, with bronzes and sculptures by Ferdinand Barbedienne and Albert-Ernest Carrier-Belleuse, not to mention Esther's original bathtub (itself a whole symbol).

Further up the avenue, the mansion of Guerlain, former supplier to the empresses Eugénie and Elizabeth of Austria, was designed by Méwès (architect of the Ritz Hotel), then updated by Christian Bérard and Jean-Michel Frank, with the aid of Diego Giacometti. Almost opposite sits Fouquet's which, founded in 1898 as a modest tavern, is today the chic restaurant of the film crowd. At Fouquet's (now a listed monument), an almost anachronistic idea of Paris is cultivated with conviction and good humor, inspired by the aviation pioneers who originally hung out there, and continued by film stars of the interwar period such as Raimu and Jean Gabin, and the track aficionados who stopped off on their way to the races at Bois de Boulogne. It is still possible at Fouquet's to imagine, one last time, what made this avenue a promenade unlike any other—the haunt of men with somewhat overly studied manners, who seemed to devote their lives to the consumption of countless cocktails and who nourished themselves on peanuts and potato chips. That golden age was followed by an inexorable decline, but recent renovation aims to restore "the world's most beautiful avenue" to its proper rank.

After the Champs-Elysées, nearby Avenue Montaigne seems strangely English. A mythical street that exudes luxury and Paris chic, it still vibrates with its perennial pleasure and *joie de vivre*. Avenue Montaigne's crowning moment of glory was certainly the 1913 inauguration of the Théâtre des Champs-Elysées, a concrete building designed by Auguste Perret based on an initial sketch by Henri van de Velde, with bas-reliefs and frescoes by Antoine Bourdelle on the outer facade, plus interior decoration by Edouard Vuillard, Ker-Xavier Roussel, and Maurice Denis. The theater's controversial programming sparked disruption and outrage which echoed the eternal quarrel between the Ancients and the Moderns: Nijinski danced his way across the huge stage almost without touching ground (to the triumph of Sergei Diaghilev's Ballets Russes Company); Josephine Baker strutted to the frenzied rhythms of the *Revue Nègre*; and Rolf de Maré's avant-garde dance troupe startled numerous aesthetes. It has remained one of Paris's most prestigious theaters, in terms of decor and acoustics as well as programming (a smaller, more intimate theater next door, was long occupied by Louis Jouvet's troupe), perpetuating the eminently French penchant for producing groundbreaking works in alternation with a return to the classics. Since that period of controversy, however,

Top left: A gilded bronze equestrian statue at the entrance to Pont Alexandre-III depicts Pegasus spreading his wings while the figure of Fame tries to restrain him. This bridge, celebrating Franco-Russian friendship during the Universal Exposition of 1900, has recently been restored, endowing the decoration with its original color and splendor.

Right: The main structure of the bridge sports a variety of lampposts, vases, dolphins, and garlands of stone or gilded iron. Over the middle arch are hammered copper sculptures representing the Nymphs of the Seine, while behind them in the distance is the glass roof of the Grand Palais.

Bottom left: At the other end of Pont Alexandre-III, on the Left Bank, is the hôtel des Invalides, the gold glitter of its recently restored dome balancing the winged horses on the bridge.

Avenue Montaigne has settled back into more peaceful, lasting joys: jewelers and *haute couture* firms still do business there, as though the spirit of the place has resisted the passing of time.

Somewhat further along, the blue-lit opalescent glass roof of the architecturally pompous Grand Palais nightly reflects the lights of Pont Alexandre-III, a bridge built, like the exhibition "palace" itself, in time for the Universal Exposition of 1900. The bridge retains a festive air with its blown-glass lamps and opulent balustrade crowning the sleek, low cast-iron arch, not to mention its four corner plinths bearing allegorical figures and winged horses. From the bridge, the gaze sweeps across the immense sky to the other bank and the hôtel des Invalides built by Libéral Bruant under Louis XIV. The simple rigor of its facade extends for some

two hundred meters, in contrast to the architectural flourishes of Mansart's dome.

Ever eclectic, on rainy days the Right Bank offers a wonderful arcaded stroll down the Rue de Rivoli, where it is possible to indulge in several essential pleasures: pastries at Angelina's tea room, books at Galignani's, foreign newspapers at W.H. Smith's, indeed antiques at the specialized gallery called the Louvre des Antiquaires.

Rue de Castiglione runs off Rue de Rivoli toward Place Vendôme. It was on 19 February 1806, that Napoleon signed the decree ordering that a street be cut from Place Vendôme to the boulevards to the north, where a Capuchin convent once stood. Ever since the Revolution, the convent gardens had become a fairground; beneath the trees and paths where the bare-legged, sandal-shod Capuchin nuns—also called Daughters of Passion—had once strolled and meditated, crowds henceforth gathered around acrobats, dog trainers, and flea circuses.

By 1814, Rue de la Paix ran north, although it was not until 1830 that fashionable stores began to appear. The Second Empire brought life and fame to the street, "where women prepared for battle." One milliner, two fashion designers, three lingerie specialists, and ten jewelers honed their wares there. Rue de la Paix was a guarantee of conquest. The court and then town society followed in the footsteps of the fashion-conscious empress. Rue de la Paix became synonymous with elegance, and will almost certainly remain so, for its layout almost imposes this role: when looking at a map of Paris, it resembles a barometer—a barometer of fashion—with Rue de Castiglione as its base and Place Vendôme as its dial.

With its cluster of luxury jewelers, Place Vendôme—flanked by Rue de la Paix and Rue de Castiglione—is a haven of femininity and luxury goods. These two pages illustrate precious objects and jewels offered by glamorous firms such as Boucheron, Cartier, Van Cleef & Arpels, and Mauboussin, names now associated throughout the world with luxury and refinement.

The grand salon of the Chaumet firm (*near right*), supplier to Napoleon I, still has David's full-length portrait of the Empress Joséphine.

The Hotel Ritz on Place Vendôme, now a hundred years young, is the epitome of a luxury hotel. Its founder, César Ritz, created an establishment with modern facilities that nevertheless scrupulously respected the grand old traditions of hospitality. A list of past guests would read like a social register crossed with the dream cast of a Hollywood film: the Prince of Wales, Marcel Proust, Alphonse XIII, Charlie Chaplin, Marlene Dietrich, Humphrey Bogart, Lauren Bacall, and others. Ernest Hemingway claimed that when he tried to imagine heaven, the Ritz came to mind. The coat of arms is engraved in the entrance way (*below*), while the Psyche Salon is a spot for Parisians who want to entertain friends in glamorous surroundings.

As the mythic source of luxury fashion for over a century, Rue de la Paix was created to stimulate desire. Although clothiers have now shifted to other locations such as Rue du Faubourg Saint-Honoré, Avenue Montaigne and Place des Victories, it was on Rue de la Paix that the leading nineteenth-century couturier, Charles-Frédéric Worth, decided to set up shop. His clients included Empress Eugénie and the princesse de Metternich. Following his example, Madame Grès founded her fashion house nearby, whereupon fine jewelers opened stores alongside (the most recent being Paloma Picasso), while firms such as Schiaparelli, Guerlain, Boucheron, Chaumet, Cartier, Van Cleef & Arpels, and Mauboussin have opened on Place Vendôme itself.

The rectangular Place Vendôme, with its angled corners, was designed by Jules Hardouin-Mansart and erected where the hôtel de Vendôme once stood. The new buildings were originally intended to house the royal library, the mint, diplomatic offices, and royal academies. At the foot of frivolous Rue de la Paix, Place Vendôme and its constellation of jewelers incarnate the splendor of feminine Paris. And the finest gem of all is the Ritz, symbol of the finest style of hotel life. As the epicenter of chic, cosmopolitan Paris, the Ritz is adored by stars, artists, and wealthy foreigners. Marie-Louise Ritz tells of a young woman who read the plaque—"This hotel was founded in 1898 by César Ritz"—only to exclaim in stupefaction: "I didn't know somebody named Ritz existed! I thought it was a word meaning chic and glamorous. How incredibly ritzy!"

Indeed, it was the Swiss César Ritz who best honored the original intentions of the marquis de Louvois and Hardouin-Mansart to make Place Vendôme a glamorous gathering spot for the elite. The hotel's Empire-style rooms are perhaps the ideal place to meditate upon the unfathomable profundity of vanity.

Place Vendôme is still haunted by La Castiglione (or "La Divine"), who was mistress to Napoleon III (as well as the favorite of Italian statesman Camillo Benso di Cavour). After scandalizing society with her obscene comments, she felt herself growing old at the age of thirty-two, and shut herself in her rooms on the square, never to go out again. For thirty long years, her furniture was draped in black velvet, and her shutters remained closed.

Strolling further north, by the old opera house—set in the city like a birthday cake—then wading through the crowds outside the department stores, the visitor approaches one of the best-preserved areas of Paris.

Of all the "villages" in Paris, Montmartre has been most successful in preserving its identity despite an invasion of tourists. It would seem that trees and plants grow better here than elsewhere, colonizing streets and facades. Visitors can either climb the hill via a steep staircase with quaint lampposts (*below*), or can follow the roughly cobbled Rue Norvins toward the ghostly, Byzantine domes of the church of Le Sacre-Coeur (*right*). They then wander aimlessly down a misty Allée des Brouillards

(*above*) to the "château" once occupied by Gérard de Nerval.

Following pages: One of the slopes of Montmartre has even clung to its vineyard, which produces excellent wine from Gamay and Pinot Noir grapes.

Toward Montmartre

Promenaders will begin to climb as they go from the Opéra district to the eminently Parisian *butte* of Montmartre—whatever route is taken, the path steepens. Rue de la Tour-des-Dames, for instance, begins next to the church of La Trinité and rises sharply to join Rue de La Rochefoucauld. The street has retained its provincial air, as has this entire neighborhood bounded by Faubourg Poissonnière, Rue de Clichy, and Rue Saint-Lazare. Dubbed "Nouvelle Athènes" in the early nineteenth century, this country-style neighborhood, though close to the busy boulevards, still provides a calm atmosphere conducive to creative work, and therefore still appeals to many writers and artists.

The skein of streets including Rue d'Aumale, Rue de La Rochefoucauld, Rue Blanche, Rue de Douai, and Avenue Frochot (this latter a haven of Gothic revival architecture)—dotted with charming gardens of boxwood, holly, and dark, metallic ivy—was once home to a constellation of up-and-coming artistic celebrities such as Gounod, Berlioz, Bizet, Chopin, George Sand, Gustave Moreau (whose house and studio can still be visited), Degas, Scheffer, Géricault, Gérôme, Manet and Paul Delaroche (whose studio-home seems to have been imported from London). The neighborhood retains the feel of a deserted stage, and has an atmosphere unlike any other. More than anywhere else, it conveys the presence of vanished souls, which is perhaps why it has been so well preserved, its charm intact.

The melancholy calm of Nouvelle Athènes is all the more strange since it is wedged between the boulevards below and the agitation at the foot of Butte Montmartre. Montmartre is a small provincial town perched above Paris, truly the most authentic and picturesque "village" in the capital. Its name alone evokes bygone images of street urchins, pavement artists, chair caners, art markets, village fairs, and grape harvests.

At the Moulin de la Galette (originally just a refreshment stall run by millers), the dazzling cabaret artist La Goulue would lead folks to the dance floor for a lively waltz, while at the foot of the *butte* the clamor of the French cancan can still be heard pouring out of the Moulin-Rouge (the real one, which burned in 1900, sent countless flaming memories up in smoke).

Once Parisians adopt a person or a place (and often the two go together, such as Casque d'or on Faubourg du Temple, Arlette la Chèvre in the Marais district, Marion in Les Halles, and the Palais-Royal laundry maid), they weave a wonderful legend around it, concocting tales with twists and turns that are in no way subject to the laws of reality.

Montmartre is a haven of this local trait, which has managed to survive the invasion of tourists and the tragedy of modern urban development. More than any other neighborhood, Montmartre, despite appearing taleworn and cliché-ridden, has managed to hold onto its authenticity. For over a century, the neighborhood has been an object of curiosity, a source of the most Parisian of myths. Nostalgia is cultivated in the "free municipality" of Montmartre with urban vigor.

It is perhaps best approached via Rue Lepic, lined with countless noisy, welcoming

shops. The hill has cliff-like borders, hidden springs, and skewed, roughly cobbled streets named after heaven knows whom (in apparent homage to stars of bawdiness, if not love—Gabrielle and Berthe, Sainte-Rustique or La Bonne). Private gardens full of oleander and spiny boxwood mask houses —each one different—which are sometimes little more than shacks.

Montmartre's minuscule cemetery opens only on All Saints' Day. Its tiny vineyard, meanwhile, yields excellent Gamay and Pinot Noir grapes; its squares are equally tiny, from the overly famous Place du Tertre to the peaceful Place Charles-Dullin in front of the Théâtre de l'Atelier, a neoclassical villa aloof from Place Pigalle with its nocturnal agitation. Pigalle, meanwhile, with blinking neon signs, night clubs, mob atmosphere (which is not all show) and an endless stream of tourist buses, has retained almost nothing of the days when Henry Miller spent "quiet days in Clichy" (a stone's throw from Place Blanche and the Café Cyrano where surrealists hung out), or of the Russian cabarets that were once so common.

Montmartre is still haunted by memories of cabaret singer Aristide Bruant (in black velvet "artist's" jacket and red scarf),

Milord Arsouille (in fact, Lord Seymour), Poulbot, La Goulue, Yvette Guilbert and other dance-hall heroines from oblivion sketched by painter Henri de Toulouse-Lautrec. It is also a favorite site for artists' colonies, worthy descendants of nineteenth-century pavement artists who sought to escape the harshness of the capital and savor their moments of despair by meeting at the cluster of buildings known as the Bateau-Lavoir (which burned in 1970). The Bateau-Lavoir served as baptistery to some of the great artistic revolutions of the twentieth century, having housed the most famous painters of the day, including Picasso, who launched cubism here.

Far left (clockwise from top left): One of Montmartre's strong points is its contrasts, from the seventeenth-century windmill called Moulin de la Galette, to the Sunday-painters' market in Place du Tertre, to Hector Guimard's Art Nouveau entrance of the Abbesses Metro station. Then there's the northern-style, red-brick Villa Legendre with its climbing foliage, the tree-shaded Place Emile-Goudeau with its village charm (the former site of the Bateau-Lavoir, where the likes of Renoir, Modigliani, Vlaminck, Van Dongen, and Picasso lived). *Left:* The Lapin Agile is the famous Montmartre cabaret where Aristide Bruant sang. *Below:* At the foot of Montmartre, the melancholy Avenue Frochot has been cut off to traffic, the better to defend itself from the agitation of the city, notably the nearby sex-shop district of Pigalle.

ROOFTOPS. Before descending the butte via aristocratic Avenue Junot, which snakes down the slope from north to south, it is worth dwelling on one of the most striking and most characteristic aspects of Paris—its rooftops. It is hard to imagine a more wonderful promenade than an airborne hop from roof to roof, such as the silent-movie hero Fantomas, high on sensual and esthetic delights. Seen from the sky—and seen from Montmartre—Paris is a sea of subtly contrasting shades, from gray slate to rain-softened, milky white zinc. This sea is edged with leafy boulevards and avenues, dotted with islands of garden greenery, and traversed by the graceful, wiry curve of the shimmering Seine.

The city's rooftops are not simply the logical and banal summit of its buildings. They also constitute a whole world in itself, a celestial halfway point between heaven and earth, composed of an impalpable, silky substance. The monochrome hue constantly changes with the passing hours and clouds. On sunny days the slate absorbs the color of the sharp blue sky, merging with it even more in contrast to the metallic sparkle of the fine ridges of the zinc guttering. The rooftops are peopled with cupolas, domes, and lead-lined terraces, with black cast-iron railings, with sentinel-like lightening rods, with silly or haughty decoration, and with metal ladders that seem to guide the chimneys upward. All their silhouettes stand out when the sky glows or threatens.

The gaze then discerns unnoticed terraces and gardens, apparently in levitation. Bell towers also sprout up everywhere, almost like Rome. Even though church bells are rarely heard in Paris, except perhaps on

Sparkling, gilded Paris sometimes chooses to dress in gray, depending on the whims of the weather. Its zinc, bronze, and lead rooftops present an infinite palette of hues that suggest a silky, rolling sea halfway between earth and sky, its waves tipped with countless highlights.

Above: The needle of the Eiffel Tower is like an elegant old lady who orders the light to change the color of her iron robe according to a subtle range of harmonious shades.

Below: A steeply sloping roof on Place Vendôme.

Right: A sea of air and light vibrates impalpably, apparently placing the church of Saint-Sulpice at the foot of the domed Panthéon.

Above and below: The rooftops of Paris constitute one of the most unusual, poetic landscapes imaginable, constantly changing depending on the time of day. Sometimes opaque, sometimes highly reflective, they orchestrate a visual ballet, whether crowding the church of Notre-Dame or flocking around an unusual tiled roof.

Right: The Pont des Arts appears even more wiry and graceful when set behind the rich perspective of monochrome rooftops.

Sunday mornings or at vespers, they constitute a large population: there are 878 church bells in Paris, not counting monasteries, which push the total over one thousand. Whether bass or treble, their delicate trills ricochet from roof to roof. Every bell also has a name: at Notre-Dame, the great tenor with its worthy F-sharp is called Emmanuel, while its counterpart at Sacré-Coeur on Montmartre is dubbed La Savoyarde.

This heavenly raft of rooftops, so vast and strange, is moored in a sea of air and light, rocked by waves of clouds. It provides a thousand and one unexpected spectacles, a complicated jumble of forms, some of which attempt to free themselves from the charming confusion like a rope-bound Gulliver. The dome of the Institut de France, for instance, is reduced to a minor turret, whereas the Panthéon manages to rise up on its hill, appearing more imposingly massive than might have been expected.

The rooftop perspective changes everything—certain buildings seem much closer than they really are, while others, previously unnoticed, suddenly bar the horizon. From here, all of Paris seems within grasp. A playful hand could reach out and move the opera house to the middle of the Invalides esplanade, or set Notre-Dame on Chaillot hill, or replace the Gare de Lyon with the church of Saint-Sulpice, or even divert the Seine in order to turn Paris into an enormous island. Paris has become a board game.

Down by the Riverside

Coming back to earth, it is worth looping through working-class Paris before regaining the Palais-Royal. There are still modest neighborhoods where "the people are gentle at play, hard at work, and have mighty fine girls in their dance halls." One poetic quarter, which has survived the urban upheavals to the east of the capital, straddles the Saint-Martin canal; this "waterfront" community is permanently associated with the film *Hôtel du Nord*, starring Arletty and Louis Jouvet. The canal broadens before the rotunda at la Villette (a vestige of the duty barriers set up by royal tax collectors, now huddling below a bend of the elevated Metro), then narrows through locks and beneath elegant iron bridges (still equipped with boxes of emergency life

Paris also likes to don the apparel of a northern, canal-lined city. Although the Seine dominates, it should not be forgotten that canals also lay claim to Paris, with banks perhaps less magnificent yet often delightful. This is Paris at a leisurely pace, a Paris that takes its time to reveal another fact of its complex, almost contradictory reality. The banks of the Saint-Martin canal (*right*) almost suggest a film-set from the pre-war years, where Arletty might pop up at any moment to cross one of the lock bridges (*left*). These watery thoroughfares nevertheless remain modest, hiding at the end of joyless streets or behind industrial buildings. While awaiting a new lease on life, they must be deliberately sought out and tracked down.

savers "in case of drowning"). Some bridges open to let barges pass, reminding everyone that Paris also has ties to the north and the misty atmospheres of Georges Simenon novels. Then this strange, dark-watered canal suddenly enters a vaulted tunnel and disappears below Boulevard Richard-Lenoir (which plays host every spring to a market famous not only for bric-a-brac but also cured hams—just one of the fairs that have enlivened Paris since the Middle Ages) and emerges again beyond La Bastille in the form of a harbor for pleasure-craft. It finally connects with the Seine, making navigation possible from Amsterdam to Marseille without ever setting foot on terra firma.

Looping back north, the outcrop known as Buttes-Chaumont (where Jean-Jacques Rousseau indulged in his passion for botany) forms the green heart of another Parisian village—narrow streets of small houses with tiny gardens, labyrinthine alleys where children play. It is perfect for aimless strolls, or for dining on a delicious steak in one of the restaurants which still bears magnificent witness to the fact that the city's central slaughterhouse was formerly located nearby, at La Villette.

Such delightful vestiges cannot undo, alas, several grim new construction projects that have absurdly carved up a part of Paris strongly rooted to its past. Fortunately, the neighborhoods around Buttes-Chaumont, built on former quarries, have largely escaped the madness of urban development.

For centuries, Paris nestled within a carefully circumscribed cluster of villages, each separated from one another by fields or empty plots. It was one big urban village, so to speak. Many Parisians spent their

entire lives within sight of their parish church, escaping it only in their imagination. (Even today, few people from the Vaugirard neighborhood visit Belleville, and few people in Belleville have any notion of the tribe occupying Auteuil.) It was not until the seventeenth century that horizons broadened, and Parisians began going from one village to another. This concept of village or quarter—not to be confused with *arrondissement*, which carries subtle geographic connotations underneath its administrative facade—has remained intact and still lends charm to everyday life in the capital.

The Parisian atmosphere has changed more in the past forty years than in the previous sixty or seventy. There are still elderly residents who remember gas lamps, ice

Street markets are an essential part of every Paris neighborhood, each with its own special attraction. They represent a colorful, gossipy, pleasant lifestyle in which human contact is easily established with merchants. Fruit, vegetables, seafood, everything is skillfully displayed beneath blackboard slates indicating the day's prices in chalk. A variety of provincial accents can be heard, all sharing a taste for harmless banter, gentle mockery, gruff affection.
Left, top and bottom: The market on Boulevard Richard-Lenoir, near the Bastille, has one of the best reputations in Paris, though every Parisian thinks that his or her own local market is the best, reflecting the tradition of village pride. *Far left*: After the market, why not grab a table in front of Chez Paul on the Rue de Charonne, in a charming setting that has barely changed in over a century.

Paris is still nostalgic for the days when it was composed of villages divided by fields, vineyards, or woods—a city in the country.

Top: On Rue Dieulafoy in the 13th Arrondissement, colorful houses hide behind cascades of ivy and wisteria, and don points on their steep, slate rooftops.

Above: Not far away, just off Place de Rungis, is the Cité Florale housing estate. Little houses bedecked with flowers line tiny alleys with botanical names—Rue des Iris, Rue des Mimosas, Rue des Orchidées.

Top right: On the Right Bank, almost up on Buttes-Chaumont, is the Mouzaïa quarter—a maze of streets; the cobbled lane called Hameau du Danube overflows with bushes and blossoms.

Bottom right: Not far from Père Lachaise cemetery, Campagne à Paris, perched atop a steep hill, unfurls its unreal streets with quaint lampposts.

Far right: On Villa Cronstadt, reeds and honeysuckle screen a red door framed in Mediterranean blue.

Extreme right, top: A grapevine climbs along the facades of these modest houses in a small courtyard off Rue de Reuilly.

Extreme right, bottom: On Villa de l'Ermitage, in Belleville, flowers sprout from purple-lacquered vases.

Far right: Nestled between bustling boulevards to the south and raucous Pigalle to the north, the Nouvelle Athènes neighborhood has managed to retain an almost provincial calm. On Rue Victor-Massé, facades that may initially seem banal compose, for an attentive promenader, striking geometries that are far from commonplace. Thanks to irreproachable balance and proportion, they convey a discrete elegance.

Above: Balconies blossom in the morning sun above

Place du Marché-Sainte-Catherine, near the Musée Carnavalet.

Below: The gold "genie" on the column at Place de la Bastille seems to fly over nearby rooftops.

delivered in blocks, and milk carts drawn by dappled dray horses. Even in the 1950s it was still possible to buy milk from a farm in Auteuil, or seek water from a spring in Vaugirard.

The city's districts often seem like "private" neighborhoods, each with its own particular savor. Collectively, they incarnate the broad range of Parisian behavior with charm and subtlety, cultivating a thoroughly French sense of taste. Indeed, it should never be forgotten that Paris is basically inhabited by people from the provinces, who have been active in forging the spirit of their adopted city over the past century. They "headed to Paris" to study, to find work, or to become wealthy (all Parisian kids have some old aunt or grandmother living in the provinces where they can spend their vacations). Newcomers usually arrived with a recommendation in hand, and therefore moved into the neighborhood where fellow townspeople had already migrated. Thus the community from, for example, Brittany stuck to the area around Montparnasse. This tradition persists even today. Therefore, unlike most other cities, neighborhoods are not organized by trade or industry—with the notable exceptions of the furniture workshops on Faubourg Saint-Antoine and the garment district in the Sentier, Paris is subdivided according to regional roots.

Foreigners are often surprised to discover that almost all the French they meet are "Parisians," as though no one lived in the provinces. In fact, these Parisians of more or less recent adoption reside in an archipelago of tiny provinces scattered across the capital.

Every Parisian and temporary resident chooses a favorite district, garden, street or spot, and often goes to great lengths to convince "opponents" of the wisdom of that choice. Everyone constructs a private dream Paris, and tries to make it conform to reality. An individual's preference for a given neighborhood can often become tenacious and implacable, depending on age and circumstance. A passionate, intimate relationship with the city is formed, expressing a determination to go through thick and thin together. Parisians are thus highly aware of the fact that if Paris is to maintain standards of taste, wit, and fine living, then they are personally responsible for maintaining Paris as it is.

Autumn in Paris is delightful. Nothing is more exquisite than a golden morn veiling the city in an imperceptible gray mist that sparkles in the gentle sunlight. A slight haze cloaks everything, softening horizons, blending forms, and smoothing out architectural aberrations and other urban heresies. Autumn is undoubtedly the ideal season for wandering through old neighborhoods, strolling down streets with the feel of cobblestones underfoot, shuffling through the dead leaves of melancholy gardens, and pausing before houses that, while often scarred, still unblushingly present fine vestiges to the public gaze.

This ongoing tour of the Right Bank now heads down toward the river to Quai des Célestins, opposite Ile Saint-Louis, where the palace of the first kings of France once stood. On the corner of Rue du Petit-Musc, the strange hôtel de Fieubet is so royally laden with ornamentation that it never ceases to charm or intrigue passersby. Yet when Jules Hardouin-Mansart originally designed

the residence for Gaspard Fieubet (royal advisor and chancellor to the French queen, Anne of Austria), there was no question of attracting attention through an orgy of decoration; all of this was added in 1850 when the building was bought by the comte de La Vallette, publisher of the *Journal de l'Assemblée Nationale*.

Near the Saint-Paul Metro station, at 119 Rue Saint-Antoine, is an alley called Passage Charlemagne, which snakes between the high blank wall of a high school of the same name and a series of dull, gray houses until it suddenly arrives at Rue Charlemagne, which boasts the surprisingly majestic vestiges of a fourteenth-century residence. Rue Charlemagne then runs below the dome of the church of Saint-Paul-Saint-Louis toward Rue des Jardins-Saint-Paul, a discreet street offering no insight into its bucolic name. All these charming little streets were laid out along the sites of the former palace, and now evoke forgotten splendors: Rue des Lions is where the royal menagerie once stood; Rue Beautreillis hosted Charles V's trellised grape arbor; and Rue de la Cerisaie marked the long lanes of cherry trees near the hôtel Saint-Paul. Legend has it that Rabelais died on Rue des Jardins-Saint-Paul, on the spot where number 9 now stands, just a few feet away from Rue de l'Ave-Maria, where the residence of the bishops of Sens was built; this noble, carefully restored building, now housing the Forney Library, is a remarkable example of fifteenth-century architecture. It was home to bishops, cardinals, and royalty such as Marguerite de Valois.

Over by city hall, known as the Hôtel de Ville, Place Saint-Gervais offers a most unusual view, for it is set on a base of steps

whose vanishing point optically suggests a theatrical *trompe-l'oeil* effect. Behind the church, the lonely Rue des Barres—narrow, severe and winding, perched above the surrounding streets—clings to an almost tragic air. It begins at Rue de l'Hôtel-de-Ville and climbs steeply to finish on a stairway of seven stone steps leading to Rue François-Miron. Rue de Barres is parallel to Rue du Pont-Louis-Philippe, yet lacks its lightness and upscale shops. Crowning the middle of Rue des Barres is the dark porch and rain-weathered columns of a portal of the church of Saint-Gervais-Saint-Protais. This austere, almost disturbing church, whose light is heavily filtered by stained-glass windows, is one of the rare churches to preserve some of the intimate, discreet charm of country churches. Writer and theologian Jacques Bénigne Bossuet preached there, the marquise de Sévigné was married there, and artist Philippe de Champaigne and playwright Prosper Crébillon are buried there.

The Marais district is a site of endless strolls of architectural interest, of quiet squares, and of art galleries, markets, and countless other Parisian curiosities.
Far left: Rue de Sévigné unveils the enigmatic church of Saint-Paul-Saint-Louis.
Left: The chiaroscuro effect of Rue Charles V evokes the setting of some popular novel.

Below: A coyly draped skirt draws gazes to this seventeenth-century statue in Square Léopold-Achille, near the Musée Carnavalet.

The ample facade at number 12 Rue Charles-V belongs to the vast seventeenth-century hôtel d'Aubray, where the marquise de Brinvilliers poisoned a frightful series of victims. The now peaceful residence, its ivy-covered walls featuring fine windows topped by grimacing mascarons, hides behind an imposing gateway with a semi-circular arch.

Not far away is another of the city's hidden treasures. At number 39 Rue de Bretagne, nestled between a delicatessen and a vegetable shop, is the entrance to a market called Enfants-Rouges. Founded in 1628, the market owes its name to the red clothes worn by infants and children housed in a nearby hospice.

Beyond bustling Rue de Turenne, at the end of Rue des Francs-Bourgeois, lies Place des Vosges. This square is the pride of Paris, and retains its serenity (if not all its luster) in the midst of the busy streets and boulevards surrounding it. Despite all the parked cars and the buses running between the Saint-Lazare train station and the Bois de Vincennes, with a little effort it is possible to imagine oneself carried back three hundred years into the past. The red seventeenth-century residences with their pyramidal roofs and the somewhat sad garden square enclosed by hostile cast-iron railings convey a nostalgia reminiscent of poetic Belgian convents and delightful Italian piazzas.

Place des Vosges, whose arcades now house antique shops, restaurants, art galleries, and book stores, was formerly known as Place Royale, and was home to the likes of Cardinal de Richelieu, the comte de Rohan-Chabot, the marquis de Breteuil, Mademoiselle du Châtelet, the great actress Mademoiselle Rachel, Ninon de Lenclos,

Above: The dome of a church rises above rooftops in the Marais neighborhood, similar to a village church.

Right: Place des Vosges remains one of the most beautiful squares in the world. Every Parisian and every tourist has dreamed of living there. The arcades of thirty-six Henri IV pavilions of brick and stone provide an elegant promenade around the square, punctuated by a gastronomic interlude at a restaurant such as Coconas, Ma Bourgogne, or L'Ambroisie, depending on one's means.

and Marion Delorme (who occupied the house where Victor Hugo would later compose poetry and his play, *Ruy Blas*). It was also here that Henri II, jousting under the colors of Diane de Poitiers against Lord Montgomery, was mortally wounded on July 1, 1559.

The facades of the private mansions scattered throughout the Marais district, in fact, constitute a stone-carved album of French heraldry. Much of the nation's history can be read in the elegantly sculpted profusion of haughty caryatids, virile entablatures, ironic mascarons, subtle framings, enigmatic medallions, and symbolic cartouches, not to mention the mood of neoclassical rigor tempered by French wit.

Bounded by Rue de Sévigné, Rue des Francs-Bourgeois, and Rue Payenne, the Musée Carnavalet (named after a Breton nobleman, François de Kernevenoy, whose widow purchased the mansion in 1578) is a museum devoted to the history of Paris. The most famous occupant of the residence, Madame de Sévigné (who was born nearby) wove the lush garland of her correspondence here. The building itself, steadily enlarged around a Renaissance core, acquired the remnants of other fine residences demolished during the furious nineteenth-century construction campaign led by Baron Haussmann. A stone's throw away, the hôtel Lamoignon, with its strange tower (standing like an eternal sentinel against the capriciousness of passing fashion), now houses the historical library of the city of Paris, accumulating layers of glorious—or at least, moving—souvenirs.

The hôtel Sully puts an enthusiastic Renaissance face on the bustle of Rue Saint-

Antoine, flanked by a crowd of shops demonstrating that the Marais district, despite thirty years of gentrification, has retained some of its working-class sinews. Now the headquarters of France's historic monuments fund, the residence was designed by Jean Androuet du Cerceau for the duc de Sully, minister to Henri IV, and it remained in the family until the mid-eighteenth century. Its French-style roofs, gleaming Italianate decoration, and majestic volume (if relatively modest scale, due to its urban location) became a prototype for residences worthy of the monarchy's high-ranking officers. Despite a certain restraint, its spirit prefigures the magnificence of treasurer Nicolas Fouquet's château at Vaux-le-Vicomte.

One residence that has forthrightly confronted the march of time is the hôtel Salé

Right: More than any other neighborhood, the Marais district contains outstanding architectural treasures such as this Medici vase with lush garlands.
Left: Still in the Marais, a fine wooden door on Rue du Foin leads to a courtyard.
Below left: Rue du Parc-Royal boasts many magnificent residences, most from the seventeenth century—not all of them restored to the same standards, alas.
Below right: The Musée Carnavalet is devoted to the history of the city of Paris; its

gate opens onto a main courtyard featuring a statue of Louis XIV by Antoine Coysevox, and a facade with elegant allegories of the seasons carved in bas-relief.

(meaning "salty," because built by the collector of the salt tax in 1656). Since 1985, it has housed the Musée Picasso, based on a collection of works given to the nation by the artist's heirs in lieu of inheritance tax. Architect Roland Simonnet adapted the interior of the residence with exemplary humility, that is, by stressing its new raison d'être. After crossing the traditional cobbled courtyard, visitors enter a setting dominated by stone, stripped of any pointless decoration, which provides a rigorous environment for Picasso's ever-surprising work. The museum demonstrates, rather than merely reflects, a troubling if unyielding fact—Picasso was the greatest classical painter of the modern era.

The almost excessive artistic heritage of this neighborhood offers yet other points of interest, such as the hôtel d'Hallwyll on Rue Michel-Le-Comte, near the Georges Pompidou Center. Its austere beauty is the sole example of a private residence by the genius Claude-Nicolas Ledoux, who built the striking city tollhouses that bore final witness to an esthetic attitude obsessed with rationality, yet never devoid of grace.

Whether by deformation or contraction, the spellings of many street names have changed down through the years. Rue du Petit-Musc, for instance, near the hôtel de Sens, was originally called "Pute-y-Musse," which might be translated as "Whore's Hideaway" and which obviously has scant connection to today's "Little Musk"! It was King Philippe Auguste who first began christening the alleyways near his palace—the one where hay was sold was dubbed "Hay Street" (Rue du Foin), the fish market became Rue Poissonnière, and so on for the

"baths" (Rue des Bains), the "old offices" (Rue des Vieilles-Etudes), the monastery of the "white-cloaked" Servite order (Rue des Blancs-Manteaux), and the lair of "ruffians" (Rue des Mauvais-Garçons).

Meanwhile, the sole medieval cloister still existing in Paris, the Cloître de Billettes, huddles behind an unprepossessing door at 25 Rue des Archives. Its low pointed arches inspire the silence appropriate to meditation and music.

The Marais district was forever separated from the neighborhood known as Les Halles by a broad avenue, Boulevard de Sébastopol, laid down by Baron Haussmann. Les Halles was originally the belly of Paris, a dazzling marketplace where wholesale fruit and vegetables were bought, miracles performed, chronicles written, streetwalkers encountered, and night birds met. The only remnants today of the old Halles are a ballet by Roland Petit, based on a libretto by Raymond Queneau, *La Croqueuse de Diamants* (The Gold Digger), or in popular novels, notably in a fine passage from Emile Zola's *The Belly of Paris*: "As dawn broke . . . the glowing dial of Saint-Eustache paled, entering its death throes like a night lamp suddenly overtaken by the morning. In the wine shop and down nearby streets, gas lamps went out one by one, like stars tumbling into the light. And Florent watched Les Halles emerge from the darkness, emerge from the dream in which he saw their pleasure palaces extend to infinity. They became solid, greenish gray, ever greater, their prodigious masts bearing the endless expanse of their roofs."

The glass-and-iron market halls built by Victor Baltard in the nineteenth century

Paris contains hundreds, indeed thousands of glamorous shops, both large and small.

Far left, top: At Mariage Frères, near the Musée Carnavalet, tea is treated as a rare and precious item.

Far left, bottom: Milles-Feuilles specialized in delicate bouquets in intoxicating colors.

Left: Serious cooks thrill at the sight of the gleaming copperware available at Dehillerin in the former Halles neighborhood.

Above: On a vaster scale, the glass-roofed Samaritaine department store boasts decorative details like this recently restored fresco by Francis Jourdain.

Left: A decorative detail from the dome of another department store, Galeries Lafayette.

Palais-Royal is another wonderful site for a contemplative promenade. Like Place des Vosges, it offers strollers a range of visual, olfactory, and gustatory delights. Depending on mood and whim, visitors can purchase a garment or accessory from Ludot, perfume from Shiseido or Rosine, and china from Jean de Rohan-Chabot, Joyce, and Muriel Grateau. Or they can indulge in a passion for heraldic decoration, dine at Muscade or the Grand Véfour, admire Daniel Buren's black-and-white striped columns, or simply read, sitting on a bench below the impeccably pruned linden trees while enjoying the subtle floral display in the central garden, re-landscaped by Mark Rudkin in 1992.

have been demolished. The church of Saint-Eustache now stands alone, sovereign, over the gutted square, rising like a vast ship over the former belly of Paris. Not far away is Rue Saint-Joseph (formerly Rue du Temps-Perdu), where Molière was buried and Zola born. The dark, narrow alleyways around Les Halles have always been among the most picturesque in Paris—many of them remain almost intact, providing a glimpse of what they once were: Rue Mondétour, Rue du Jour, Rue Vauvilliers, Rue Sauval, Rue du Cygne, and Rue de la Grande-Truanderie (where Gracchus Babeuf, the somewhat crazed revolutionary who plotted the overthrow of the Directorate, was arrested in 1797). All of Paris teemed in these streets bursting with shops, bistros, restaurants, and prostitutes. And still teems today—just as in old days, crowds still circle around an acrobat, a rapper, or a mime.

The Seine leads us, one last time, back to the Palais-Royal, which is just as seductive as ever. The history of the Palais-Royal, all by itself, sums up the Parisian art of fine living. The palace was begun in 1629 by Cardinal de Richelieu, who was appointed chaplain to Marie de' Medici in 1615. When Richelieu bequeathed the palace to the crown on his death, what had initially been the Palais-Cardinal became a "royal" palace, although never a royal residence.

For several hundred years, the grounds behind the Palais-Royal were an unrivaled temple of business, fashion, entertainment, flirtation—in short, of Paris life. The eighteenth-century chronicler Melchior Grimm wrote, "It would be hard to depict the spectacle presented by this promenade when

Above: The hôtel de La Vrillière, near Place des Victoires, just opposite the Bank of France, is one of the most attractive architectural specimens in Paris, as demonstrated by this corner tower whose balconies are decorated with graceful cast-iron railings.
Right: In the center of Place des Victoires is an equestrian statue of Louis XIV, which stands out against the pure, sun-lit facades designed by Mansart. The fashion world has moved into this neighborhood—first Victoire, followed by Kenzo and Thierry Mugler. Aloof from the hubbub of Les Halles and the Opéra district, the quiet quarter now attracts an elegant, leisured clientele.

the sun, sinking toward the horizon, allows women to come out for a breath of fresh air, to enjoy the pleasure of seeing and above all of being seen in the gardens. Double and triple rows of chairs, placed along the spacious lanes, barely suffice to receive this crush of women, almost all of them pretty; the most beautiful and elegant among them stroll along the paths with an easy grace further enhanced by the simple and graceful form of garments now adopted by fashion. . . ."

During the Second Empire, luxury shops opened in the arcades flanking the garden; Mellerio, Boucheron, and Oudin drew crowds of playboys and nouveaux riches who frequented the many cafés and restaurants offering the most extravagant culinary wonders to be found in Paris. The windows of Chevet's featured artistic mountains of lobster, crayfish, foie gras, stuffed turkey, and so on, attracting hoards of window shoppers.

At the turn of the century, freed of the vices that had made its reputation, the Palais-Royal went into a virtuous slumber, as though exhausted from so much debauchery.

In a strange turnaround, given that it had once been a haven of the most undisciplined behavior, the palace became the seat of France's constitutional court, or Conseil d'Etat, charged with laying down the law, defining rules, and arbitrating conflicts between citizens and government. Later, one wing was attributed to the Ministry of Culture. Then, in 1986, artist Daniel Buren authoritatively and rightfully planted his striped columns in the main courtyard, which the government's usual inattention to heritage had allowed to become a parking lot. The arcades, once again home to bou-

tiques, have recovered some of their former animation. On the corner of Rue Montpensier, the Théâtre du Palais-Royal has retained its traditional gold and red velvet decoration, just as the famous restaurant Le Grand Véfour has kept its 1740 neoclassical decor, which catches the summer sunlight from the gardens. The likes of Colette and Jean Cocteau used to dine here, for both lived in this strange palace which, when evening has fallen and its gates have closed, is enlivened solely by the cries of the birds wheeling overhead and the water tumbling in its fountain. It is almost like being in Rome.

Colette wrote, "The Palais-Royal slumbers. A lone pigeon, blue as a western storm, huddles in a ball on the cold-scorched lawn."

To which Cocteau replied, "Sometimes when I return to the nocturnal Palais-Royal, a kind of intricate town slotted between walls that tilt in the moonlight, I marvel at this square where the chandeliers of the Comédie-Française glow through the windows, where the globes of the lamps resemble lilies of the valley around the fountain."

This promenade through Paris draws toward its close at Place des Victoires. The duc de La Feuillade commissioned Mansart to design the elliptical "square" in 1680, in honor of Louis XIV, whose central statue in the middle is placed at a strange angle, as though he is preparing to charge the Bank of France. The duke must have owed the king a great deal.

No one knows exactly how many of the old private residences were demolished by urban development, but the original appearance of Paris was permanently effaced during its nineteenth-century transformation

Right: The lantern topping the Printemps department store, built in 1881.
Below: On Avenue Rapp, not far from the Eiffel Tower, Hector Guimard transformed this door into an ode to curving lines and women, via a lavish weave of wood, stone, and wrought-iron.
Far right: The Musée Jacquemart-André on Boulevard Haussmann was built in the late nineteenth century in the then-fashionable eighteenth-century spirit. The interior is enriched with items from other magnificent residences

demolished due to urban development. The grand, spiral staircase rises amid marble columns, while the luxuriously appointed bathroom in the private apartments (*bottom*) are not far from the glassed-roofed conservatory.

(which foreigners, familiar with the fact that Paris has never suffered the ravages of war, are often surprised to learn). On the other hand, it thereby acquired a certain unity, harmoniously linking the center to outlying neighborhoods without incurring too much damage.

The most significant peripheral neighborhood is the Parc Monceau district. It is crisscrossed by streets such as Rue Fortuny, Rue Henri-de-Rochefort, and Rue Ampère, featuring small town houses with picturesque facades, all aligned in a row that shields their charming private gardens in the back. Exactly one hundred years ago, Rosa Bonheur, then living in her studio in the Fontainebleau Forest, recalled what the area had been like during her childhood, prior to development: "While my father was giving lessons, I would work from nature, out in the open air. . . . You have no idea of what that elegant and luxurious neighborhood was like back then. Boulevard de Courcelles, Avenue de Villiers, Place Malesherbes and Avenue de Messine were all countryside, real countryside! You could see crops there."

Thus the former "plain of Monceau," which might initially appear soulless, is in fact one the most mysterious quarters in a city already full of mystery. Here, more than anywhere else, it is easy to imagine fin-de-siècle Paris, or Paris during the First World War, the Paris of Proust peopled by fashionable ladies, recent millionaires, charming yet vain aristocrats, women of uncertain virtue and the rising professional classes that constituted the new elite of the Third Republic (1870–1940). Every one of the quarter's highly varied houses is an architectural

pastiche, whether done in an invented Gothic style (notably the house built for actress Sarah Bernhardt), imagined Renaissance taste, or supposed Enlightenment sensibility crossed with Romantic sentimentality, not to mention more surprising touches such as Norman half-timbering, Italian marble, and exotic imports from just about anywhere. These sedate streets can nevertheless make a promenader feel uneasy, as though the facades are hiding something. Something perhaps not as respectable as appearances would suggest. Indeed, many of these houses were once temples of lust. So there remains a certain something in the air, despite the reassuring bronze plaques of doctors and lawyers who have adopted the neighborhood with a strange enthusiasm.

Paris is a city of seduction, which explains why it needs to be observed, watched, and studied—with loving eyes, desiring eyes, yearning eyes.

Paris and Parisian behavior bear observation. They often turn out to be much more exotic than initially realized. Everyone must construct a private version of Paris, creating it in the desired image by using scattered fragments to build an imaginary landscape that will subsequently be transformed into reality. For the true Paris is the one which people invent for themselves—in its profusion, it can fulfill the most fanciful dreams. Paris has to be loved passionately, that is to say with hypocritical indulgence, seeing certain things yet refusing to see others (though without harboring too many illusions). And should reality truly appear too shocking, it can always be replaced with a few pages from the past—Paris, after all, is an open book.

INTERIORS

Parisians are passionately stylish.
Everything testifies to their unerring
sense of taste, ranging from
eighteenth-century woodwork and
Art Nouveau interiors to Art Deco furniture
and contemporary design.

Two imperatives govern interior decoration in Paris: a great deal of taste and a little boldness. This is why true Parisians always think it inappropriate to heed an interior decorator slavishly. And should they be tempted to seek advice, they treat it merely as useful help to avoid egregious error; metaphorically speaking, they apply a rule of etiquette similar to an engraved invitation that indicates desired dress, all the while leaving everyone the freedom to dress as they see fit, in their own style. Parisians have a natural sense of taste, and openly assert it. Ever since the seventeenth century, the famous French sense of taste, epitomized by Parisian fashion, has survived multiple upheavals which in fact constitute signs of fidelity. French taste owes its survival to a certain lifestyle tolerant of successive—and often contradictory—realities.

This taste springs from a powerful determination never to be trapped by the fashionable whims of a specific period or place. It is generally innate to the Parisian character, and every person graced with it receives it as a perfectible gift. Although every epoch has had its own idea of "perfect taste," they are now blended, in subtle doses, in interiors not always accessible to the public.

Without daring to claim, as did aristocratic author Barbey d'Aurevilly, that "democracy is the monarch of baseness," admittedly refined taste was originally an aristocratic affair. Indeed it still is, provided that it is expressed naturally and unstubbornly, by refusing to adhere rigidly to outdated forms, allowing new lines to create new pleasures (on the sole but imperative

Preceding pages: Figures in stone decorate the apartment of interior designer Jacques Grange, who coordinates refined alliances of objects. Parisians are innately passionate about interior decoration. Whether enthusiastic about past styles or about contemporary creativity and furniture, they all share a quest for rare or unique objects. It therefore seemed logical to discuss not only homogeneous interiors (revealing a strong personality or an addiction to a given style) but also public places that display an attraction to a particular aesthetic.

Above: A row of chandeliers with crystal pendants lights the antechamber to the apartments of the duc de Morny at the Louvre.

Right: The grand staircase of the Nissim de Camondo residence, with its fine, late nineteenth-century gilded wrought-iron banister.

condition that such lines be pleasant and dignified). For just as habit can enfeeble judgment, so taste may be subject to aging. It needs tireless revitalization by discreet yet efficient signs of warmth; Paris, for instance, is such an oasis of refinement that a small lapse in taste is often necessary to forestall a perfection that displays the simple fault of being faultless. A comfortable lapse allows personality to emerge; it is a way of making a mark on a world in love with both logic and image.

It is all a question of appearances. Decorating an apartment, home, mansion, studio, or even office is—or perhaps should be—a self-portrait of the person inhabiting it. Interior decoration is a success (whatever that means) when it reveals the personality, roots, profession, and hidden desires of an individual more efficiently than the most thorough handwriting analysis or astrological chart.

Contemporary interiors make little use of French classical or baroque models. A few pieces of furniture or decorative elements may grace interiors that usually defy the laws of harmony, though on rare occasions they brilliantly compose a coherent setting. The reason is simple: rare are the apartments or residences in Paris whose architecture and space resonate to neoclassical or baroque cadences. Those aesthetic options can only be comfortably exploited in a rural or provincial setting, such as country houses typical of the Bordeaux region.

Baroque decoration sprang from the Counter Reformation, spreading its exuberance through Italy, Austria, Germany, and Spain, though temporarily overlooking

France where local classicism had become law. It was nevertheless this ostentatious climate that produced the leading French cabinetmaker, André-Charles Boulle, who broke with the architectural weightiness of earlier furniture. Boulle's work was later disdained during the reign of Louis XV (1710–1774) and ignored during the Directorate, Empire, and Restoration, only to be snapped up during the Second Empire (1852–1870).

"Grand taste," or the art of proportion on a disproportionate scale, was imposed by Louis XIV (1638–1715), who saw it as a means to his political ends. The French universe at that time was organized like an eminently sophisticated solar system, with mechanisms structuring society all the way down to the private life of every individual. This new situation sprang from the monarch's desire to be surrounded by nothing but excellence. Aesthetics, in those days, was the expression of a political aspiration for divinity.

The Seventeenth Century

Overlooking Parc Monceau is the private residence of a family that has been in the banking business since the Second Empire. Its interior decoration is so accomplished that even a simple description (because it cannot be pictured here) serves as a kind of mirror of the seventeenth-century aesthetic ideal. For once, successive heirs have at least managed to keep the furniture intact—or, more precisely, have perfected it by progressively acquiring more authentic

The magnificent private residences, or *hôtels particuliers*, of the seventeenth century are among the most interesting in Paris. Almost all of them are found in the Marais district.

Thus, the hôtel de Châtillon on Rue Payenne has an entrance hall marked by a delicate iron gate decorated with chimera and foliage (*far left*), in harmonious contrast with the geometric pattern of the banister, also in wrought iron. The staircase of dressed stone (*left*), rises in an ample and elegant half-turn, with every detail reflecting balance and charm. In the center, a hanging lantern gracefully echoes the entrance gate. Elsewhere, a staircase on Rue de Bac (*above*) begins with winding steps in an elegant volute form.

pieces. The soberly furnished entrance hall, paved with white tiles and black cabochons, leads to a spiral staircase with a stone balustrade. On the left is a fine, massive Louis III table, and on the right are plaster replicas, artfully painted and patinated, of sculptures by Antoine Coysevox. Opposite them are two upholstered benches. On the walls are engravings in the austere style of French painter Nicolas Poussin.

Still on the ground floor is a study bearing shelves filled with calf-bound volumes in a full range of autumnal tones, from the palest ochre to the darkest burnt sienna. The large desk is adorned with bronzes such as those produced by Boulle for the Elector of Bavaria. Some fine Louis XIV chairs and Régence armchairs occupy the room—rich, harmonious, virile furniture, worthy of an individual of a certain rank who brings an air of respectability to the room. The study not only extends into a billiard room, but also gives directly onto a small garden, to which the foliage of Parc Monceau confers an unexpected, dreamy air. Straight off this room is a bedroom boasting a canopy bed draped in floral brocade. A door decorated in *trompe l'oeil* leads to the boudoir.

Upstairs are the reception rooms. The walls of the landing and the wide, semi-circular corridor remain bare, apart from gilded bronze appliqué lamps that alternate with stone plinths bearing imposing bronze animals.

A large salon overlooks the trees in the park, which seem within reach of the stone balcony. On the walls—painted in a subtle pale gray pattern simulating large chalky

Above: Certain legendary buildings spark envy and curiosity concerning the lucky occupants. This is the case at number 1 Avenue de l'Observatoire, which simultaneously overlooks the Luxembourg Gardens, Boulevard Saint-Michel, and beyond. Stained glass windows decorate the main staircase.

Right: A staircase in a grand bourgeois home in the Faubourg Saint-Germain neighborhood rises in a perfect spiral. The white landing tiles, interspersed with black cabochons, date from the seventeenth century.

slabs—are symmetrically hung ancestral portraits of no particular monetary value, along with two hunting scenes by André Max Leroy and another painting, by Nicolas de Largillierre, that miraculously escaped preemption by the national museums when it surfaced in the sale rooms. The Louis XIV parquet floor is generously covered with Aubusson carpets, while several fine, austere pieces of furniture complement armchairs and sofas from the same period, covered in petit-point upholstery from the Beauvais tapestry workshop. What was long called the "grand genre" has here found a refuge. It conveys order, serenity, power.

THE CHALLENGE OF RECONSTITUTION. When obliged to leave the Eure-et-Loire region (where they had been living in an old mill) and to return to the capital, a family of Parisian stock decided to pursue its dream of "getting away from it all," of mapping personal space onto imaginary continents, of recovering vanished charms— namely those of provincial life, and in particular the appealing austerity of the Lozère region. The challenge was to recreate, in a duplex right in the heart of Paris, a setting that artfully evokes the desired change of scenery, which for many is an essential condition of domestic contentment. Here it entailed reconstituting—without pastiching—the special atmosphere of a fourteenth-century Lozère château, the fixed point around which a timeless interior was anchored. This "early period" style is, alas, all too rarely associated with the idea of comfort that many think indispensable to personal happiness.

A family of Parisian stock gambled on being able to recreate the atmosphere of a Lozère château right in the heart of the capital. Impeccable care was taken with every detail: the quality of the furniture and objects, the harmony of colors, the choice of artworks and flooring (of imported materials). The "early period" furniture was chosen with great discernment. The dining room (*left*) includes an easel holding a painting of fine dimensions. A fifteenth-century manuscript is placed on the gueridon table (*below*) inlaid with Renaissance marquetry. In the large salon (*right*), a setting sun softens the imposing atmosphere.

Without succumbing to the tendency to obsessively accumulate and systematize everything, this family undertook a relentless hunt designed to flush out furniture and objets worthy of their reconstitution, which entailed a whole ethic rather than a specific aesthetic. Since success was far from certain, the master of the house pulled out all the stops: having found a traditional cabinetmaker who he felt could execute his dream, and learning that this craftsman was about to close his workshop on Faubourg Saint-Antoine, he bought out the business and installed the carpenter in Lozère, near his own château. The desired alchemy subtly took effect. The move was doubly ideal for the craftsman in terms of easy access not only to the high-quality wood required for the project but also to his favorite pastime, trout fishing. Here he

could reveal his talent for crafting forms which, in the style of that early period, were more important than decorative details, insofar as the interior decoration reflected a certain Jansenist austerity.

The inner shutters, stairway, and doors were thus produced on the spot, not far from the models of inspiration (rather than slavishly copied), before leaving for Paris. The result is an extraordinary coherence, a perfection of forms representing a reaction to the Italianate taste of the Valois dynasty. The relentless precision of detail is accentuated by the presence of high-quality paintings and tapestries. These features are not only a mark of authenticity but also instill a sense of emotion detectable only in an interior with true soul, one where every object—book, silver piece, bouquet of flowers—is neither useless nor pointless, but has its own necessity.

Louis XV Intimacy

By the dawn of the eighteenth century, Paris had become the unchallenged capital of elegance and good taste. The almighty Louis XIV had wished it thus, and so it came to pass, despite the monarchy's move to Versailles.

Following the death of Louis XIV, cabinetmakers to the regent—Cressent, Criaerdt, Dubois, and Lebas—excelled in certain types of furniture such as flat desks and bowed commodes with curved legs. Then came the Louis XV style, which perfectly corresponded to the reign of "the Well-Beloved" king, and which was typified by the rococo style, a harmonious and

softened form of baroque. This French version of a foreign style represented a revolt against earlier taste, a transition toward a logic revamped from top to bottom, resulting in the creation of many pieces of furniture unknown till then. The curve reigned supreme, as seen in the fine collections of the Musée Nissim de Camondo. Opulent, teeming curves combined form and decoration into a single object, prevailing on harmony to determine the quality, comfort, and aesthetics of a piece of furniture. This approach culminated in a chair, salon, or bedroom that subtly blended concern for form with necessity of function, fearlessly embracing the femininity characteristic of a monarch who identified himself, right from

The decor of the Musée Nissim de Camondo, near Parc Monceau, recreates the intimate atmosphere sought by the marquise de Pompadour, the arbiter of eighteenth-century taste. Built in 1910–1912 to house the eighteenth-century collection of Moïse de Camondo, the museum (named after the founder's son) offers one of the purest examples of the style of that period, not only in the confident choice of furniture and objects but also in the way they are arranged, capped by a selection of fabrics and harmonious bouquets that enliven the salons. The extensive use of gilding is exemplified by a mirror (*far left*) with gilded bronze clock and candlesticks beneath a portrait of *ancien-régime* politician Jacques Necker. Meanwhile, a Louis XV chaise longue (*left*), known as a *duchesse brisée*, basks in the play of shadow and light.

the start, with the mythological figure of Eros rather than Mars.

The invasive sensuality of these curves could perhaps be seen as the unspoken desire to feminize the lifestyle at court. Indeed, the king's obsessive relationships with the fair sex all too often distracted him from his obligations. He even placed the object of his desire, Madame de Pompadour, beyond the reach of court, thereby investing her with terrific power. The marquise de Pompadour—whose brother, the marquis de Marigny, was Superintendent of Royal Buildings and, following a voyage to Italy, the advocate of a return to classicism—had a significant impact on the taste of the day. She was the first to break with the tradition of stately salons, retreating to more intimate rooms propitious to flirtatious games, in which she excelled and for which she had new types of furniture created. Reading stands, small writing desks, wine coolers, and coffee tables were developed with light, flowing lines and decorated with gilded bronze scrolls, Coromandel lacquer, marquetry, or elegant japanning.

The art of fine living had reached its height, becoming synonymous with the "sweet life" that aging French statesman Charles Maurice de Talleyrand would later remember so nostalgically.

Paris furnishings thus came to represent "French taste" par excellence and spread beyond the kingdom's borders. The Electors of Bavaria and Saxony, the Palatinate princes, the king of Poland, and, later, Catherine the Great of Russia all sought furnishings from Paris. The truth is that even today the furniture coveted by the wealthy is supplied by famous Paris cabinetmakers, whose work continues to command extravagant prices.

Rococo decoration drew its inspiration from endless interpretation of floral and mineral motifs, to the point of saturation. Yet it miraculously avoided derivativeness, and managed to express seductiveness by lyrically and eternally linking abstraction to sensuality. Even today it contributes a touch of refinement to contemporary settings, surfacing naturally to either convey a festive air or underscore the sensual, feminine side of fine living, the essence of Paris. For this reason, it is almost impossible to enter a modern Paris apartment without detecting a few echoes, however discreet, of the Louis XV style: the wood of bergère-style armchairs, now upholstered in leather, may be painted to accentuate curves without exaggerating them, so as to harmonize with a sofa of simple lines, a low table generally of glass, and other furnishings in the same spirit. All will be arranged casually yet with distinction, eschewing the studied elegance that is the very opposite of real elegance (French author Balzac claimed that studied elegance was "to true elegance what a wig is to hair").

Among Parisians least bound by the laws of classicism, there unconsciously arises a desire for superior refinement, which is often expressed by the acquisition of an item of Louis XV furniture, whether woodwork, or object. Even if it is soon relinquished, the item incarnates a taste that obstinately resurfaces from one generation to another, in a clear attempt to generate the greatest possible harmony within a single space.

Above: The bedroom of the Musée Nissim de Camondo is adorned with a gilded bronze and steel bed dating from the 1790s.

Far left: The walls of the small study, with its Louis XV sofa, are lined with the cherry red Indian silk often used for a "cabinet of curiosities."

Below left: A fine vase sits on a plinth in the midst of the flowery foliage in the garden.

Village Atmosphere

THE SPIRIT OF A PLACE. Just as a chance encounter may make or break a person's life, so a trip, object or conversation may lead to a change in surroundings that will, in turn, alter other attitudes. This is because people do not behave in the same way in a loft as they do in a wood-paneled apartment.

In the case of interior decorator Josy Broutin, it was her love at first sight with a seventeenth-century apartment that led to a change in surroundings. She is one of those rare, demanding individuals who stops at nothing in their quest for perfection, hunting for perfect specimens like a passionate entomologist. After their marriage, Monsieur and Madame Broutin first lived amidst a turn-of-the-century decor enlivened by some 1930s furniture, then they evolved toward Second Empire furnishings. Finally, a new home dictated their ultimate style: everything would be late seventeenth or early eighteenth century. Josy Broutin favors the aesthetic value of a building over its actual pedigree. She is sensitive to its power of literary evocation and its ability to blend with other objects, because objects enjoy indulging in conversation— for their true nature tends to emerge from the quality of their dialogue as much as from their intrinsic value.

The most important aspect of successful interior decorating is correctly grasping the spirit of the desired period. Since it is essential to eliminate any strange, parasitical trends that might threaten the whole operation, a decorator must remain constantly on the lookout for impostors. The source of all incongruities, according to Broutin, resides in the temptation to succumb to aestheticism, whereas style is basically an ethic and an overall harmony.

In Broutin's home, Nantes floor parquetry determined the arrangement of the entrance hall. Below two late-seventeenth-century wall lamps are aligned six Portuguese chairs from the same period, with painted decoration. Opposite them is a shapely sideboard on which sits an eighteenth-century Venetian gilded wood reading stand, flanked by two pairs of ecclesiastical taper holders from the same period, as well as a painting of Jesus and Mary Magdalen. The whole setting is escorted by armchairs of the same origin as the chairs. On the ceiling, the colors of a largish, early-nineteenth-century chandelier of painted metal echo the Renaissance-style portière (door-hanging) in fabric designed by Mariano Fortuny. The salon, meanwhile, which boasts an imposing, nineteenth-century crystal chandelier, is organized around a gilded wooden Louis XV bed and a seventeenth-century Venetian console table with its leg bracket carved in an angel motif. This setting seems more village-like than Parisian. Whereas the details and choice of fabrics and objects reflect a feminine spirit, the overall climate is masculine, due to a somewhat rugged look, a calmness tending

Above: For interior decorator Josy Broutin, an interior should reflect an entire ethic. For her clients, she creates furnished landscapes in the image of the inhabitants. She is known for delicate proportions and a timeless sense of intimacy, as seen in this bedroom, where an early-seventeenth-century Dutch canopy bed is garnished with an eighteenth-century silk valance and a tester in Fortuny fabric.
Lower right: The bed, which dominates the room, nevertheless leaves enough space for two nicely curved eighteenth-century Italian armchairs in painted wood, plus a table, covered in fabrics from the same period, that hosts a collection of gilded wood boxes.
Far right: In the entrance hall, a still life of fruit is organized around Louis XVI candlesticks and place settings, while in the kitchen (*extreme right, top and bottom*), a large upright cupboard receives the last rays of the sun.

Above: A highly artful disorder reigns in the home of Dominique and Pierre Bénard-Dépalle, allowing objects to exist in their own right. They merely have to coexist with their neighbors in a setting whose harmony defies every law of order and symmetry.

Far right: In the dining room, a seventeenth-century French chandelier lights the cage-door cupboards designed by the owners themselves. The shelves hold various items unearthed in France, revealing a penchant for cream-colored Pont-aux-Choux porcelain.

Below: In the garden courtyard, objects are tested before being assigned a role indoors or offered for sale.

toward austerity. An uninformed visitor would perceive this interior as the refuge of a scholarly traveler, so diverse is the origin of the various objects.

THE HEART OF MOUFFETARD. At the back of a discreet courtyard on Rue Mouffetard, in one of the most typical "villages" within the Latin Quarter, Dominique and Pierre Bénard-Dépalle have a large house which serves as a shop of old objects and antiques. They claim to sell bric-a-brac, but they do it with the conscientiousness of the finest antique dealers. Their store, like their home, feels haunted by fictional characters. Figures straight out of Abbé de Brantôme's memoirs or Oscar Wilde's stories—dandies for whom detail is paramount—seem to lurk everywhere. Here, time has come to a halt. Evocative memories, real or invented, abound.

Luminous Louis XVI

Depending on the period, the Louis XV style was sometimes awarded pre-eminence over Louis XVI, and sometimes vice versa. Final judgment is as impossible today as it was for our predecessors. Just as it is not necessary for a Parisian of old stock to give the impression of high social standing in order to win recognition from his or her peers (having a respectable air suffices or, even better, being respectable without assuming that air), so it is for the Louis XV and Louis XVI styles. Their authenticity is so rife with imitation that they now need simply retain that authenticity in order to win respect.

Major aesthetic shifts, of course, rarely heed history, so it is not too surprising that

Above: The candles stacked in this hanging box (as though in some "cabinet of curiosities") reflect the assorted, unmatched feel of country homes.

Right: The crackling fireplace adds life to this interior, frozen in time and space. The strange still life over the mantle seems to come straight out of the shed or attic of some overlooked country house.

Far right, top and bottom: In other rooms, skillfully disparate objects mingle with personal items in the cupboards of Dominique and Pierre Bénard-Dépalle's home which, doubling as an antique shop, is open only on Thursdays.

the "Louis XVI style" predates the reign of that monarch by a good twenty years. Discoveries from excavations at Pompeii and Herculaneum spurred a renewed taste for antique decoration throughout Europe, although French neoclassicism lagged somewhat behind England, where the aristocracy adopted the neoclassic rage en masse. For the first time, Paris had lost the lead, as a result of its indifference to the spirit of travel. People's enthusiasm for furnishings continued to grow. It was good taste to make a gift of furniture, and people were infatuated with novelty. Not only was fashion more than ever a question of "the style of the day," but furniture had to submit to the hard rules of hierarchy, not unlike the gentlemen at court as described in duc de Saint-Simon's memoirs.

Once on the throne, the chaste Louis XVI made no contribution to the new stylistic direction, much less lead it. There was, however, a very real "Marie-Antoinette taste" that had a marked influence until it turned out to be fatal to its instigator. Like the marquise de Pompidour, Louis XVI's queen developed a veritable cult for furnishings and objets d'art throughout her reign, a cult she shared with the king's brothers and many other aristocrats, aesthetes, and financiers in France. Marie-Antoinette had her own personal warehouse; the inventory of her goods reveals the sureness with which she shaped fashion and taste in her day, by ordering pieces from the finest cabinetmakers—the Jacob brothers, Weisweiler, Reisener, Roentgen, and Oeben. These artisans' foreign names illustrate the extent to which Paris was able to attract the best talent from all over Europe.

Marie-Antoinette, much in the spirit of today's thinking on interior decoration and overall harmony, influenced architects who then became more attentive to the organization of space. Furniture and paneling, relieved of the weighty gold of previous reigns, were edged in delicate pastel shades—mauve, daffodil, sea green—usually against a white background, which reminded the queen of her native Austria and represented the final fling of the "grand genre." The contrasting personalities of king and queen were greatly responsible for that period's original ability to ally stately decoration with a taste for comfort. That alliance, however, would soon degenerate.

Lack of awareness of her tragic destiny seemed to drive the fascinating boldness with which the queen imposed her style, pushing decorators to reach ever further in the interpretation and variety of propositions arising from a single theme. This taste then attained the elegant perfection of a civilization that was unknowingly entering its twilight.

The Louis XVI style has certainly been the one most commonly employed in Parisian interiors ever since the Second Empire. The most famous example, of course, is that of fashion designer Christian Dior. Dior, whom Françoise Giroud described as "warm if distant," adored the Louis XVI style. He had his friend Victor Grandpierre decorate his bedrooms and library, while the living rooms were handled by another friend, Georges Geffroy. These same interior decorators were responsible for Dior's fashion house on Avenue Montaigne, still symbolized by an armchair with a gray and white medallion motif. As the incarnation of Parisian chic and luxury, Dior is now associated throughout the world with this decor, which is nothing other than a bourgeois pastiche of an

Above: A half-moon Louis XVI commode, signed Dubois, with white-on-blue japanning depicts *putti* at play. It is found in the showroom of Jean-Marie Rossi, an antique dealer of great stature, due to his size as well as to the unique eighteenth-century objets d'art found in his shop on Faubourg Saint-Honoré.
Right: A Louis XV commode, stamped Joseph, in oak with ebony veneer, decorated with lacquered panels.

Above the gilded bronze frieze with a lion's head is a very rare clock set on an elephant of Saxony porcelain, flanked by two eagle-head candelabra of gilded bronze.

aristocratic style. True enough, in the meantime the aristocracy had become purely ornamental, its offspring becoming the playthings of *haute-couture* designers.

PASSIONATE ABOUT STYLE. The most extravagant and poetic example of addiction to the Louis XVI style, however, is the case of Madame D. She inherited—along with many wonderful pieces of furniture, paintings, and objets d'art—a magnificent Louis XVI commode stamped with the mark of famous cabinetmaker Jean-Henri Riesener. It was love at first sight. When Madame D delivered the commode to a specialist for minor restorations, the restorer discovered a secret drawer holding a letter whose contents cannot be revealed here without betraying the illustrious family to which it belongs. From that day, however, the letter has governed Madame D's life. Her devotion to the Louis XVI style became total, as though inspired by divine grace. She scoured antique shops and auction rooms in search of chairs (by Jacob), tables, desks (she owns an admirable one by Weisweiler), beds, clocks, appliques, and any other curio in that style, simultaneously relegating other pieces of furniture to her secondary residences or selling them off.

She even moved, having bought the finest neoclassic mansion on the Paris market, and in five years reconstituted the most accurate and balanced Louis XVI interior imaginable. The edged paneling and the damask silk fabrics, specially woven in Lyon (from original workshop models) to harmonize with the upholstered chairs and generally blue pastel walls, create a climate of surprising, indeed troubling, authenticity.

Only the outstanding furniture and objects that pass though the hands of the grand Parisian antique dealer Jean-Marie Rossi can give any idea of this effect.

Thrilled by the idea of living in a setting this perfect, she instructed her cook to prepare meals dating from the eighteenth century, supplying him with a rare culinary library. Then, little by little—almost imperceptibly, according to her friends—her vocabulary began to change, her phrasing took on a different rhythm. When she very courteously received the author for an interview during the preparation of this book, she was dressed in a floor-length tea gown of French-blue moiré taffeta, with a stole of Liège lace across her bosom. Her hair, powdered and piled high, was offset by a scarf. It hardly needs pointing out that she served tea in a Sèvres service that once belonged to Marie-Antoinette.

While it is impossible, alas, for readers to visit this residence, they can always go to the Musée des Arts Décoratifs where the famous Bariolle Salon, which boasts numerous items originally decorating the hôtel de Serres, has been superbly restored thanks to the generosity of baronne Marie Hélène de Rothschild. In fact, Madame D's salon is very accurately evoked via the decorative woodwork in shades of sky blue, gold, beige and white, the pier-glasses and bas-reliefs in biscuit, as well as the upholstery, tapestries and armchairs in shades of harmonious blue.

By their very nature, Parisians make an obsession of flaunting their liberty. It is hardly surprising if readers, when leafing through these pages, are stuck by the eclectic, free-wheeling way that Parisians combine ideas and styles. Most of those

styles harmonize and coexist comfortably, as long as they echo the specific character and lifestyle of a given individual. Even if certain mysterious trends and styles transcend changing fashions—the notorious "current taste" which interior decorators cannot totally ignore—there are a few essential guidelines that must be respected: sobriety, unity, and harmony of materials, colors, main lines, and volumes. The only error is pointlessness. Given those rules, nothing outlaws combining Italian straight chairs with English armchairs and a Louis XV sofa, as long as proportions, floors, and walls create a setting that successfully harmonizes the whole.

From Empire to Restoration

The Empire style, though highly valued in the provinces for its perfectly homogeneous suites of (generally) mahogany furniture, is rarely found in Parisian interiors. While this may represent an unconscious rejection of Napoleon, the real reason is certainly aesthetic and functional. Indeed, "domestic" Empire furniture is simultaneously austere and unsociable, insofar as it blends poorly with other styles, due to the specificity of its highly pronounced decorative vocabulary, which is as dry as a Napoleonic code of decoration.

Direct descendant of the neoclassicism of the *ancien régime*, Empire style is strongly marked by the "Egyptian revival" trend, whose pharaonic symbolism haunted the young General Bonaparte's dreams of absolute power. But, similar to the victor of the battle of Arcole, it would get flabbier as the reign progressed. Sphinxes, griffons, chimeras, and elaborately crowned

Right: A Louis XVI console table with curved corners orders this marvelous ensemble arranged by antique dealer Jean-Marie Rossi. The decoratively edged marble shelves and top hold an outstanding Louis XV service in soft-paste porcelain from the Sèvres and Vincennes manufactories. The floral service contains no fewer than 147 plates and several rare dishes, such as a pair of tureens used for stews and ragouts, known as *pots à oille*. In the foreground is a wooden Louis XVI armchair, painted pale gray and upholstered in a fine tapestry from the Beauvais workshop.

pharaohs appeared on the arms of chairs and the legs of tables and commodes.

After the Consulate period, however, Egyptomania swiftly faded in favor of ornamentation conveying—with no ambiguity this time—the imperial epoch's thirst for monumentality and power. Stars, bees, eagles, and swans as well as winged one-foot lions, caryatids, and war trophies began decorating objects, woodwork, and furniture. The most popular items were the chaise longue made fashionable by Madame Récamier and the cheval glass (a free-standing swing mirror) that became the Empress Joséphine's fetish piece of furniture.

The volute became as typical of the Empire as the straight line was of Louis XVI style. But despite a search for suppleness, Empire furnishings and settings remained stiff and rigid, betraying the taste of a society that had no aesthetic tradition of its own, no art of fine living. Those in power simply mimicked an extinct class; the style of its furniture was nothing but pastiche, guaranteed a long life insofar as it appeared eminently "suitable." The furniture of the day soon renounced heroism (like many imperial generals) in order to become unconditional disciples of comfort. The hôtel de Beauharnais (now the German Embassy on Rue de Lille) best expresses these aesthetic aspirations in all their grandeur.

The nostalgia that Parisians have for a comfortable rural lifestyle—houses set among greenery, salons and bedrooms opening onto floral balconies and terraces—has rehabilitated the Restoration style associated with the reigns of Charles X and Louis-Philippe. The most significant contributions of those reigns, which hardly

The choice and arrangement of objects in the home of fabric merchant Dominique Kieffer clearly betray a woman's touch. She is a true Parisienne-by-adoption, who still dreams of the attractions of life far from the city. She evokes these attractions in her house in the 16th Arrondissement by artfully combining rustic furniture from various periods, mostly Louis-Philippe and Restoration, with numerous objects and fabrics of her own design.

aspired to glory, are perhaps the "Voltaire" armchair (a comfortable mutation of the "bergère" chair) and the mirrored wardrobe (a rather chubby heir to the cheval glass). Although lacking rigor, these styles encourage a mix–and-match approach that occasionally yields felicitous encounters. They are comfortable and practical (an important new piece of furniture entered salons at that point—the work basket) and were marked by a certain flabbiness, like the kings themselves, dully accepting the invasion of countless, often opaline, knick-knacks. Indeed, people liked to stack and cover things—clocks and dried flowers were placed under globes, and tables and pianos were covered with carpets. Yet the Restoration styles cannot be rejected, given their seductive qualities. The wealth and variety of potential interpretations, along with a compatibility

with other styles, often produce ensembles of irreproachable charm and comfort.

A fine example is provided by Dominique Keiffer's house, in the 16th Arrondissement of Paris. The two-story house is surrounded by a quiet garden with paths lined with boxwood and acanthus, shaded by chestnut trees and a large ash. To the right, off the entrance way, is a spacious kitchen, with the dining room to the left. The salon, overlooking the garden, is furnished with Louis-Philippe and Restoration furniture made of fruitwoods, as well as linen-upholstered sofas. The paintings have been chosen more for their association with friends or with places visited than for their intrinsic or artistic value—family items, related once again to the vagaries of vacations and souvenirs of friendships.

Capricious Collections

Fashions for the home can have an impact on living space, choice of site, and selection of one neighborhood rather than another. Similarly, they spur various transformations and derivations.

In recent years, there has been a renewed interest in displaying art at home in the seventeenth-century manner, which gave rise to the domestic "painting gallery." In those days, collecting paintings was in the best of taste, as Monsieur de Coulanges assured the marquise de Sévigné in a letter: "Paintings are all the rage . . . when you have enough for every bedroom, you can decorate your courtyards and forecourts." In the eighteenth century, the collecting mania spurred the development of what was called the "cabinet of curiosities" (a

This page: A collection of portraits and miniatures of ancestors creates a mildly nostalgic atmosphere in the home of fabric merchant Manuel Canovas (*top*). His workspace is adorned with orders of chivalry inherited

from the family. The severe if elegant Louis XVI desks bask in the soft light of a French window (*bottom*), while a terra-cotta statue (*left*) sits on an eighteenth-century stand.
Far right: Interior decorator Jean-Louis Riccardi has created a theatrical atmosphere in his own home by combining eighteenth-century Italian and nineteenth-century furniture, along with the objects he enjoys collecting.

small room of art works and curios). In both cases, special rooms—galleries or studies—were designed to house the collection.

WINDOW ON THE PALAIS-ROYAL. Jacques Grange, an interior decorator solicited by the likes of fashion designer Yves Saint-Laurent and French actress Isabelle Adjani, moved from his apartment near Place Saint-Sulpice to lodgings overlooking the Palais-Royal gardens, once inhabited by novelist Colette. Given this setting steeped in memories, Grange respected Colette's cozy, whimsical tone, all the while including the results of his fruitful hunts for rare, unique, surprising objects. Each object enters into an intriguing conversation with its neighbors. Since modern apartments are not always large enough to house collections worthy of

Jacques Granges is a genius at mixing and matching. He tames rare objects by providing them with a serene setting. Refinement is never flashy in his Palais-Royal apartment. His attitude is most apparent in the arrangement of items, which are the fruit of endless quests to acquire the right object, enabling a nineteenth-century buttoned plush chaise longue to cohabit peacefully with a seventeenth-century Portuguese rug and an early-twentieth-century English stool in mahogany (*top left*). Similarly, "Egyptian revival" candlesticks accompany a painting by Osbert, not far from busts by Janniot and La Gandara, and a photograph of Colette (in a frame by Ettore Bugatti), who once lived in this apartment (*lower left*). The bedroom, meanwhile, features a Louis XVI canopy bed (*right*) adorned with fabric from the Jouy factory. The bedside table is a gueridon that once belonged to Chateaubriand.

Interior decorator Martine Dufour, known for her tact and professionalism, fully adopted the taste and personality of her long-time friend Marin Karmitz when decorating his house. Here the goal was to organize a comfortable space that could also house the art works that Karmitz has long collected. Beneath a bush in the kingwood-floored garden (*left*) hides a sculpture by Germaine Richier, while the adjoining dining room (*right*) boasts a totem figure by Gaston Chaissac opposite a Chinese screen. Thonet cane-backed chairs filter the light.

the name, recent taste has favored vast spaces such as factories, schools, theaters, and print shops, converted into museum-apartments. These new spaces should not, however, be confused with the rage for lofts in the late 1970s and early 1980s, imported from New York and now synonymous with "politically correct" housing.

PRIVATE MUSEUM ON THE LUXEMBOURG GARDENS. Moreover, upper middle-class houses and large bourgeois apartments have undergone certain transformations that permit them to receive and display art works in worthy fashion.

When the collector is a cultured and inspired art-lover, such as film producer Marin Karmitz, such collections can rival commercial galleries and even museums. His house, built by the architect who designed

Works of art govern the organization of space in the home of Marin Karmitz.

Above: A work of art in paper by Chilida hangs above a desk by Alvar Alto.

Right: An oil painting by Bernard Dufour dominates the staircase leading from the entrance and dining room to the living room, while shelves cleverly provide space for smaller works by Bonnard, Gonzalez, Goya, Spoerri, and Arnulf Rainer.

Far right, top: In the living room, wood-and-metal bookshelves by René Herbst encourage a dialogue between art works by Germaine Richier, Tàpies, and Boltanski.

Far right, bottom: The bedroom features works by the likes of Giacometti and Soulages.

the Salpêtrière Hospital, sits opposite the Luxembourg Gardens. Furnishings by Pierre Chareau and striking bookshelves designed by René Herbst accompany art works by the likes of Tapiès, Degottex, Bernard Dufour, Henri Michaux, and Germaine Richier, not to mention nineteenth-century Japanese bronzes, simple Chinese tables adorned with sensual lacquerwork, a seventeenth-century Dutch burgomaster's armchair, and Anglo-Indian armchairs from the days of the British Empire. Everything here reflects the deepest instincts of a collector whose taste turns simultaneously toward the classical, the modern, and the contemporary. Karmitz's ideal is attained thanks to the quiet coexistence of works clearly chosen by a true connoisseur, a discerning aesthete able to appreciate and combine diverse styles, a lover of forms which forge discreetly original alliances. This meant that his interior decorator, a long-time friend of Karmitz, had to fulfill a double imperative: she had to open up the reception space, and at the same time encourage a dialogue between the individual works of a collection carefully built with the specific intent to engender a subtly harmonious relationship between the objects, and thereby lend them soul.

The garden, a largish rectangle spreading over a courtyard with foliage-covered walls, is planked with deep-red kingwood—the one truly striking note of color in this residence of subtle monochromes (stemming from choice of materials as well as choice of colors). Although outdoors, the garden does not completely break with the interior; there is an invisible border between these two worlds, which entertain an ongoing dialogue that evolves with the season

The so-called Maison Opéra, built by Charles Garnier, who designed the Paris opera house, is a model of Second Empire style. It boasts a skillful combination of colors and overabundant furniture, objets d'art, carpets, tapestries and paintings (*right*). The indoor garden (*above*) links the blue salon to the dining room. Flower tubs decorated with Nevers porcelain contrast nicely with the low, buttoned plush chairs.

and the light. The same goes for the dining room, which rises into an elegant staircase flanked by clever shelves for displaying small paintings (an oil by Bonnard, two gouaches by Gonzalez, a collage by Spoerri, a chalk drawing by Goya, a work by Arnulf Rainer). Everything here, from the hallway to the attic, serves as a discreet setting for art works that never destroy the feeling of intimacy. They nurture a meditative mood with every glance, weaving a skein of paths propitious to vagrant musings that never contradict a desire for coherence between thought and action. A determination to turn art works into life's special companions (rather than a show of images) reigns with both discretion and rigor, whether in the office, the children's room, the master bedroom, or a modest corner. They accompany a life devoted to action as well as to acquiring a broader perspective on existence.

Second Empire Opulence

Paris, the capital of good taste—these words have a certain stiffness and ostentation about them, incompatible with the very idea of taste. They nevertheless bespeak a tradition, and refusing to acknowledge that tradition would plunge the world into uncertainty and obliterate the memory of all those brilliant, capricious, lively souls who forged this taste down through the centuries. Without all that feminine talent, people today would not be so free in matching furniture to curtains or choosing a garment.

Yet this is also tyrannical Paris, the city of Parisiennes who raised it to unmatched levels of excellence and hedonism.

Ever since the Renaissance—more precisely since the days of Catherine de' Medici and the princesse de Clèves—no Paris salon could survive without a feminine presence. For instance, Madame d'Epinay, a woman of much feeling and even more intellect, was not only friend and patroness of Jean-Jacques Rousseau but was also highly regarded by Voltaire, who delightfully described her as, "my philosopher, the brilliant eagle in a gauze cage." She played hostess to the entire mid-eighteenth-century philosophical crowd, including Diderot who became a regular visitor after initially avoiding her, and German writer Melchior Grimm, who was her lover for over a quarter of a century. Then there was Madame du Deffand, who needs no introduction, and the duchesse de Berry; more recently, the same role has been played by the vicomtesse Marie-Laure de Noailles.

The "First Estate" clearly coalesced around the salons of cultivated women, who received guests in harmonious settings that were more than just magnificent, insofar as they conveyed an exquisite savoir-faire that made it seem as though the armchairs themselves knew how to engage in conversation. Such women played a primordial role in the growing renown and influence of Paris. In addition to the famous salon hostesses, there were the contributions of royal favorites like the marquise de Pompadour and queens such as Marie-Antoinette and Empress Joséphine, all of whom left a major mark on the taste of their times. And there was the correspondence of the princesse Palatine, sister-in-law of Louis XIV, whose judgment she was able to inflect through intelligence and diplomacy as well as

through her strength of character and Rhenish turn of phrase.

Yet the truth of the matter is that everything remained within a tight circle until the Second Empire. Wit and taste were shared among the members of a closed society that the French Revolution never succeeded in totally dismantling.

Although now appreciated for its decorative qualities and comfort, the Second Empire style was the unfortunate outcome of a long series of poor imitations that ultimately yielded an accomplished form of thoroughly debased taste. Three hundred years of emphasis on taste served to elevate this debasement into a veritable orthodoxy. The cause of this situation was straightforward: desperate for legitimacy, the bourgeoisie aped the aristocracy which, like the emperor himself, imitated the bourgeoisie in turn. The melange of genres was fatal to refined taste, which settled into the "coarseness" of comfort. The Second Empire plumped heavily and enthusiastically for a "nouveau riche" style that would constitute an aesthetic as much as a sensibility or ethic. It nevertheless exported well. Every epoch has the Medici it merits.

After successive pastiches of styles that were vaguely Renaissance, troubadour, Gothic, and archaeological (fashionable in the days of Louis-Philippe), Parisian homes suffered the invasion of the Louis XVI "Empress" style—a pure invention on the part of Empress Eugénie, who wed fashion designers to cabinetmakers in her frantic passion for padded chairs, and whose major obsession was the rehabilitation of Marie-Antoinette. This gave rise to new types of settee with names such as *confident* (seated two) and *indiscret* (seated three). There was also a

four-seat divan which in fact was an even earlier development, since the duchesse de Berry had ordered one for the Tuileries Palace as early as 1821 (it is also worth noting that it was the duchess who first launched the fashion for period furniture, which has survived down to our day, for better or for worse). During the Second Empire, upholsters got the upper hand on cabinetmakers, and would henceforth set the decorative tone—it was a golden age not only of indoor plants, but also of buttoned plush upholstery.

MAISON OPÉRA. When Charles Garnier presented his design for the new opera house in Paris, the prudish Empress Eugénie was appalled by its lavish profuseness. Yet she was ultimately converted beyond all expectations, becoming a fervent advocate of the "all Louis" style (Louis XIV, Louis XV, Louis XVI). It was in this context that Garnier built the hôtel de Bourlon de Rouvre (also known as Maison Opéra), the private residence of Nicole Toussaint du Wast, who has maintained the interior in a

Far left, top: The grand salon of Maison Opéra is sturdily based on red and gold, with decorative floral panels set in gilded frames, impressive bronze chandeliers, upholstered Louis XVI "Empress" sofas and chairs, and a lacquered gueridon table with mother-of-pearl inlay. Nothing is missing, not even the piano.

Far left, bottom: A massive pseudo-Renaissance fireplace dominates the Henri II dining room. Below a candlestick, the sideboard holds nineteenth-century silver and baroque shells. *Left*: In a corner of the salon, a Napoleon III sofa in Louis XVI style flaunts its lavish floral pattern.

state of perfect conservation. Built between 1865 and 1870 in the new residential quarter of Miromesnil, the house represents the apotheosis of Second Empire decoration.

THE APARTMENTS OF THE DUC DE MORNY. Unlike Marie-Antoinette, whose sense of taste was both innate and the product of a venerable heritage, Empress Eugénie nurtured pretensions that often provoked sniggers behind her back. Obviously, no one dared rival the empress, but the princesse Mathilde Bonaparte (initially betrothed at an early age to her cousin, the future Napoleon III) desired to reign over the taste of her times. Supported by her companion Nieuwerkerke, Superintendent of Fine Arts, as well as by the duc de Morny, she influenced cultural developments by holding a double salon,

Right: The grand salon—or Turgot salon—in the duc de Morny's apartments in the Louvre is a perfect example of the stately Second Empire style. Organized around a circular sofa topped by a palm tree and a 180-light chandelier by Barbedienne, the salon incarnates all the archetypes associated with the Second Empire: Louis XV furniture, plush chairs around gilded or lacquered gueridon tables, lighter chairs with lyre backs, Sèvres china, wall paneling and Corinthian pilasters gilded with gold leaf. The curtains are of damask silk, with fringed valances.
Left: Painted ceilings in the duke's apartments include the dining room with its panoramic garden arbor, and the grand salon depicting the various ages of the Louvre.

Above: The famous Lucas-Carton restaurant on Place de la Madeleine is a magnificent example of the foliage-inspired inventiveness of Art Nouveau as practiced by Louis Majorelle, one of its major French advocates. A sideboard topped with shelves and a wicker flower vase dominates the main dining room, infinitely reflected in its mirrored walls.
Right: The decorative handles of the sideboard are in gilded bronze.

emperor and empress painted by Franz Winterhalter.

Once adapted and softened, the permissive Second Empire style allowed for unsuspected combinations, superimpressions, and juxtapositions of fabrics. Prayer rugs could be used as upholstery, and petit-point tapestry was matched with densely patterned wallpaper against which were hung architects' drawings, sepia photographs, oriental-style paintings, and family—or purported family—portraits.

It was warm and comfortable, and exuded wealth on a large or small scale. It was difficult to go wrong—or, in fact, very easy. The style was falsely gay because, in fact, it was as lugubrious as an Offenbach operetta. In short, Proust's bourgeois Madame Verdurin would soon be transposed into his elegant princesse de Guermantes.

both literary and artistic, which drew leading figures such as Prosper Mérimée.

The duc de Morny's apartments at the Louvre now make it possible to admire one of the finest Second Empire style ensembles still intact, along with Maison Opéra. Its stately gilded woodwork, chandeliers, thick carpets, and dense braiding are accompanied by furniture composed, in the grand salon, of a circular settee crowned by a palm tree, Louis XVI "Empress" armchairs, and comfortable gilded wood chairs and poufs upholstered in deep red damask. All seats were strangely low, for the true monarchs of the day were the courtesans, and their habits colored everything. Tables and stools—as well as decorative woodwork in the form of Corinthian columns—were all gilded with gold leaf. In the antechamber opposite are copies of the portraits of

From Art Nouveau to Art Deco

Mired in the Second Empire style, good taste was about to expire when there suddenly emerged, from England (for once!), the Arts and Crafts movement, which subsequently inspired Art Nouveau. William Morris launched the trend in London, and Charles Rennie Macintosh developed it in Glasgow, until its floral shoots were extending into Germany, Belgium, and France. Although its exuberance met with praise in France (notably for taking nature as its source), the movement was condemned for its very excessiveness or, more chauvinistically, for its foreign origins.

Several major artists and architects of various nationalities working mainly in

Paris and Nancy—such as Guimard, Gallé, Majorelle, Grasset, Carabin—seized on these ideas and produced dazzlingly inventive ensembles. In Paris, Hector Guimard in particular designed a large number of buildings and houses, the most striking of which are two private residences, one on Rue Fontaine in the 9th Arrondissement and the other at 8 Villa-de-la-Réunion in the 16th Arrondissement. His architecture displays unbridled virtuosity, not only in the lines of thrust that define facades and determine the distribution of interior space, but also in the boldness of materials. He harmoniously combined ceramics with both plain and varnished brick, rough-hewn and dressed stone, and cast and wrought iron—in short, he called on every convention.

In addition to these examples, Art Nouveau influence—which owes its French title of nobility to Guimard's decoration of the Paris Metro—can be seen on numerous apartment buildings and private residences. Thus at 14 and 16 Rue d'Abbeville (see page 6), two buildings present two decorative themes, in different materials, in a turn-of-the-century style. On Avenue de Wagram, meanwhile, the Céramic Hôtel boasts a facade entirely covered in polychrome tiles.

Although it returned to fashion in the late 1960s, Art Nouveau never truly conquered contemporary interior decoration, having been designed for a totally homogeneous context, in which architecture also played a role. On the other hand, it is not rare to encounter handsome objets d'art or furniture in the turn-of-the-century style decoratively echoing contemporary items or—in certain country-style town interiors—responding to rustic furniture made of fruitwoods.

Right: Bob and Chesca Vallois have created an ideal setting for their collection of Art Deco furniture and contemporary art work. Their apartment flanks a lush indoor garden, and hosts art by Jean-Pierre Raynaud, César, and Sol LeWitt, alongside furniture by Ruhlmann, Chareau, and Frank.
Left: An armchair by Jean-Michel Frank, sculptures by Bernard Venet and Miklos.
Below: Detail of a polychrome chair by Miklos.

While examples of apartments decorated in an Art Nouveau style are rare or even nonexistent in the Paris of the 1990s, the same is not true of the Art Deco or "1930s Modern" style. Since comfort is part and parcel of its classical beauty, this style has justifiably endured. It is admired for its balanced volumes, elegant details, and sensual materials. At home almost everywhere, it can provocatively impose itself as the tasteful bridge linking bold combinations of styles. Two homes provide outstanding examples of this gambit—that of Bob and Chesca Vallois, and that of Denis Doria.

RUE DE SEINE ANTIQUE DEALERS. Located not far from their antique store, the apartment of Bob and Chesca Vallois runs along a greenhouse-garden sporting a fountain and stream. They were among the

first Parisians to successfully assert a passion for furniture from the interwar period. Their secret was their ability to reconcile their fundamental aspirations with the randomness of object-hunting—a subtle type of hunt, if there ever was one.

Of the incredible number of objects, furniture, sculptures, and paintings that have passed through their hands, they have been able to hold onto those which, if not the most spectacular or most timelessly perfect, are at least finely tuned to one another. For this is the home of veritable collectors, that is to say within the humanist tradition—which despite the vicissitudes of time has survived to the present. The Vallois collect in a spirit of historical accuracy and excellence, combined with the pleasure of sharing their discoveries. In this respect, they have had a marked influence on the taste of their contemporaries by providing a new way of seeing and understanding.

The front of the apartment, bathed in light, is perfect for bronzes, sturdy furniture, and rugs. Further back, where the light is softer, works on paper are hung and the more delicate furnishings and objects (in terms of presence, as well as of material) are arranged. In the same way, given the recent effects of economic recession, social hardship, and a return to supposedly timeless values that favor renovating places to their original appearance, Bob and Chesca Vallois demonstrate that a certain late-twentieth-century art of fine living can remain in tune with its times.

ART DECO MOOD. An Art Deco approach, which tends to become an obsession for a period or more precisely for a given designer or decorator (Robert Mallet-Stevens,

Left: In the home of Denis Doria, interior organization reflects an ascetic rigor that stems from the very structure of the space. A large metallic staircase rises freely through the various levels, including the salon with its chairs by Francis Jourdain and Pierre Chareau.

Above: Doria's bedroom, by Chareau, is in sycamore.
Below: The library furniture is signed by Hoffmann and Mackintosh.

Pierre Chareau, Francis Jourdain, or René Herbst), governs the rigorous and somewhat ascetic interior of Denis Doria's home. Here, the collection of objects is transcended by the firmness with which each piece of furniture, each object, each painting, each sculpture and each drawing has been chosen—to respect its creator's mood and philosophy, as well as to attain an absolute harmony that itself conveys an emotion, makes an aesthetic impact, tells a story, radiates contentment. The architecture of the house and the care with which each detail participates in Doria's determined effort at coherence ultimately constitute an overall ethic.

Harmonizing Styles

BACHELOR PAD. Another Parisian tradition is the bachelor's hideaway, known in French as a *garçonnière* even though the age of its occupant does not always accord with the college-student connotations of *garçon* (boy). Instead, Paris bachelor pads are the realm of shameless egocentrism.

Many sites in Paris bear the stamp of great Art Deco designers. Denis Doria's place, for example, harbors a living room dominated by the forms of architects Pierre Chareau and Robert Mallet-Stevens (*top left*). In one corner is an illuminated globe (*top right*). The living room gives onto the dining room, which features applique lamps by Jacques Le Chevallier and a chandelier by Adnet (*lower right*), as well as a glass port decanter and glasses by René Lalique (*lower left*).

Thus, Monsieur G has established his private hermitage not far from the Champs-Elysées. At an early age, given his family background, he attained a key post in the fashion industry, and has subsequently commuted between his Paris office, his country home, and meetings in major international cities. His apartment is composed of a large living room, a bedroom, a large entrance hall, and a kitchen with raised dining room. A woman friend who is an interior decorator has organized Monsieur G's space around a flat Régence desk, creating a business universe that oscillates between fantasy and reality; spaces are etched with the rigor typical of a woman of action. The living room, divided into two areas by a few steps, inevitably evokes a retreating sea which has left the shore scattered with objects and furniture (both practical and whimsical). These items appear to have been flushed out during long hunts in antique shops, but in fact come primarily from Monsieur G's family.

Decorator Andrée Putman turns the dreams of Parisian bachelors into reality, thanks to her sure touch and attentiveness to the inhabitant. The living room (*top*) is organized around a large rug by Eileen Gray, a flat Régence desk, an armchair made of horn (detail, *bottom right*), and an eighteenth-century wine cooler by Canabas. The walls are hung with works by Barceló, Kabakov, Garouste, and Twombly. In the bedroom (*bottom left*), a folding door opens onto the bathroom.

Modernists

Innovative decorative artists of the 1920s and 1930s were among the most classical—Jacques-Emile Ruhlmann (justly considered a twentieth-century Riesener), Armand Rateau, Louis Süe, and André Mare designed furniture and interiors in the tradition of eighteenth-century cabinetmakers. They were nevertheless cheered by advocates of the Modernist movement.

Sixty years after the birth of that movement, the hopes of Robert Mallet-Stevens, Pierre Chareau, Charlotte Perriand, René Herbst, Le Corbusier and others are now apparently coming to pass. All were determined to reinvigorate contemporary aesthetics with a beneficent modernity able to pick up the broken thread of a long tradition of elegant taste. A promise fulfilled!

Independently of those two schools, other designers—now highly fashionable—have attempted to reconcile a modern, therefore timeless, style with classical tradition. The most rigorous among them are Jean-Michel Frank and André Arbus.

Frank's taste evokes ascetic discipline and best expresses itself in the invisible, the sole guarantee of true elegance. With

Far left: This screen by Olivier Gagnère evokes paper cut-outs of tribal origin.
Top left: The cubist-style living room features paintings by Aki Kuroda and José Maria Sicilia, a horse by Braque, a Calder mobile, and other art works that converse with the furniture designed by Gagnère.
Bottom left: Gagnère also designed this metal kitchen chair (*left*), whereas the triangular glass lamps in the bathroom were devised by Yoyo Maeght.

Arbus, the evocations are more complex, and his style is more related to his fascination with neoclassical architecture.

Architects, interior decorators, and furniture makers—whom the French now call *designers*—conceived the modern living space as a whole. Each element should contribute to its unity and generate a sense of balance. These enduring ideas continue to inspire Parisian designers and interior decorators, because a style is defined more by overall lines than by items of decor; in this regard, furniture provides the best testimony to a given period, because it determines overall profile or silhouette.

The name of Olivier Gagnère is often associated with a diagrammatic, austere approach. Yet just when everything natural is expunged, it returns in force. Thus for the home of Yoyo Maeght, daughter and granddaughter of famous art dealers, Gagnière profitably perpetuated family tradition by

Architect Jean Nouvel is also an interior decorator. For the owners of the Bailly Gallery on Quai Voltaire, he employed a sophisticated play of mirrors and lacquered walls to create endless reflections of the light falling from a glass-and-metal ceiling, yielding multifaceted, disconcerting lines of vision. The only exceptions to the rigorous monochrome are the teak flooring, a few colorful chairs by Wink, a sofa by Mario Bellini, and a rug by Hilton McConnico. The bathroom (*top and bottom left*) features a bronze sculpture by Wierick.

Right: Hubert Le Gall is a whimsical artist who enjoys mixing the real and the fake, reality and illusion. His *trompe-l'oeil* chimney is an ironic homage to Jean Cocteau and to the interior decoration of the interwar period.

Above: In front of a sideboard that looks as thought it might be the pride of a concierge's apartment, Le Gall has negligently installed a bicycle. The mounted butterflies add an unexpected, colorful note.

Far right: The chairs are by Le Gall, who turned the fireplace into a giraffe which, like every good Paris denizen, is covered in graffiti.

discreetly planting a few traces of its enormous collection in the midst of a heavily geometric space. What might have come across as spectacular is, to the contrary, quiet and almost cozy.

For an apartment over the Bailly art gallery on Quai Voltaire, architect Jean Nouvel chose colors that pay homage to the great Mexican architect Luis Barràgan. Nouvel created a rigorously defined space by playing on light effects to dramatize relentless simplicity.

Hubert Le Gall not only designs furniture and objects, he scatters them across his apartment with rare abandon. One chimney becomes a giraffe, while another is merely a *trompe-l'oeil* effect (although the candelabra are equipped with real lights); the backs of the chairs around the table are decorated with landscaped enamels. Everything startles, everything intrigues, and above all everything seduces, sparking admiration at such unbridled whimsy.

Few Parisians have the luck or desire to live on a river barge on the banks of the Seine. Yet renovated boats can be veritable floating retreats. Jean-Jacques Beaumé's barge combines work by major Art Deco artists with African art and with his own creations.

There are various ways to invoke the role of taste in everyday life: "It's all a question of taste," or "every taste springs from nature." Nevertheless, timeless good taste, constantly evoked, remains indefinable. Approaching the question from the opposite angle, it might be argued that the one thing going for poor taste is that, like an elephant, it is hard to describe but easy to recognize. Poor taste is the worst of crimes, with the exception perhaps of an absence of taste.

Left: Artist Jean-Jacques Beaumé displayed an early interest in Art Deco, successfully marrying that style to his own creations on his houseboat. Beaumé is one of those rare Parisians who actually lives on the Seine, benefiting from a waterfront lifestyle along the quays of the Arsenal harbor near the Bastille. His own work strongly recalls African art, and is more literary and visionary than real (*lower right*). The walls of the dressing room (*lower left*) are covered with raffia on which African fabrics are hung. The sculpture set on Beaumé's rugs in the living room (*right*) is by Jean-Pierre Augé, while the furniture is by Beaumé himself and Jean-Jacques Arguerolles.

PARKS AND GARDENS

Fountains, gazebos, and statues
decorate islands of greenery in the
midst of a realm of stone.
Parisians seek breathing space
and the delights of country living.

aris is an archipelago of villages, each with a patch of green that acts more as a magnet than would a real village square with church and bakery. These parks and gardens—whether formal, hanging, gone to seed, or just recently planted—are miraculous havens of rural scents and fresh air, evoking dreams of the countryside and—height of luxury—a vacation spot in the heart of town. True urban buccaneers are able to seize private spaces, create unlikely hideaways in little-known neighborhoods, and navigate down anonymous streets harboring countless wonders. They are able to carve out a perfect lair that combines the attractions of the city with the peaceful charms of field and wood.

A marked taste for gardens has been a constant feature of this city of stone, one shared by individuals and government alike. From the *ancien régime*'s tradition of royal domains to the Second Empire's (1852–1870) concern for urban health and renewal, the number of parks and gardens grew steadily. Although this trend seemed to wane at the end of the nineteenth century, it has resurfaced all the more strongly in the past fifteen years. Whether miniscule or immense, countless gardens now provide oases of luxuriance, peace, and pleasure.

The squares and parks of Paris embody a poetry whose grace is more sophisticated than might first appear. Like all poetry, it has its own rhetoric and its own tropes: rows of wrought-iron chairs (with their flaking paint); little hoops bordering lawns; heavenly, swinging gates that so fascinate children (similar to every game invented out of nothing); bandstands; merry-go-rounds with wooden horses, creaky old swings,

Preceding pages: One of the most magnificent fountains in Paris is called Les-Quatre-Parties-du-Monde (The Four Parts of the Earth). It was designed by Gabriel Davioud and executed by Jean-Baptiste Carpeaux. Forceful jets of water partially veil the spirited horses, providing a sparkling culmination to the vista down the Jardin de l'Observatoire.

Above: The timeless legend comes true every day: lovers love Paris parks. When in love, the rest of the world ceases to exist—who cares if anyone is watching?
Right: In autumn, sweeping chestnut trees with their yellowing leaves lend a melancholy air to the Luxembourg Gardens.

and sandboxes where first loves are born; gardeners' little cabins of simulated logs; statues representing former heroes; and finally, those notice boards, densely criss-crossed with wire, that display incomprehensible rules and regulations intended for children's nannies and pratical jokers. Everything transpires under the watchful eye of guards—sometimes grumpy, sometimes good-natured—who blow their whistles at unruly children, at lovers, and at closing time.

There is also something indefinable in the air, not unlike that special feeling of being backstage—a headiness that comes from the surrounding harmony, that circulates among the trees, accompanies the rustle of leaves, and escorts the racing children. It swells with the strains of a local brass band that mounts the bandstand after lunch on the first Wednesday of every month (and on Sundays in summer), occupying the octagonal platform with long, stork-like struts that support an immense umbrella aping the dome of the opera house.

Landscape Gardens

Every Parisian has his or her own idea of what a park should be, whether in landscape or formal style. Although space is as a rule extremely limited, a local taste for abundant foliage paradoxically tends to favor "English" landscape gardens over "French" formal gardens. The former prevailed during the Second Empire, the last period of major urban development in Paris, and still largely dominates park aesthetics,

Above: A mascaron in the form of a lion's head adorns a courtyard on Rue Monsieur-le-Prince, not far from the Luxembourg Gardens. It is one of the city's countless decorative details noticed only by the curious.

Below: English philanthropist Richard Wallace donated some sixty-six drinking fountains to Paris in 1871, many of which still exist, notably in Montmartre. They may no longer have a metallic cup and chain, but you can still quench your thirst.

Right: The first rays of sunlight strike the ivy-covered quays of Square Jean-XXIII, at the foot of Notre-Dame, on a hazy spring morning.

even though its detractors claim that its goal of reproducing nature with no apparent ornament requires above all a great deal of space, air, and luxuriant vegetation. Attempting to reproduce this atmosphere in a narrow plot or on a small mound enclosed by four walls is virtually impossible. Yet that is what urban life is about—conquering space, maintaining links to a countryside constantly pushed further away (more ardently desired the more inaccessible it becomes), and drawing energy from these contradictions to spur an inventiveness that adds charm to the city's infernal rhythm.

The trees of Paris are attuned to the sky—that immaterial, light-studded medium—and channel it to solitary souls enchanted by nature's bucolic passions (both wild and civilized). Parks are archipelagos of Edenic inventiveness, of dreams fleetingly come true to the pace of changing seasons, of timeless reveries that thrill the soul.

At the junction of Rue de Sèvres and Rue de Babylone, almost opposite the Hotel Lutetia, a discreet alley named Rue Récamier leads to a square so withdrawn that it seems to be private property. Home to a few fine specimens of rare trees, it is the sole remaining fragment of a garden once belonging to the convent of the Annunciates of the Holy Spirit. Entering this delightful copse almost seems forbidden. And if a sense of melancholy hangs over the strangely terraced maze, that is perhaps because it was also once the garden of the residence overlooking Rue de la Chaise, where Madame Récamier held her glamorous salon, hosting geniuses of the day such as Delacroix, Stendhal, Lamartine,

Musset, and Chateaubriand, who clearly enjoyed many amorous adventures in this neighborhood, despite its prudish image.

Completely different is the working-class neighborhood of Batignolles, to the north of Place Clichy and the distinguished Parc Monceau, as though demonstrating that Paris changes even as it stays the same, from one village to the other. Square des Batignolles seems to be a vestige of the nineteenth century; conceived as a thoroughly nostalgic landscape, the square is right at home in the mist that so often forms at the foot of Montmartre, and its atmosphere is unique. Although called a square, it is actually a miniature park, with a little lake and small waterfall made with rocks hauled from the forest of Fontainebleau. A tiny isle in the middle serves as the base for a somewhat absurd statue of birds. Winding paths create a feeling of vast space, accentuated by little hillocks forming an almost alpine pasture. The square triggers reveries and dreams of voyages, underscored by the rumble of nearby trains heading for Normandy. Designed during the Second Empire by Adolphe Alphand, chief engineer of the Promenades and Plantations Department (established expressly for Alphand by Napoleon III, on Baron Haussmann's advice), Square des Batignolles looks like a small-scale version of Alphand's masterpiece, Parc des Buttes-Chaumont, built on the site of a former quarry where ruffians used to hide out.

Buttes-Chaumont, representing some fifty acres of greenery, is adorned with artificial rocks and grottos, a lake, and a rocky hill crowned by French architect Gabriel Davioud's pastiche of the Sibylline temple

on the grounds of Emperor Hadrian's villa at Tivoli near Rome. Buttes-Chaumont, one of the finest accomplishments of its day, was intended by Baron Georges Eugène Haussmann to open up the northeast sector of Paris, which was slowly asphyxiating. Inaugurated in 1867 for a Universal Exposition, over a hundred years later it remains one of the capital's most surprising parks. It reflects social ambitions strongly influenced by philosopher Saint-Simon's utopianism, and evokes both the sea and the mountains. On the Rue Manin side, every afternoon a clutch of kids thrills to the steep hills and cliffs of artificial rocks, the barriers and benches of simulated wood (as though carved by a Parisian counterpart of the whimsical artist Le Facteur Cheval). Over by Rue Botzaris, the mountains dominate even more, the slopes leading up to the temple magnificently planted with tall trees. This part of the park was inspired by the Jura Mountains in terms of the gravity of its lines, the acuity of its faults, the ruggedness of its relief, and its overall serenity. It offers attractions generally reserved for mountain climbers and hermits, who commune in a rather elegant asceticism. A notorious suspended footbridge arching over the void of a Wagnerian waterfall creates sculptural and aquatic effects appropriate to the precious strangeness of this park, which should be entered, according to writer Louis Aragon, "with a feeling of conquest and the true intoxication of an open mind."

Two other parks landscaped during the Second Empire form pendants to Buttes-Chaumont: Montsouris on the southern rim of Paris, and Monceau in the heart of the residential neighborhoods to the west.

Far left, top: Square Le Gall, not far from the Gobelins Manufactory, offers welcome shade and hooped arbors in a neighborhood worthy of exploration.

Far left, bottom: The cascading foliage of this arbor-staircase flows down a new park on a hillside overlooking the Belleville neighborhood.

Left: The vast park at Buttes-Chaumont boasts not only grassy slopes and winding paths, but also a Roman temple perched on an artificial cliff. On hot days, the "beach" underneath is occupied by local residents as well as visitors from afar who come to enjoy the waterfall, rocky landscape, and hanging bridges.

Above: Square Edouard-Vaillant in Belleville is planted with handsome plane trees around a central gazebo flanked by this unusual greenhouse, which in fact houses only public benches.

Parc Montsouris, not far from the Cité Universitaire where college dorms are located, was also carved out of a former quarry with an unsavory reputation. As distinct from its two companions, it exudes an English charm. Relatively large, its forty acres include gentle slopes around a small lake with still waters ruffled by a rumbling waterfall; the strange atmosphere is underscored by the suburban railroad line that runs down the middle from north to south, cutting the park into two sectors with distinct personalities. Still romantic in feel, it was even more so when graced with a weather station that was a small-scale reproduction of the Bardo Palace in Tunis, built for the Universal Exposition of 1867; unfortunately, it burned to the ground and not a trace remains.

Here, Paris feels distant, even though the bustle of Montparnasse is just a few minutes away. It seems as though only locals frequent the park, as though it were a gigantic square. Parc Montsouris is like a village green in England—the hub of an entire geography of small streets and secret alleys leading to it. Urban sounds fade into the generous mass of foliage shielding all the small houses surrounding the park, giving the neighborhood such a special appeal that its inhabitants, whether here by choice or by chance, no longer think of leaving. Montsouris, the most sentimental of Parisian parks, offers its charms to those intoxicated by solitude. Letting the mind flow with the little stream and waterfall creates an impression of security—here more than anywhere else; every anonymous passerby could well be a friend, by sharing one of Paris's best-kept secrets, untouched

Above and right: Parc Montsouris was the work of Baron Adolphe Alphand, who designed most of the city's parks. A naturalist down to his bones, Alphand created benches, bridges, railings, and other furnishings in the form of artificial vegetation made of reinforced concrete. Here a bridge of artificial tree-trunks spans a stream (*above*). Parc Montsouris with its rolling landscape would seem cut off from the world if the balconies of several high rise buildings did not overlook the bandstand near Rue Gazan (*right*). Further north, near the mysterious mound that masks the Montsouris water reservoir, are alleyways famous for their floral villas.

by changing fashion. More than any other park, Montsouris was designed to delight promenaders—its curving paths reveal unexpected vistas at every turn, its colors shift with every season and from every angle, whether seen from hill, valley, or lake (which, when the park was inaugurated in the presence of the emperor, emptied like a sink).

Villa Gardens

The enchantment of Parc Montsouris extends to certain nearby rustic streets. Lined by wisteria-covered villas, these streets echo the park's attractiveness. Many artists have chosen to reside in this neighborhood. On Rue Nansouty, architect André Lurçat's Villa Guggenbühl is next to painter Georges Braque's red-brick studio with its tall north-facing windows (designed by Auguste Perret, the architect of the Théâtre des Champs-Elysées).

Not far away, at 53 Avenue Reille, more tall windows betray the presence of another artist's studio, namely that of Amédée Ozenfant, who had his friend Le Corbusier design the building. At 101 bis Rue de la Tombe-Issoire is a dead-end alley called Villa Seurat that is lined with houses not only designed for the most part by Lurçat but also inhabited by artistic and literary ghosts—Henry Miller and Anaïs Nin lived there, as did Salvador Dali, Antonin Artaud, Chaïm Soutine, Chana Orloff (whose studio was built by Perret), and Jean Lurçat, who had brother André design his studio-house.

Parisians adore private or hidden gardens, as countless impromptu patches of green confirm. Scattered across the capital are tiny paradises sheltered from the surrounding concrete, often bearing idyllic names such as the Hermitage, Petite Alsace, and the Cité des Fleurs which, situated off Avenue de Clichy, is a lane of houses with gardens full of fragrant shrubs—the heady scent of jasmine and forsythia has replaced the gardenias of old.

In the Mouzaïa quarter, sandwiched between Parc des Buttes-Chaumont and the delightful square of Butte-du-Chapeau-Rouge, lies an enticing skein of cobbled slopes dotted with street lamps. The colors of the doll's-house dwellings artfully match the vegetation—purple lilacs against a lavender wall, golden honeysuckle against a brick wall, violet wisteria against pink plaster. This Lilliputian quarter was built over a quarry whose gypsum was exported as far away as Louisiana.

Somewhat further south, not far from Père Lachaise cemetery (that city within a city), is the butte called La Campagne à Paris. The tiny village at the top, reached by a flight of steep stairs, is composed of two or three winding streets. Hibiscus and rose bushes reign along these seemingly vast lanes whose facades—whether plaster, brick, or buhrstone—boast delightful ceramic ornamentation in the form of shiny cabochons or garlands of roses. Here, even buhrstone has class.

Nostalgic for the days when the outlying quarters were still rural, Parisians love adding bucolic touches to their urban pleasures. Most of the time, such touches are within easy reach.

Far left, top and bottom: Parc Montsouris is surrounded by attractive houses bedecked in ambient foliage.

Left: Some lucky people can open their windows onto park greenery as though it were their own garden, like this mansion overlooking Parc Monceau on the Right Bank.

Above: The Cour du Bel-Air, where this bookstore is located, is one of the most attractive courtyards along Rue du Faubourg Saint-Antoine, near the Bastille.

Right: Not far away is Passage du Cheval-Blanc, where plants seem to rise from cobblestones to enliven the bordering workshops.

Artists' and Writers' Gardens

To give tiny gardens some breathing room—especially in working-class neighborhoods where nature has invaded a courtyard, veranda or shack—they may be bordered with sand or lined by low walls. Shrubs are often shaped onto an arbor, and a lilac may be planted at the corner of a building—that wonderful flowering tree, herald of spring, breaks the harshness of straight lines while simultaneously shielding occupants from prying eyes.

The true elegance of Paris resides in these modest patches of color which greet the promenader from one bank of the Seine to the other. They are an unpretentious demonstration of a commitment to beauty, one that insists on remaining discreet—indeed, self-effacing—even when it deserves to be noted.

When the gentle sun of spring stirs trees to yield their first notes of pale green, gardens and balconies awaken with light poetic touches of color. The first fragrant breaths of May caress romantic bowers where balmy breezes take hold of bodies and minds. It is the season most conducive to visiting artistic and literary haunts.

In Faubourg Saint-Germain, for example, the garden of the Musée Rodin (formerly the private residence of the duc de Biron) was haven to a constellation of artists from Rainer Maria Rilke to Jean Cocteau, not forgetting of course the sculptor whose name was given to the museum and who lived there until his death in 1917.

The garden has lost its Anglo-Chinese follies typical of the eighteenth century, yet still retains its ample trees, its rigorously geometric lawns, and, above all, its charm—which is no mean feat for a classical setting that now hosts sculptures of extreme dramatic tension.

Over on Chaillot hill on the Right Bank, meanwhile, the garden of the Musée Balzac is a fine example of a mixed flower-and-vegetable garden, heady with the scent of wisteria. Its delightful, almost provincial simplicity is startlingly reminiscent of the Loire Valley, where Balzac set many of his novels. This small suburban retreat, where Balzac penned *Scenes of Parisian Life*, betrays the writer's taste for the countryside. It conveys the true subject of his cycle of novels, *The Human Comedy*: nostalgia for a simpler world, a paradise lost through the unleashing of passions, pettiness, and treachery.

The garden adjoining the Musée Bourdelle, on a crooked street near the Montparnasse train station, is a room of greenery inundated with skylight. Rather than a garden in the strict sense, it serves as vestibule and logical extension to a house and studio that are largely open to natural light.

With the approach of summer, such sites host a rising mist, iridescent and spidery, full of the scent of moss, dampness, bark, and young growth. They demonstrate why Paris is still a favorite haunt of writers and artists, as do the Cité Fleurie (a green isle of artists' studios on Faubourg Saint-Jacques) and the garden of the Musée de la Vie Romantique (which honors the memory of George Sand and Frédéric Chopin).

Located in the heart of a chic Right Bank neighborhood, Parc Monceau has always been highly romantic. Approached from

Left: The Musée Bourdelle presents the sculptures of Antoine Bourdelle, a friend of Rodin, in a studio-garden that is a haven of foliage within sight of the modern Montparnasse Tower.
Above: On Rue de Babylone, La Pagode is in fact a movie theater and tea room. Its miniature garden is a miracle of "chinoiserie" with rocks, shrubs, and wooden paths.
Below: Not far from Parc Georges-Brassens (a successful transformation of former city slaughterhouses), painters found a haven in La Ruche (The Hive) on Passage de Dantzig. This famous artists' residence with studios arranged in a circular "honeycomb" notably housed Fernand Léger, Ossip Zadkine, Marc Chagall, and Chaim Soutine.

Rue de Prony, there rises a rotunda, like some antique relic, marking the main entrance to the park (the building was originally a toll-house designed by Claude-Nicolas Ledoux at the former city limits).

It was in 1783 that Louis Carrogis, better known as Carmontelle, laid out a landscape-style garden for the duc de Chartres (who became known as Philippe-Egalité during the Revolution, and whose son became King Louis-Philippe). Without slavishly copying the landscape model from England, which was all the rage at the time, Carmontelle skillfully orchestrated the finest accomplishments of the gardener's art. Of his many picturesque inventions in the inimitable eighteenth-century style, there survive only a pyramid, grotto, and naumachia (a pool for mock sea-battles).

By 1785, Parc Monceau was already being called "the Chartres pleasure gardens," for it had become an enchanting site covering nearly fifty acres—one of the marvels of Paris, complete with a Chinese kiosk, waterfall, marble temple, "lost" tomb hidden in a copse, lake, obelisk, Egyptian pyramid, and many other "follies" and objects designed to amaze.

It outraged the philosophers and other leading thinkers of the day precisely because it was designed to amaze rather than teach, as symbolized by the colonnade of the naumachia, a fragment taken from the former mausoleum of the Orléans family in Saint-Denis. The grounds lacked nothing—not even the phony ruins of which the Enlightenment was so enamored. The mansion itself overlooked Rue Monceau, where the gate to the Musée Nissim de Camondo currently stands.

Parc Monceau still seems haunted by the muses of Romanticism, such as Gounod (*left*). It has nevertheless become a playground for affluent children; the social status of the neighborhood can be read on the facades proudly ringing the park (*above*), protected by imposing gates with ostentatious gilding.

Right: Reflecting the taste of his day, Carmontelle originally dotted Parc Monceau with many follies, such as a Chinese kiosk and a hidden tomb. All that survives today, however, is the colonnaded "naumachia," or pool for mock naval battles. The classical architecture seems to inspire students, generations of whom perpetuate the pretense of studying on a bench beneath the trees that endow this park with a certain spiritual energy. *Above*: That same energy was incarnated by Chopin, whose marble statue shows him at the keyboard, drawing tears from a swooning allegory of Music.

The modern park, which in fact dates from 1867, after having been first revamped (still in the landscape style) and then seriously amputated by Baron Haussmann's urban development schemes, is another example of Adolphe Alphand's work. It has retained its typical Second Empire charm with lush, opulent greenery evoking the hoop-skirted damsels in straw hats seen in paintings by Franz-Xavier Winterhalter. This image is reinforced by the lavish residences ringing the park, impassive speculative dwellings that embodied recent, questionable wealth; Emile Zola's *La Curée* (*The Kill*), set in this neighborhood, was a cruel and visionary testimony of those times.

During the Third Republic (1870–1940), the park was endowed with statues glorifying Gounod, Maupassant, Chopin, and some lesser lights. Here exotic specimens seem to be at home among the abundant greenery. Once autumn comes, winged maple seeds flutter to the lawn beneath the coppery blaze of chestnut trees and the velvety blue of cypresses.

Orchestrated around banks of flowers and stands of trees, around pathways and statues, Parc Monceau is a landscape version of the world of Marcel Proust. It is quite different in spirit from other Paris parks, themselves distinct from those in England, where grass dominates all, and from those in Italy, where intensely architectural plots cannot be dissociated from the buildings for which they were designed.

Formal Lanes

Strangely, formal gardens are generally underrepresented in the capital of the nation that made "French-style" landscaping so famous. Very few of the city's parks display the straight lines, vistas, ornaments, box hedges, and statues that are the gardening equivalent of French enthusiasm for classicism, rhetoric, and the oratory arts.

Summer best suits these large gardens, when dense foliage provides the necessary coolness and respite from the sun. It is during summer that Parisians like to stroll, laze, and idle in the floral sanctuaries dotting the city.

On the Left Bank, the Luxembourg Gardens extend from the Observatory to Odéon, crisscrossed by joggers every dawn. In spring, the smell of roses floods the open windows of the adjoining Palais de Luxembourg, where the French Senate is

The Luxembourg Gardens put a handsome face on urban parks by alternating stands of trees with clipped lawns and colorful flower beds. Season in, season out, it good-naturedly welcomes a varied public with equally varied attractions, from statues representing real or allegorical figures (*far right, top:* social reformer Frédéric Le Play and a "Mask Seller") to La

Pergola—a delightful spot for a leisurely breakfast on a summer's day (*far right, bottom*).

housed, and mixes with the scent of leather-lined desks. The terrace of the palace offers a view unique in Paris, one that the eye cannot embrace in a single glance. The carefully laid-out lawns, adorned with generous beds of flowers, form a multicolored carpet dotted with chairs and orange trees in summer, flanked by shady lanes of chestnut and linden trees. Another dense hoop of splendid trees masks the iron fence in the distance. This mass of greenery also screens a puppet theater, tennis courts, and the romantic Medici fountain.

Although the Luxembourg Gardens do not offer the grandiose vistas of the Tuileries, they are more conducive to reflection and intimacy. Daydreaming on a tree-shaded bench on a fine summer's afternoon gives rise to countless ideas. Philosophers Diderot and Jean-Jacques Rousseau would stroll here, painter Antoine Watteau would sketch, and Victor Hugo had the heroes of *Les Misérables* promenade here. Furthermore, it is the garden of queens and poets—harboring statues of Anne of Brittany, Anne of Beaujeu, Blanche of Castille, Anne of Provence, and Mary Stuart.

Far left: The Medici Fountain inevitably evokes Florentine magnificence, an impression enhanced by the row of vases so typical of grand Italian villas. Yet it creates a thoroughly Parisian setting, where countless students come to study and flirt.

Left: The bandstand in the Luxembourg Gardens probably has the best acoustics in Paris. Every summer, crowds sit on green park chairs in the comforting shade of the trees, listening to military marches, Viennese waltzes, and Jamaican steel bands.

Whereas philanthropists, scholars, and statesmen might seem out of place here, poets are right at home insofar as they remain childlike. The children in the Luxembourg Gardens are perhaps freer, more confident, and relaxed than those— more affluent—seen in Parc Monceau, the Champs-de-Mars, or Ranelagh, accompanied by English-style nannies (except that the dark blue cloak has evolved into a green Loden coat which nevertheless retains the air of a uniform). Seeing how these children all dress alike, or almost so, it is hard not to think of the classic description of financial success recounted in Maupassant's *Bel-Ami,* which so dazzled provincial readers in 1890. In contrast, the parents of the children in the Luxembourg Gardens seem to belong to the worthy gentry of the university, now mixed— changing neighborhoods oblige—with the sometimes no less aristocratic and cultivated milieu of leading lawyers, film producers, and senior civil servants.

On the other bank of the Seine, anyone lucky enough to occupy the royal suite of the Hotel Meurice is able to appreciate the fine formal lanes of the Tuileries Gardens. Long and straight, they pass between tall trees that brush the sky. When the Paris sun is high, intense scents permeate a semi-torpor untroubled by the din of cars on Rue de Rivoli and the river expressway situated below.

On turning a corner, the sudden sight of a marble statue may make the promenader pause long enough to reflect on the continents of asphalt that the parks of Paris manage to hold at bay. Indeed, what else do people seek in gardens if not the mythical purity that encroaching urban development attempts to absorb little by little? As a simulacrum of paradise lost, the Tuileries powerfully evoke another universe—one caught between city and countryside, between heaven and earth. In addition to serving as fence and natural border, the roads that ring the park sharply define it: a green-cloaked island of repose whose history faithfully mirrors the history of the whole country.

Indeed, the Tuileries Gardens have undergone several incarnations since they were first laid out on the orders of Catherine de' Medici (who refused, for that matter, to live in the château overlooking them). People came from afar to admire the maze, the menagerie, the echo chamber, the fountain, and the copies of antique statues, not to mention the tree-lined lanes, the mosaic flower beds framed by boxwood hedges endlessly repeating royal monograms and coats of arms, the sun dial, and the grotto decorated with ceramic animals by the famous potter Bernard Palissy, who had his kiln near the current site of the Carrousel arch.

Toward the middle of the eighteenth century, to make the gardens an elegant meeting spot once again, the governor of the Tuileries château, Monsieur Bontemps, had the bright idea (which he attributed to his mistress, Mademoiselle Allard) of installing thousands of chairs in the park. Promenaders loved this new convenience—"the benches were abandoned, it seemed almost disreputable to use them." The traditional chairs have recently been replaced by a new model designed by Jean-Michel Wilmotte.

Also bordering the Seine, upriver, is the Jardin des Plantes, or botanical gardens. An heir, in its own way, to the splendor of the monarchy, this park views the chaos of passing time with a certain disdain—it was designed for serious study, and has eternity on its side. Even though its layout initially appears straightforward, its private geography is not immediately obvious. It was set in fields that were then outside Paris, near the Bièvre River.

Time seems to have come to halt in the Jardin des Plantes, with its sharply defined lanes, its botanical gardens, and the exuberant leaves of its venerable trees (most of which are over a hundred years old).

Far left: Rising from the yellow-strewn lawn, three bronze leaves are etched with three versions of a *Nocturne*, a poem by Saint-John Perse.
Left: The drainage grate of this nineteenth-century fountain opens like a fan.
Below: A deserted lane of plane trees—"Will he ever show up?"

Above: At the back of the Jardin des Plantes is the recently restored Museum of Natural History, where architect Paul Chemetov has magically renovated the exhibition space to accommodate thousands of stuffed animals. The unstuffed pigeons, meanwhile, struggle to survive here just like everywhere else.

Below: The alpine garden draws visitors to its vast cascade of mountain shrubbery.

Far right: One of the well-ordered lanes in the Jardin des Plantes.

Henri IV (1553–1610) first suggested bringing rare varieties of plants and trees together in a single place, ranging from medicinal plants to those useful for manufacturing or culinary purposes. Thanks to the boom in trade with Holland, bulbous flowers made their first appearance in France and became objects of unbridled speculation.

Henri's son, Louis XIII (1601–1643), then carried out the plan by founding the Jardin Royal des Plantes Médicinales, based on a model already established in Montpellier. The park assumed its botanical vocation, shaped by the Enlightenment's penchant for classification: impeccably divided into four sections, it catalogued specimens into evergreen trees, evergreen bushes, common plants, and aquatic plants. Artificial embankments of detritus and gravel along the borders kept out harsh winds. A maze was laid out, crowned by a belvedere, a highly symbolic feature that had been fashionable since the early seventeenth century.

The combination of seriousness and whimsy, along with a dash of the unexpected, lend a great deal of charm to the Jardin des Plantes. Ten, twenty, or thirty little gardens will surface depending on the chosen itinerary—whether along the central flower beds or down the shady lanes, whether over to the stuffed animals in the Museum of Natural History at the back, or through the grand eighteenth-century buildings along the side.

Each item is obsessively identified in French and Latin on little metal plaques. No less than 15,000 species are inventoried here: flowers abound in their diversity, and the most humble among them, once named, are transformed into rarities; the shrubs always seem bizarre, and even the most common become enigmatic; the widely differing trees all share a strange craze for growth and immortality, vying to see which will be the tallest, have the widest trunk, survive the most revolutions.

A special microclimate must favor superlative performance here. Modesty is nevertheless maintained, for the place is far too popular to tolerate arrogance and snobbery, its scientific caretakers having included the likes of Georges Louis Buffon (who headed the garden in his day), Antoine de Jussieu, and Georges Cuvier. It is a garden of delights with old-fashioned charm, which still boasts a zoo founded by Bernardin de Saint-Pierre, author of an eighteenth-century best-selling novel, *Paul et Virginie*.

This enchanting, ever so slightly melancholy park also has an alpine garden, and a grandiose paleontology hall that measures time on a grand scale. The greenhouses have everything imaginable in the way of exotic plants (inspiring the artist Le Douanier Rousseau); all of them seem to be carnivores, with forms that curve in such fascinating ways that they must all be involved in some plot—if not against humans, then against the insects flitting indecorously overhead.

CRAFT SECRETS

With full respect for tradition,
master artisans perpetuate the fame
of glamorous fashion houses and
rejuvenate the Parisian sense of taste.

The sky over Paris welcomes every kind of weather, accommodating soft light and harsh sun in turn, tirelessly washing the cityscape with chromatic variations and contrasts. Subtle shades of blue, gray, and pink evolve unpredictably, like old-fashioned postcards whose chemical magic mimicked the uncertainties of nature by naively imitating a bold palette. Similarly, Paris has always known how to accommodate one of its most glittering, variegated assets—equal to its most precious monuments—namely, its motley population of master artisans.

The very word "artisan" evokes the creative, magnificent, unusual, unsettling, frivolous extravagance of Paris. Although these traits might seem contradictory in another context, none are incompatible here, since they are married in so many elegant—that is to say, obvious—ways. An item made in Paris, even the most ordinary one, is often endowed with an allusive grace that has inevitably developed in a city where a show of beauty too often distracts the eye from the true essence, namely a taste for perfect detail.

Those who indulge in a nostalgia as repetitious as it is unfounded should take a closer look at the show currently running in the streets, boutiques, and workshops: here, at least, the end of the twentieth century in no way rhymes with resignation and decline. Should those bitter souls ever abandon their self-complacent chagrin, they would find nothing more pleasurable than a stroll down Faubourg Saint-Antoine to visit cabinetmakers, gilders, bronzesmiths, and mirror cutters. An equal if more personal pleasure can be had—with more

Preceding pages: A plaster cast of Louis XIV, made by a master artisan as an element of interior decoration.
Above: Catalogues of patterns are to a fabric decorator what a herbal is to a botanist.
Right: Interior decorators Elisabeth Garouste and Matthias Bonetti have created an oasis of calm for fashion designer Christian Lacroix within the hustle and bustle of his *haute couture* firm. Rejecting the eternal white-lacquered Louis XIV medallion chair, they have created a dreamy, unreal interior, perfectly in keeping with the fashion world's image as a place where dreams take form. They have conveyed Lacroix's taste for bright colors and unusual shapes, and reflect as well his whimsy and mastery of materials.

easily accessible objects—at the luxury and fashion trades, centered originally in a "golden triangle" formed by Place Vendôme, Rue du Faubourg Saint-Honoré, and Avenue Montaigne, but now also taking root in the Marais district.

These workshops with their customs and objects constitute a whole new continent for visitors. This world should be discovered without obsessive reference to a guide book in an attempt to identify the style of a piece of furniture, the name of a statue, or, more prosaically, one's location in the maze of unfamiliar streets and alleys forming the nervous system of an age-old organism of creativity and know-how.

The pleasantness, malleability, and suppleness of French life endow Parisian artisans with a less dogmatic though perhaps more attentive, lively, inventive, and colorful attitude than those in other capital cities (where talent is by no means lacking). That is because, once again, Paris offers something different—an atmosphere and local spirit that are simply not exportable. A true setting for creativity goes deeper than a film set. Today's master artisans are no better than their forebears, nor are they any less good—in fact, they are not much different. Indeed, certain workshops have been operating since the days of Charles X, Louis-Philippe, and Napoleon III. As to more recent firms, they have often been in business for over fifty years.

Most of the major houses such as Dior, Cartier, Hermès, Lancel, and Vuitton—whose names are synonymous with refinement the world over—are more than one hundred years old. Yet their fame is due not to their venerable age, but to their

ability to innovate while remaining faithful to tradition.

Where would the "luxury goods trade" find itself without the traditional skills of Parisian artisans, now that, in the realm of elegant taste, dangerous offensives are being launched by France's talented, dynamic neighbors? Not only do Parisian specialists maintain extremely high traditional standards, they also continually improve them by proposing new forms. They imitate their forebears by adopting the motto: "Never imitate anyone, including yourself." This idea is perhaps just a subtle, artistic variant of the political adage, "Change so that nothing changes."

These artisans' attitude, ambition, and philosophy all participate in the same quest: perfection. Thus modern members of the craft knighthood, whose swords are chisel and gilding iron, continue to take up the venerable gauntlet.

Left: André Lemarié has played a major role in *haute couture* even though his name is known only to a privileged few. His firm, specializing in feathers, was founded in the days of Charles-Frédéric Worth and since that time has never ceased to supply the fashion industry—even though the raw materials for his art are becoming increasingly difficult to find.

Right: Madame Louyot (*top*), a traditional laundress, knew how to restore dignity to the most fragile of fabrics. Wielding her old-fashioned flat-irons (*bottom*) like a virtuoso violinist, she would prepare wedding gowns and christening dresses with all the fluting, flounces and other subtleties of fancy linen.

Artisans of Fashion

As the fashion capital of the world, Paris has been able to sustain craft specialists whose talent and skills enable that industry to survive.

Opening the door of number 2 Boulevard de Strasbourg feels like entering Empress Eugénie's fan conservatory: chandeliers topped by a crown hang from a coffered ceiling in what was the Parisian temple of the delicate art of fan-making during the Second Empire. Anne Hocquet, the last fan-maker in France, reigns over a realm of mother-of-pearl, lace, and paper, producing objects that evoke the wonderfully feminine world of modesty and enticement.

Henri II furniture and blue tapestries (with gold-embroidered fleur-de-lis patterns) provide an appropriate setting for a vast range of fans, some of which spread open in showcases while others cower from light and dust in sized drawers. Although fans are not a specifically French accessory,

Anne Hoguet is the last fan maker in Paris. In the magnificently old-fashioned setting of her workshop-museum—open to the public—she makes and restores these key tools of seduction. Time has frozen here. The din of the street is left behind as the Paris of the Second Empire and Balzac returns to life. A realm of tortoiseshell, mother-of-pearl, feathers, lace, and paper slumbers in showcases and drawers, protected from harsh light (*left*). Henri II furnishings harmonize boldly with the blue wall fabric woven with gold fleur-de-lis (*right*).

Above and lower right: The François Lesage firm fervently maintains the tradition of fine embroidery, serving as a conservatory of subtle techniques. François is carrying on the name of a firm founded by his father, and with an eye to the future he is training his successors with extreme care and bemused good-will; they can thus benefit from his unequaled know-how and magnificent collection, illustrating arcane aspects of a trade known for its countless tricks. As an embroiderer, Lesage has helped fashion designers to

make their wildest dreams a reality, combining total technical mastery with humor.
Far right: Silk, velvet, linen, and damask all have their special embroidery stitch. Every period has a special fabric, every style its special patterns.

having been introduced into the country by Catherine de' Medici, they soon became an inevitable element of French seductiveness. They long inspired not only fashion, but also elegant compositions from turn-of-the-century artists such as Pierre Bonnard, Edouard Vuillard and Edgar Degas, and even served as advertising space. Whether hand-painted or printed, in feather or lace, with a base of ivory, tortoiseshell, mother-of-pearl or lacquered wood, a fan remains "a lost object of love"—how wonderful it would be to hear once again the snap of a fan being opened in a box at the opera, or the impatient flutter of a fan in a courtesan's hand.

On Rue Vivienne, the less specialized Marescot firm supplies an impressive range of lace to fashion designers not only from Paris but also from the United States and Italy. Claude Coudray, who joined the firm in 1958, remembers vividly when Cristóbal Balenciaga came to the shop to choose the lace that he employed so wonderfully in his *haute couture*.

Intricate and skillfully made lace adorned nineteenth-century court dresses, as depicted in paintings by Winterhalter and often designed by the likes of Charles Frédéric Worth and Jacques Doucet. Little by little, fashion called for the addition of embroidery employing sequins and madroños, in which the Michonnet workshop excelled, thereby becoming the official embroiderer of the Second Empire. After the First World War, Albert Lesage bought the venerable firm, launching a dazzling career in embroidery to which his son, François, has proved a worthy successor.

In the 1920s, pearl-embroidered dresses were all the rage in Paris, and designers

Jeanne Lanvin and Jean Patou had Lesage frantically adorn the busts and flounces of evening gowns with them (even though Paul Poiret preferred fluid, pleated, printed layers, Madeleine Vionnet opted for the strict geometry of dresses cut on the bias, sometimes discreetly decorated with pearl-embroidered patterns, and Alix—the future Madame Grès—favored skillful draping). The most extravagant embroidery, however, appeared on clothing by the inspired, eccentric Italian designer Elsa Schiaparelli —figurative pockets depicting elephants, acrobats, lovers drawn by Jean Cocteau, or giant lobsters imagined by Salvador Dalí. Then fashion designers Christian Dior, Jacques Fath, and Pierre Balmain called on the talents of the Lesage firm, followed more recently by Yves Saint Laurent, Karl Lagerfeld, Christian Lacroix, Hubert de Givency and Jean-Louis Scherer.

Balenciaga, meanwhile, has retained his penchant for embroidered trim evoking traditional Spanish dress, as well as feather embroidery, for which he calls on another fashion wizard, feather specialist André Lemarié. Lemarié has created extraordinary, magnificent models for Yves Saint Laurent, Nina Ricci, and Christian Dior. In recent years the firm, founded in 1880, has

added the fragile florist craft to its specialties—Lemarié fashioned the legendary camellia for Chanel in 1994, producing 20,000 copies.

Raymonde Pouzieux, another veritable artist, designs ornamental trimmings for *haute couture*, sometimes going so far as to concoct entire garments with incredible virtuosity, as she did for Christian Lacroix. As the unchallenged specialist in bourdon lace and braid, she has long produced the distinctive trimming of Chanel suits.

Coco Chanel was one of the first fashion designers to produce her own costume jewelry, which she had designed by Paul Iribe. Peerless jewelers Josette Gripoix and Georges Desrues, meanwhile, have worked with the greatest fashion designers for three quarters of a century, enriching garments with costume jewelry and ornaments which inventiveness and technical perfection elevate to the status of fine jewelry without expensive gems.

Geneviève and Gérard Lognon, meanwhile, are the mathematicians of fashion, for nothing is more complicated than the art of pleating, of which they are past masters. First of all, a precision drawing must be made on paper of every three-dimensional cardboard mold to be produced. Then the

fabric is placed between two molds and "steam-cooked" in a large oven. Every type of pleat has its advocates and its specialists—sunburst pleats, herringbone pleats, flat pleats, round pleats, accordion pleats, Watteau pleats, couched pleats.

For ladies going to a ball, shoemaker Raymond Massaro will "handcraft your feet." Massaro handles leather the way fashion designers handle fabrics. He works it with such ease that this stiff and apparently austere material surprisingly lends itself to every kind of fanciful idea and combination. Although major private clients are a vanishing breed, Massaro is able to give free reign to his imagination by working with fashion designers—thanks to his skill, models elegantly glide down runways. His father made the famous beige and black pumps for Coco Chanel.

Far left and upper left: Shoemaker Raymond Massaro, working out of a mezzanine on Rue de la Paix, remembers the time when certain clients would buy pumps in batches of identical pairs in different colors. The comtesse Bismarck ordered six pairs per week. The days of such madness have passed, but the spirit lives on thanks to Massaro's total mastery—a shoe from his hands never resembles any other, even if made by the most conscientious workshop.

Massaro works with fashion designers such as Karl Lagerfeld.
Below: The tradition of making objects, boxes and furniture of shagreen, taken up by artists such as Jean-Michel Frank and André Groult, is perpetuated in this workshop near the Bastille.

Decorative Crafts

As one ages, more and more places in Paris become unbearable to visit, due to changes they have undergone. Entire streets have occasionally been subjected to humiliating transformations. That is why it is crucial to show intense, non-nostalgic appreciation for the city's craft workshops, where framers, tapestry weavers, instrument makers, gilders, bookbinders, woodworkers, china restorers, mirror makers, lacquer specialists, and other artisans are perpetuating skills with passion and elegance (elegance being the sole entirely pleasing quality insofar as it is totally disinterested, with no goal other than its own attainment). Some of these workshops are age-old, maintaining intact a tradition as well as an enchanting place where time stands still.

Cabinetmakers, the aristocracy of the craft trades, have enjoyed a privileged role since the eighteenth century. They constituted veritable dynasties, notably the Boulle, Saunier, Dumoulin, and Jacob families. While all were not sons of masters, they all, without exception, began as apprentices and journeymen to a master on Faubourg Saint-Antoine. They acquired unchallenged authority only when the guild wardens, extremely strict in assessing work, conferred the title of master on them, thereby accepting them into the club. Some of this craft nobility still rubs off on today's furniture makers.

In the eighteenth century, Paris was the European capital of culture, elegance, and decorative arts. The language and taste expressed in the salons in Paris and court in Versailles held sway everywhere. Their

Above: Old wooden armchairs, more or less bearing the scars of time, are stacked in a workshop a stone's throw from the Bastille. Metamorphosis is imminent, however, for Monsieur Gouin will revive their former splendor by respecting age-old gilding methods, notably using a secret patina to soften the excessive shininess of gold leaf.

Right: The master gilder in his workshop. On his bench is the gilder's pad holding the gold leaf, which is so light that it flutters away with the tiniest breath of air. *Below:* Leaves of gold used for gilding furniture.

Above: Wood carver and furniture restorer Jean Renouvel, shown in his workshop on Rue Elzévir in the Marais district, was awarded the title of Master Artisan by the French government in 1994. His hands can transform beech, oak, and linden into magnificent forms worthy of Marie-Antoinette's boudoir in Versailles (which he helped restore to its original beauty).

Right: These rococo shapes, just emerging from the raw wood, still convey the spirit of journeyman artisans. *Below*: A furniture workshop on Faubourg Saint-Antoine, drenched in light and stacked with carved wooden pieces ready for assembly.

reign went long unchallenged, and has never completely disappeared. Even though excellent furniture was made throughout France, true veneering—the prerogative of cabinetmakers—was done only in Paris. And if by chance foreign masters attempted to imitate their Parisian colleagues, they cruelly lacked the gilded bronze decoration that contributed so much to the success of a piece. This primacy is moreover evident in the "foreign" names of the great cabinetmakers, who came from all over Europe to set up shop on Faubourg Saint-Antoine, not far from the Bastille.

What might be called the "Paris school" of furniture enjoyed unchallenged preeminence throughout the eighteenth and nineteenth centuries, and still does today thanks to the workshops on Faubourg Saint-Antoine which, though they practice only restoration, remain faithful to tradition. These unprepossessing alleyways house experts who know how to restore all the hidden—sometimes disfigured—splendor to afflicted furniture, tarnished bronze, damaged gilding, and shattered marquetry. Such resuscitation has been made possible only by perpetuating sophisticated techniques. These same skills are now enabling the French art of furniture, after decades of decline, to recover part of its past glory, thanks to a talented generation of new artisans weary of the sclerosis displayed by industrial objects.

Of all these skills, marquetry is certainly the one that shines the brightest in Paris. Whatever people may think, it is not just a charming, old-fashioned thing of the past. Even though Parisian cabinetmakers no longer create furniture embellished with

wood inlay, they intelligently pursue the grand art of eighteenth-century marquetry. Simon-Pierre Etienne, for instance, specializes in restoring marquetry furniture and objets d'art, assisted by five journeymen. The same goes for Michel Germon, president of Les Grands Ateliers de France, and the Mahieu firm, founded in 1895, one of the last companies authorized to practice mercury gilding, whose secret has been handed down since the eighteenth century—one gram of melted gold is alloyed to eight grams of mercury, giving bronze a golden green shade that is "browned" with agate prior to being patinated to the client's wishes (which may range from "shiny like Versailles" to "aged by two centuries of existence"). At the bronze-and-iron Meilleur firm, meanwhile, fourteen restorers labor in a thousand square-meter workshop for clients such as Fontainebleau château, the Musée des Art Décoratifs, and the Comédie-Française. Similarly, master cabinetmaker Henri Desgrippes has trained many talented apprentices. And, Vincent Corbière, who is both instrument maker and cabinetmaker, produces furniture from surprising materials such as slate.

All of these artisans work according to their own special methods, favoring historical accuracy over aesthetic interpretation, thanks to their confident expertise in styles and techniques (where secrecy still rules). Someone like Jean-Marie Montagne, for example, spends many hours at the Louvre because "studying paintings accurately informs us about the setting and atmosphere in which the furniture was used." Steeped in a didactic atmosphere generated by his father (who was a cabinetmaker with

the Jansen firm), Montagne brings a new tone to contemporary restoration, in which sensitivity and observation count more than the intrinsic value of a given piece of furniture. In this respect, he shares Baudelaire's rejection of rigid systems because, in the poet's words, "a system is a kind of damnation that forces us into a perpetual oath . . . I have arrogantly resigned myself to modesty, and am content merely to feel."

On Rue Beautreillis in the Marais district, Georges Glaser fashions objects in another material—metal. His storefront workshop is filled with an acrid odor as he performs the infinitely precise motions of a brazier, a trade that dates back to the thirteenth century (and was practiced by twentieth-century decorative artist Jean Dunand until he concentrated on lacquered wood). Glaser takes a rigid sheet of copper, brass, or silver and transforms it into a vase, a tray, or a shop sign by hammering tirelessly. "If the gesture isn't sufficiently accurate," he

Left: Nectoux is a venerable firm that restores the traditional zinc countertops in Parisian cafés. It employs the last artisans who still have the skills required for the task, which is much more sophisticated than the average café customer imagines.
Far left: Claude Kern, awarded the national title of Master Artisan for perpetuating the tradition of mercury gilding on metal, holds a fine recently completed sphinx.
Below: A red-hot ball of glass takes shape in a glass-making workshop.

Above: The Montmartre workshop (*above*) of Guy Goudgi, who left his native Georgia to practice metalcraft in Paris, produces objects that are veritable sculptures.

Far right: The hilt, blade, and scabbard of a ceremonial sword rest on Goudgi's preparatory sketch prior to assembly.

Below: Semi-precious stones of various colors await cutting and setting.

explains, "the metal suffers. Because if the molecules are crushed rather than pushed, the material becomes inert and dull." This is the skill shared by all metalsmiths, including Guy Goudgi, who was taught the *repoussé* technique (hammering designs in relief) by an old master in his native Georgia. Yet it is in Paris, where Goudgi has chosen to live, that he now creates sculpted objects and jewelry harking back to the Mesopotamian, Etruscan, and Scythian civilizations.

Statue casting, an art related to sculpture, has a master in the person of Michel Lorenzi. Nothing seems to have changed in Lorenzi's workshop on Rue Racine since 1871. Various generations of Lorenzis have cast every type of statue and bas-relief, from ionic capitals to chained slaves, and from lewd fauns to the Victory of Samothrace and San Marco lions. In order to make plaster casts from original works, Michel Lorenzi constantly travels to Italy, Egypt, and the French provinces, not to mention the Louvre, where his path has certainly crossed that of Emile Rostain, a picture restorer of genius.

Giovanni Morelli stresses the key role played by restorers when it comes to attributing a painting to an artist. A restorer is above all a true artist, armed with a perfect knowledge of materials and able to share the most personal emotions of the original artist of the work.

Every painting needs a frame. The rarest, most varied frames are to be found at Havard Père & Fils in Montparnasse. Since the end of the nineteenth century, countless artists have come to this "frame maker." Henri Matisse, Nicolas de Staël, and Fernando Botero spent hours pensively examining some eight hundred different frame

Top: Preparatory drawings and models for rococo decoration to be cast in plaster.
Above: The workshop of Lorenzi Frères, on Rue Racine, not far from the Luxembourg Gardens, has become a veritable museum harboring masterpieces of statuary and casting.
Right: Stuc & Staff is a firm specializing in molds for quality renovations—the walls of its workshop constitute a catalogue of the history of ornamental art.

models that clutter the walls, testifying to four hundred years of this art. And let there be no mistake, framing *is* an art, as confirmed by the work of Philippe, the Havard grandson, as well as other highly esteemed framers of contemporary art such as Guy Mondineu and Bernard Frappat.

Finally, it is impossible to discuss Parisian crafts without mentioning the Gobelins Manufactory, a historical site now considered to be a national monument. The Gobelins family from Reims set up a tapestry workshop in Paris in the mid-fifteenth century. In 1667, French statesman Jean-Baptiste Colbert turned it into the official supplier of furnishings to the crown, and appointed the famous artist Charles Le Brun as its director. Le Brun recruited talent such as Blin de Fontenary and Baptiste Mannoyer, while Pierre Mignard, his successor, added a drawing school to the workshop, as an indispensable part of an artisan's artistic education. During the Régence (1715–1723) and Louis XV (1710–1774) periods, Charles Natoire, Carle van Loo, and Jean-François de Troy supplied elegant new decorative models, which were more graceful and less solemn than those preferred by Louis XIV (1638–1715).

The Gobelins Manufactory can still be visited today, and a tour of the premises reveals the various complexities and stages in producing tapestries, carpets, and upholstery—infinite patience is required. The artisans here are veritable artists whose mastery is displayed in the adjoining museum, which features many outstanding pieces and cartoons by major painters such as Raphael, Correggio, Le Brun, and Boucher, as well as more recent artists such as Chagall, Matisse, Max Ernst, Rougement, and others.

Right and below: The production of braiding, trimming, frogging, tassels, and fringes requires thread, fabrics, cord, and skeins of silk, plus a constellation of tools. Yet the most irreplaceable element required to accomplish this craft, and one of the constant features of French decoration, is the human hand.

Far right: Ever since it was founded by Colbert, the Gobelins Tapestry Manufactory has continued to produce woven versions of cartoons designed by great artists who turned their talents to this slow and painstaking art. Given a lengthy production period, most tapestry orders are now placed by government organizations—the manufactory's output continues to honor an eminently French craft.

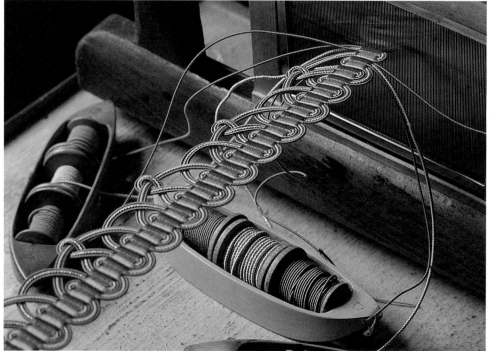

RENDEZVOUS

The places where real Parisians
like to go: glass-roofed shopping
arcades, hidden museums,
cafés, bistros, even luxury hotels.
Places that, once discovered,
are visited again and again.

*I*t is a mistake to assume that Paris is always Paris, a homogeneous, harmonious city running from the center to the outskirts. Paris, in fact, is a cluster of villages, each having retained its own appearance, character, customs, and even fragrance. A true Parisian can sniff the air, eyes closed, and identify, say, Place de la Madeleine or Parc Montsouris. This feat is no urban myth—it is a fact. Each neighborhood has its own style, faces, storefronts, organization, provincial flavor, hierarchy, and rituals. By resisting the centralizing tendency and lethal appeal of standardization, Paris has managed to retain a feeling of intimacy.

Only through habit, or long experience in the capital, is it possible to acquire that special attention and sensitivity to little things necessary to really experience *living* in Paris. This is because Parisians are always on the lookout, despite themselves, for something exceptional or original. True Parisian chic entails not only discovering a quaint restaurant where the cuisine is better and the interior more attractive than anywhere else, but also knowing enchanting streets untouched by time, boutiques where rare items are cultivated like hothouse orchids, and charming courtyard gardens far from urban noise and bustle.

Inveterate promenaders claim part of Paris as their own by wandering tirelessly through town. Whether melancholy or slightly euphoric, meditative or adventurous, such aimless strolls lead to constantly evolving discoveries, and are the privilege of genuine cities. Meandering throughout the city's streets, promenaders constantly reinvent their own Paris, and etch their own

Preceding pages: In 1864 an Alsatian named Bofinger launched a still-thriving fashion when he founded the brasserie that bears his name. The restaurant, with an interior largely decorated by the Alsatian artist Hansi, has become a favorite meeting place after performances at the nearby Bastille Opera House. The cuisine accords with the setting—sincere and respectful of tradition, as might be expected of what has become a veritable institution.

Above: Certain arcades, such as Passage Bourg-l'Abbé, no longer function as shopping galleries.
Right: Many others, however, survive as places of exciting hunts for the rare object or book, as is the case with Passage Verdeau, located near the Drouot auction house.

personal and emotional map of the capital. Paris appears irreconcilably different to everyone. A kaleidoscope of villages, pedestrian arcades, tiny shaded squares, gardens, and canals, all these places are equally poetic and authentic, if often modest and unsophisticated. They are simple, private spots that remain completely faithful to the city, revealing its truth most radically: Paris is not composed solely of majestic views and monumental buildings whose very perfection sometimes seems like a theorem writ in stone.

Arcades

The local glass-roofed arcades, or "passages," are unique to Paris. Not because other European cities lack them—Milan has the Victor-Emmanuel Gallery and London boasts the Burlington Arcade—but because those in Paris have a different feel. They are more casual, less ostentatious, and are often the last refuge of a working-class lifestyle that extends back to the interwar period.

Most of the Parisian arcades date from the nineteenth century, though they are in fact heir to an older tradition. They retain a subtle mixture of bourgeois confidence, of social and commercial ambivalence, and of an almost crude banality tinged with a taste for the bizarre. This is why the surrealists found them so fascinating—Louis Aragon claimed that they were called "passages" because it seemed "as though, in these corridors concealed from daylight, no one was permitted to halt for more than an instant."

Although now in decline, one easily senses the former glory of luxurious shops,

Above: The L-shaped Passage des Panoramas, linking Rue Montmartre to Boulevard Montmartre, will soon celebrate its 200th birthday, and yet remains the most lively of all arcades because it has remained faithful to its modest origins. *Right*: In contrast, Galerie Colbert, despite its magnificent if somewhat flashy restoration, has not attracted the public it deserves (notwithstanding its excellent brasserie, Le Grand Colbert). Like the nearby Galerie Vivienne, this arcade dates from the 1820s. It then languished and went into a long decline, until it was recently refurbished to its original appearance; it now houses exhibition galleries for the Bibliothèque Nationale next door. A statue of *Eurydice Bitten by a Serpent* stands beneath the fine renovated rotunda.

elegant cafés, and refined decoration which flourished daily beneath a glass and metal sky. Sunlight filters through the strikingly graceful webs of glass that are perhaps the most attractive products of that revolutionary building technology which still largely governs modern taste.

The first arcade, Passage Feydeau, opened in 1791. It was modeled on the now-vanished wooden galleries in the Palais-Royal, which had been the focus of Parisian social life throughout the Enlightenment. After the Revolution came Passage des Panoramas and Passage du Caire which, though near one another, experienced quite different fates. Located in the midst of working-class Paris, Passage du Caire was never very glamorous; from its inception it housed humble artisans and wholesale suppliers to the garment trade (even today this neighborhood, known as the Sentier quarter, is still a teeming garment district).

In contrast, the Passage des Panoramas was one of the most prestigious arcades, even though its modern vestiges only fleetingly reflect its former prosperity. Its initial success—which led to the spread of arcades along the broad boulevards that served as the social nerve center of nineteenth-century Paris—was largely due to an experiment in 1799 by American inventor Robert Fulton who installed a panorama at the entrance to the arcade which took its name. The attraction proved to be enormously popular. Each canvas of the panorama—ninety-seven meters in circumference and twenty meters high—depicted an exotic view that aroused wonder among beholders. Even the celebrated painter Jacques-Louis David, although skeptical, admitted that, "One can

Above: Passage Jouffroy is certainly one of the leading arcades when it comes to high-quality curio shops, and is greatly appreciated by its varied, loyal clientele.
Far right: The same applies to Galerie Vivienne, with its more elegant Empire decor and a tearoom whose tables spill out into the arcade itself.

Below: Not far from the entrance to Passage Verdeau and the restaurant Chartier is a confectionery and dry goods store called À la Mère de Famille. It offers a vast selection of treats in a wonderfully old-fashioned turn-of-the-century setting.

go to the panoramas and make sketches from nature." Chateaubriand, in his preface to *An Itinerary from Paris to Jerusalem*, wrote: "The illusion was total. Right from the first glance I recognized the buildings that I'd mentioned. Never was a traveler put to so rude a test. Jerusalem and Athens would have had to be transported to Paris in order to convince me of illusion or truth." Passersby could thus indulge in this entertaining fiction (long since abandoned) and simultaneously discover the latest fashion or chic trend, all the while sheltered from the weather. Arcades seemed both private and public, providing a modernized response to the defunct salons. They functioned as a showplace for a high society built on commerce (and therefore still excluded from the last remaining sanctuaries of the *ancien régime*). Everything seemed possible: lucrative ideas floated, success was proudly sported, unbridled wheeling and dealing yielded gastronomic and carnal rewards. All kinds of merchandise were bought and sold in the arcades, which also served as a sort of back room to the boulevards, where schemes were hatched in a thrillingly semi-clandestine way. "Passages" led to and from the boulevards in a complex circulatory system, some as major arteries and others as minor veins. Born in the era of industrialization and the rise of the bourgeoisie, the arcades incarnated an active, agitated, unstable lifestyle in which everything was geared toward exchange, trade, speculation.

The Passage des Panoramas offered a little of everything, pandering to various pleasures: Marquis sold succulent chocolate ice-cream and flavored teas, Félix specialized in lemon and Malaga pastries, while Susse, a stationery and antique dealer, was where Alexandre Dumas the elder discovered a Delacroix drawing for 600 francs, which he resold for 50,000. Susse was subsequently taken over by Dewambez & Stern and now offers fine engraved business cards, elegant letterhead stationery, and fancy menus, in a setting reminiscent of a Romantic-era reading room, to a far-flung clientele from Venice, Marrakech, New York, and Hong Kong.

Across Boulevard Montmartre, at number 10, is Passage Jouffroy. Its arcade is framed by the Ronceray Hotel, formerly the Grand-Hotel de la Terrasse Jouffroy, whose fourteen windows once opened onto the sidewalk. The Italian composer Gioacchino Rossini lived nearby in the residence of fellow composer François Boieldieu, a veritable "artist's pad" which had formerly served as the Embassy of the Ottoman Empire and the home of Prince Tuffiakin, an eccentric and extremely rich Russian boyar. The harem has long since deserted this arcade but, in a final incarnation of that sensual tradition, it is still possible to purchase erotic books and bawdy images (depicting excessively fat women pretending to converse with mustachioed, enterprising soldiers). Actor Michel Simon was often seen here. More conventional shoppers can buy masks and marionettes in the arcade, where children dash from the nearby wax museum, Musée Grévin, to admire old-fashioned toys displayed in a store named Pain d'Epices. Other promenaders muse on faraway places in the shell-lined back room of Thomas Boog's boutique, which specializes in boxes and curios whose purpose is as

mysterious as their origin, along with a selection of baroque objects every bit as strange as the collection of canes displayed by Frères Ségas at shop number 34.

Arcades and galleries often functioned in pairs. Galerie Vivienne and Galerie Colbert are next door to one another, yet have distinct personalities. Galerie Vivienne, though less majestic in architecture, swiftly became the favorite arcade of Parisians, remaining so until the Second Empire (1852–1870), when its relative distance from the grand boulevards led to its steady decline. When inaugurated in 1828, the arcade housed elegant shops of various kinds: a bookstore, two print dealers, fashion and novelty shops, and a delightful café. Following numerous vicissitudes and progressive dilapidation, Galerie Vivienne finally came back to life some twenty years ago. Wine merchants Legrand Filles & Fils expanded and took over a former print works just in front of the central rotunda, while Christian Astuguevieille, a designer of furniture and objects d'art, moved into the shop once held by Valentine, who did ironing work (a flatiron in each hand, she did business at the sign of Les Demoiselles Sarrazin). A tearoom and a crafts store soon followed, while other more venerable businesses took a new lease on life. The Siroux book store, for instance, founded in 1826, is now a magnet for lovers of rare and unusual books. The faithfully restored and architecturally protected arcade has thus become a fashionable gathering spot, preserving some of the intimacy which shelters it from nearby shabbiness. Not everyone who passes through the gallery today realizes that they are following in the footsteps of such

literary figures as Colette (who lived next door), Alfred Jarry, Louis Aragon, and Paul Léataud (not to mention those of corrupt constable François Vidocq, whose underworld memoirs made him the gallery's most famous resident). Gracefully nostalgic, with soft overhead lights which caress the mosaic floor, the delicately restored and varnished woodwork, and the display windows decorated with monochrome bas-reliefs, Galerie Vivienne has returned to elegant if unpredictable life.

Galerie Colbert, meanwhile, built by Billaud on the site where the stables of Philip of Orleans once stood, was intended to be more majestic than its neighbor Vivienne, which it never managed to dethrone. It boasts a magnificent rotunda, graceful clusters of opaline globe lamps, and fine frieze decoration. Restoration has recently transformed it from a sordid wreck into a bright and shiny corridor—though now it is too bright, too cold, and too perfect, so that even the free-wheeling whimsy of Jean-Paul Gaultier's boutique and the immaculate tablecloths of an excellent brasserie, Le Grand Colbert, do not manage to generate much warmth. It is a pleasant arcade to pass through, but hardly conducive to stopping.

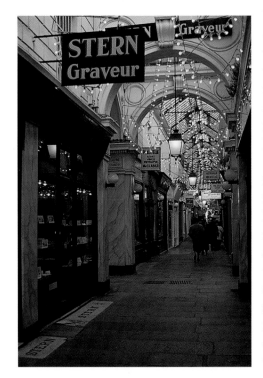

Passage Véro-Dodat and Passage du Grand-Cerf are somewhat removed and somewhat different from the other arcades. Passage du Grand-Cerf (*right*) was built in 1825 on the site of an inn bearing the same name, which served as the starting point for the royal stagecoach service. Recently restored beneath its high glass roof, and featuring passages linking the upper-floors, it has not yet rediscovered its former vigor.

Passage Véro-Dodat (*below*) is exceptional in that it has been spared the vicissitudes of time. It boasts two of the capital's leading antique dealers, Eric Philippe and Pierre Passebon, as well as a number of glamorous, internationally known boutiques.

A little further up Rue des Petit-Champs is Passage Choiseul, which runs north toward Rue Saint-Augustin. Built on the site of the former residence of the marquis de Gesvres, governor of Paris in 1703, the arcade has become a literary fixture. Alphonse Lemerre, a nineteenth-century printer and bookseller, had his premises there and promoted the avant-garde of his day—the "Parnassian" school typified by François Coppée, Leconte de Lisle, José Maria de Heredia, Barbey d'Aurevilly, and a moody young poet named Paul Verlaine. Novelist Louis-Fernand Céline, who lived at number 64, alluded to Passage Choiseul in a few furious pages of *Journey to the End of the Night*: "In [the passage], everyone knew everyone else in each of the little shops. It was like a real provincial village of its own, stuck for years between two streets of Paris,

which meant that everyone spied and humanly slandered each other to the point of lunacy."

In the 1960s, Passage Choiseul regained its former prosperity. Actress Sophie Desmaret opened a curio store named Fleur de Cactus, which was the title of a popular comedy that had played for years at the Théâtre des Bouffes-Parisiens. Then Catherine Harley set up her famous modeling agency there. Perhaps exhausted by so much agitation, Passage Choiseul has of late become dormant, though it still draws crowds and could reawaken at any moment.

Passage Verdeau, meanwhile, has been able to retain its dignity. Inaugurated in the mid-nineteenth century beneath its high, pointed-glass arches as an extension of Passage Jouffroy, it has remained a Mecca for collectors of all types: La France Ancienne, which has replaced La Malle des Indes, deals in extremely rare books and post-cards, while stamps and rare comic books are sold by Roland Buret, and cameras can be had from Monsieur Latou. In many respects, Passage Verdeau merits its witty description as "a branch of the Drouot auction house," which sits nearby.

However, the arcade with the finest decoration is undoubtedly Passage Véro-Dodat. Its name comes from the two entrepreneurial pork-butchers who built it, and has retained all its old charm (featuring a ceiling painted by Théodore Chassériau, strict white and black floor tiles, burnished brass trim, and mezzanine windows with slatted wooden shutters). Passage Véro-Dodat houses a range of traditional shops including a book store—Le Troisième Faust—and a number of antique dealers. Pierre Passebon's

windows, for instance, display intriguing objects and furniture, while those of Eric Philippe reflect his philosophy, refined over the past twenty-five years, that objects should enter into a dialogue with one another. There is also Christian Louboutin, a more recent arrival, who artistically fashions footwear; his shoes, displayed in Emilio Terry's inspired interior, become precious objets d'art in their own right.

Hidden Museums

Paris is full of hidden spots that are far less crowded than its arcades. Architects such as Hector Guimard, Robert Mallet-Stevens, and Pierre Chereau, anxious to leave a trace of their skill and their aesthetic (which was also often an ethic) bequeathed their houses to posterity, constituting a heritage that Paris still boasts. In a similar way, several artists and writers also transformed their homes into museums, sparking an irreversible and fragile process of commemoration. All these houses dotted across Paris constitute an itinerary tinged with melancholy, one that modestly if forcefully testifies to a vanished way of life, which —though on public display—retains its intimate quality.

North of the broad boulevards and their arcades stretch the quiet streets of Nouvelle Athènes—dubbed "New Athens" in honor of the political and artistic Hellenophilia of its inhabitants. It became a village of artists, writers, theater people, and finally courtesans. At number 16 Rue Chaptal, at the end of a tree-lined, cobbled lane, stands a beige house with green wooden shutters.

Below and right: The Musée de la Vie Romantique on Rue Chaptal is housed in the former residence of an unjustly forgotten painter, Ary Scheffer. The museum recreates rooms frequented by the likes of George Sand, Franz Liszt, and Frédéric Chopin. Jewelry, manuscripts, and paintings (by Scheffer and others) are exhibited in this intimate, sober yet nostalgic setting, thanks to interior decorator Jacques Garcia, who was able to rejuvenate the house

and its old-fashioned charm with impeccable fidelity. It was once the focus of the "Nouvelle Athènes" neighborhood. Over the fireplace to the right is a portrait of George Sand, "the good lady of Nohant," by Auguste Charpentier.

Top: Dappled sunlight filters through the foliage in the garden of the Musée de la Vie Romantique, evoking the memory of George Sand, Lamartine, Delacroix, and others.

Above: Meanwhile, the footsteps of Renoir, Van Gogh, Suzanne Valadon, Maurice Utrillo, and the cat-loving T.A. Steinlen still ring on the cobblestone path leading to the Musée de Montmartre on Rue Cortot.

Right: In the home and studio of Gustave Moreau on Rue de La Rochefoucauld, a stairway spirals with the grace of a large ribbon. The unchanged decor of Moreau's residence is intimately linked to the work of that singular artist, whose spirit remains wonderfully present.

Far right, top: A terra-cotta statuette of George Sand in the Musée de la Vie Romantique.

Far right, bottom: The office of composer Gustave Charpentier—whose "musical novel," *Louise*, was a hit in 1900— is reproduced in the Musée de Montmartre.

As though lost in its garden, the house presents itself with straightforward simplicity, aspiring to nothing other than contentment. Built in 1830 as a private residence for the painter Ary Scheffer and his brother Henri, it was later occupied by writers Ernest Renan (Henri's son-in-law) and Ernest Psichari (Henri's grandson). Now transformed into the Musée de la Vie Romantique, the house still seems haunted by some of its famous guests—not only George Sand, who came accompanied in turn by Franz Liszt and Frédéric Chopin (whose statue in the indoor garden faces a rock pool), but also Lamartine, Turgenev, Delacroix, and many others.

Not far away, at 14 Rue de La Rochefoucauld, artist Gustave Moreau set up his home and studio. The facade is by André Lafon, but it was Moreau who designed the interior with extreme precision in his choice of volumes and ornamental details. Moreau's own works are still hung just as he decided they should be, and the furniture was all selected by him with the passion of a connoisseur. The large chests and hinged cabinets holding some 5,000 drawings and 350 watercolors were also designed by Moreau. Novelist Georges Charles Huysmans described Moreau as "a great artist who stands head and shoulders above the common crowd of history painters."

Further up on Montmartre is the Musée de Montmartre (12 Rue Cortot). Wonderfully faithful to its past, and again tucked in a garden with a stirring variety of colors and scents, the museum occupies a mansard-roofed house that was long the oldest private residence on the hill. Its stones must have a special soul, for the house has attracted a surprising succession of glamorous residents. It was built in the seventeenth century, then bought as a country home by Roze de Rosimon, an actor who followed Molière in performing the roles that the playwright made famous (Rosimon even imitated his mentor to the extent of dying on stage while performing in *The Imaginary Invalid*). In 1875, the house was occupied by painter Auguste Renoir (his first residence in Paris), and by Emile Bernard, an unjustly forgotten artist who invited painters Vincent Van Gogh and Paul Gaugin to stay. Subsequent inhabitants included Maximilien Luce, Suzanne Valadon and her son Maurice Utrillo, Léon Bloy, André Antoine (founder of the Théâtre-Libre), Raoul Dufy, and illustrator Francisque Poulbot (a Montmartre artist par excellence, if only because of his drawings of local street urchins, now known as "poulbots"). The museum also evokes the heyday of singer and satirist Aristide Bruant at the cabaret Au Lapin Agile, and presents a reconstitution of the office of composer Gustave Charpentier. On the walls are posters by Steinlen, Suzanne Valadon, Modigliani, and Marie Laurencin.

In a neighborhood with a completely different appeal, novelist and poet Victor Hugo bought the house on 6 Place des Vosges in 1832. It was here that he wrote *Les Misérables* and a volume of poetry, and also where he fell in love with Juliette Drouet and threw parties for his friends in the Romantic movement. The miscellaneous jumble of furniture and objects is of dubious taste, to say the least, but there are admirable drawings and ink-and-coffee

washes done by Hugo in quantities that match his verbal effusions.

The exquisite little Place Furstenberg, shaded by four paulownia trees standing guard around a fin-de-siècle lamppost, is tucked away in the Saint-Germain-des-Prés neighborhood. Here, behind an anonymous door and in a former abbey outbuilding, sits the artist's studio of painter Eugène Delacroix, which he called his "lair." He spent the last six years of his life in this house, living upstairs while working on his *Descent to the Tomb* and *Road to Calvary*, two of the strongest and most dramatic works in a career full of strength and drama. During this same period, Delacroix was working on the paintings for the walls of the church of Saint-Sulpice. Once again, a house has been transformed into a museum without losing its soul.

A short distance from the heart of Montparnasse, on a street named after sculptor Antoine Bourdelle, is a museum devoted to this artist, respectfully run by his daughter,

Left, top and bottom: Places full of memories, such as the home of Victor Hugo on Place des Vosges, induce a strange feeling of nostalgia. The writer still seems to haunt the suite of rooms displaying not only his collections but also many of his own watercolors and pen-and-ink drawings.

Right: At the Musée Bourdelle in Montparnasse, the sculptures in the studio almost seem asleep, awaiting a final tap of the chisel by artist Antoine Bourdelle. The sculptor's dwelling faithfully reflects his oeuvre.

Above and far right, top: The bathroom and bedroom of Jeanne Lanvin, a woman of wit, intelligence, and talent—including the talent of discovering people such as Armand Rateau, who decorated these rooms, now reproduced in the Musée des Arts Décoratifs.

Right: The Palais de la Porte dorée, at the edge of the Bois de Vincennes, has reconstructed the office of Maréchal Lyautey, decorated by Jacques-Emile Ruhlmann. It is typical of Ruhlmann's style in its mastery of volumes and its subtle harmony of materials and colors.

Far right, bottom: Parisian treasures have been accumulating for over a century at the Musée Carnavalet, devoted to the history of the capital. It includes numerous interiors saved from destruction, notably an Art Nouveau interior designed for the Fouquet jewelry firm (*left*) and the former ballroom of the hôtel de Wendel, with frescoes by Catalonian artist José Maria Sert (*right*).

on the day's news. Such places provide outposts for observing the habits of the original Parisian tribe with its highly codified customs. Le Cochon à l'Oreille is an authentic café where customers can order simple dishes and a variety of sandwiches, just as market porters did in the old days of Les Halles.

Above, below, right: Le Cochon à l'Oreille, Rue Montmartre. Cafés are every bit as Parisian as baguettes—the very baguettes spread with butter and consumed at the bar with a cup of coffee in the morning, amidst comments

Rhodia Dufet-Bourdelle, and her husband, furniture maker Jean Dufet. Bourdelle's vast old workshop, recently revamped by architect Christian de Portzamparc, harbors the virile lines and flawless volumes which once again revive those swinging interwar years when Montparnasse was the haunt of leading Parisian artists—Bonnard, Matisse, Germaine Richier, Alberto and Diego Giacometti, and Vieira da Silva.

Cafés

Nothing is more Parisian than a café—a place to chat, to daydream, to work, to relax, and to meet. Even if cafés elsewhere merit great affection, such as the Caffé Greco in Rome, the Florian in Venice, the Pedrocchi in Padua, and the Central Café in Vienna (where so many delightful meetings, not to mention love affairs, have taken place), cafés were born in Paris and have become a symbol and an essential part of everyday life here. London can keep its pubs, Brussels its taverns, Munich its *Bierstüben* and New York its bars; Paris boasts countless little spots waiting to be discovered. Although all apparently the same, each one has its own personality shaped by local neighborhood rituals. Even though a great many have been devastated by costly and inappropriate "modernization," it is almost always possible to find a seemingly nondescript café where the whole life of the neighborhood is re-lived at the bar, in a verbal gazette of constantly updated local incidents and events. The zinc-lined countertop—logically known as "le zinc"—littered with stacks of coasters and empty

glasses, is the ideal place for a certain kind of conversation hard to imagine anywhere else but in Paris. In a few relentless sentences, the world is put right, while stinging shafts of wit put politicians in their place. Cafés breed certainty, offering little room for doubt. It is here that Parisians gather, temporarily declaring a truce on social distinctions and differences of opinion. Everyone hammers home his or her vision of the state of things in the most categorical way. Indeed, one of the charms of café life is the idea that merely affirming something makes it true—for as long as a beer or espresso lasts, at least. In short, the world is made over every morning at the bar.

Borrowing Saint-Simon's simple technique of "sketching a small [literary] portrait with swift strokes," it is possible to trace the impact of the advent of cafés on Parisian behavior, followed by their close cousins, bistros, and restaurants. Cafés were not mere watering spots—history was often made there and, prior to the development of twentieth-century techniques for molding public opinion, cafés were the site of obstinate maneuvers designed to spark insurrection and revolt, or to spread new ideas and fads.

It was at the Palais-Royal, which Blaise Pascal called "a luxurious little town enclosed in a big city" (never were open-air cafés more graciously depraved), that Francesco Procopio dei Costelli invented the modern café in the seventeenth century. Along with coffee and hot chocolate, patrons enjoyed a surprising variety of beverages with bewildering, enigmatic names: cream of orange flower, orange peel liqueur, oil of Venus (an artful blend of

cinnamon water, carnation, vanilla, and sugar), and hippocras (sweet wine spiced with cinnamon, ginger, cloves, and mace), not to mention various scented and flavored soft drinks, frangipane juice, Queen of Spain liquor, and even pickled walnut liqueur. This last was invented by an old lady from Grenoble whom Choderlos de Laclos used as the model for the character marquise de Merteuil in *Les Liaisons Dangereuses*; the marquise's peremptory comment to Valmont might even serve as the motto of Parisian wit—"Believe me, viscount, one rarely acquires qualities one can do without."

Purveyors of brandy, mineral waters, and lemonade-like soft drinks then formed a guild called the *limonadiers*, which became so successful that in 1704 Louis XIV, always in need of cash, abolished it and sold five hundred hereditary licenses in its stead. Cafés flourished in both Paris and the provinces. Waiters, often dressed in "Armenian" coats (then the height of fashion), served a highly eclectic crowd composed of society ladies and gentlemen, clergymen, soldiers, provincial visitors, and so on.

Cafés became the official headquarters of the publicizers, that is to say men particularly well-informed in politics, literature, religion, economy, and even human interest stories, who compensated for the almost total absence of newspapers by dispensing their knowledge at places such as the Pont-Neuf, the Arsenal, and the Cordeliers monastery, as well as in public parks and gardens such as the Palais-Royal. They received greater attention, however, in cafés, where conversations could be conducted with great liveliness.

Above and left: The Café de Flore, along with Les Deux Magots, constitutes the social epicenter of Saint-Germain-des-Prés. The two cafés are not really rivals, however, since right from the start each attracted its own distinct clientele with an accuracy that no ethnologist could explain. It is a simple fact—the Flore is more cosmopolitan than Les Deux Magots, which in turn is sunnier and less intellectual. The shadow of Jean-Paul Sartre still hovers over Café de Flore, even if there are now fewer writers and more public relations officers from nearby publishing houses.

Along with the Café Procope, the Café de Foy (also located at the Palais-Royal) soon became highly renowned. Promenaders of all kinds—financiers, officers, nobles, and more modest folk—would stop there to discuss the latest news in a clamor rising above the music played by the house orchestra. Also famous was the Café du Pont-Neuf, better known as the Café Conti because of its location on the corner of Quai Conti and Rue Dauphine. There was also the Café de la Régence, praised by Diderot in *Rameau's Nephew*: "Whether the day is fine or nasty, it is a habit of mine to take a stroll in the Palais-Royal at five o'clock. . . . If the weather is cold or rainy, I seek refuge in the Café de la Régence, where I enjoy watching the chess players."

During the First Empire (1804–1814), cafés encountered stiff competition from the new pleasure-gardens (Tivoli, Ranelagh, Frascati) which offered all kinds of amusements in addition to beverages. The cafés then moved toward the boulevards (Café Riche, Café Helder, and many others) or toward the Champs-Elysées (Café Velloni, which also specialized in ice cream).

Toward the end of the nineteenth century, in addition to the literary cafés on the Left Bank (Café Serpente, Café Voltaire, Café de Buci), many establishments opened on Montmartre: La Nouvelle Athènes, Abbaye de Thelème, Café de la Place Blanche, Le Clairon de Sidi-Brahim, and Le Rat Mort, which featured an old lady customer nicknamed Fleur de Pipe, who was reputed to have inspired a Balzac character.

In *Le Paysan de Paris*, author Louis Aragon painted a picture of Le Petit Grillon, the café in Passage de l'Opéra where the

surrealists would meet, as well as Café Certa. Yet the most famous twentieth-century cafés—which fully merit their reputation —are, on the Left Bank, Les Deux Magots, the Café de Flore, La Rotonde, Le Dôme, and Le Sélect; on the Right Bank are the Café de la Paix, La Colisée, and the Café de Paris on the Champs-Elysées.

Three hundred years after their invention, cafés still perform their original role. The beverages served have barely changed since the late nineteenth century. The atmosphere has evolved along with fashion and consumer habits, and every decade adopts its specific model—Café de Flore and Les Deux Magots for the 1920s and 1930s, La Palette in the postwar period, Le Clichy in the 1950s, Café Beaubourg (designed by Christian de Portzamparc) for the 1980s.

Even the 1990s has its trendsetter: the Café Marly, designed by Olivier Gagnère for the Louvre, where a skillful use of space and volumes, handling of walls, and choice of materials reconciles a sense of monumentality with a desire for intimacy. This café

Far left: With admirable persistence, La Palette on the Left Bank has remained a favorite haunt of art students and gallery owners. Its tables regularly invade the sidewalk of Rue Jacques-Callot.
Top left: This more modest café, still steeped in its straightforward 1960s decor, is a comfortable student hang-out.
Bottom left: In contrast, the Café de l'Industrie, near Place de la Bastille, draws a more upmarket, indeed more "in" crowd.

Located in one of the eastern quarters of Paris, which are slowly coming back into fashion, Café Charbon has taken advantage of its age. Founded over a century ago, it was originally surrounded by the workshops and factories of local artisans, who constituted a local clientele. This clientele has remained faithful, yet has now been joined by new, more urban, customers. It is a reliable stop for breakfast, a lazy Sunday brunch, or a quick workday lunch composed of a plate of mixed cheeses or cold cuts as indicated on a slate hanging from beer kegs (*above*). Other customers stick around late at night, having a final drink at one of the longest bars in Paris, lit by lamps on accordion brackets taken from a nighttime fishing boat (*right*). The silhouette painted on the mirror (*left*) is by Jérôme Mesnager, whose "white bodies" can been seen on walls and bridges all over Paris.

Right: Café Beaubourg is one of two notorious modern cafés that opened near the Georges Pompidou Center (the other, Café Costes, no longer exists). It has become the favorite stamping grounds of contemporary art lovers. Designed by architect Christian de Portzamparc, the interior of Café Beaubourg is skillfully handled to make it feel almost like a club. *Below and far right*: Following the closure of

Café Costes, Gilbert Costes opened Café Marly under the arcades of the Louvre, opposite the glass pyramid. Olivier Gagnère's interior decoration brings a little Italian warmth to Paris.

responds to its glamorous architectural setting, developing a stylistic idiom of strong harmonies shrouded in soft light, in counterpoint to the bright terrace beneath the Venetian-like arcades facing I. M. Pei's pyramid. It strikes a subtle balance between the need for a certain privacy and the need to be seen. And, like every other Parisian café, it offers "snacks" at all hours of the day, though its refined fare goes beyond the usual range of salads and sandwiches, given its upscale location.

Also worth mentioning are cafés in and around the former Les Halles neighborhood (now situated halfway between two highly strategic poles, the Georges Pompidou Center and the Louvre). Le Cochon à l'Oreille on Rue Montmartre, for instance, thrived in the days when the neighborhood was livelier by night than by day: two dis-

tinct groups of customers would meet here, and only here, over a ham sandwich and bowl of onion soup at dawn (marking the end of the working day for one group, and the start for the other). These cafés still display their striking ceramic frescoes depicting, with naive application, scenes from local life in the late nineteenth century. La Cloche des Halles on Rue du Bouloi only feigns ordinariness, for behind its banal appearance hide simple but delicate treasures of bistro-style gastronomy: perfect ham, delicious quiches, and succulent tarts. Finally, on Rue Tiquetonne, in a globe-trotter's decor that would have appealed to Karen Blixen or Ernest Hemingway, a café simply called Le Café maintains the fine tradition of a back room where, once drinks have been served, the backgammon and chess boards come out. A whole "in" crowd, dressed in black, has thereby revived the *ancien régime* tradition of the nearby Palais-Royal—customers play, smoke, drink, swap ideas, and eat one of the best *croque-monsieurs* in town (a grilled ham and cheese sandwich, made here with goat's cheese and cinnamon).

On the Left Bank's Boulevard Saint-Germain, a bookstore called La Hune is flanked by Café de Flore et Les Deux Magots. These false Siamese twins are in fact as different in style as they are in appearance, yet for three-quarters of a century they have been the focus of the social life of the Saint-Germain-des-Prés crowd, a tribe of diverse origins bound by mysterious and intangible rituals and codes. Whereas Café de Flore has a more solid literary reputation, Les Deux Magots is more cosmopolitan. Such distinctions are however of little importance, for one establishment is meaningless without

the other, even if their customers rarely cross over (except at certain times of the day, when the sun appears more generous with one than with other). In both cafés, breakfast is selflessly transformed into a working meal—publishers and their press attachés in the Flore, the film and fashion crowd at Les Deux Magots (where thirty different types of whiskey are on offer). The Café de Flore, on the other hand, proposes an English-style Welsh rarebit which has its own charm, especially if served at the table just left of the door, where the customer can exchange local news not only with the white-aproned waiters but also with the cashier perched in her glass sentry box, all the while keeping one eye on a newspaper and the other on the stairway leading upstairs (where no regular would be caught dead, unless committing social suicide or displaying a form of snobbery bordering on nihilism). Indeed, knowing the right cafés is not enough in Paris—it is important to know where to sit and what to drink, which inevitably varies with the time of day (and not merely for dietary reasons). Whereas a discreet greeting is considered good taste at the Flore, people ignore one another at Les Deux Magots. At La Palette on Rue de Seine,

Right: In the foreground is the large percolator at Le Square Trousseau, a typical Paris bistro.

Far right: Le Clown Bar, near the Cirque d'hiver, is a fine example of a turn-of-the-century café: a long, curved bar, high stools, a large skylight, and tiles in geometric pattern. In one corner stands a plaster clown's head; pictured below is a very rare two-tiered gueridon table rimmed in brass, with wooden chairs sporting studded leather seats.

Far right: The Baratin, on Rue Jouye-Rouve between the Rue and the Parc de Belleville, maintains the tradition of the Parisian bistrot. The wine menu will tempt even the most radical of teetotalers, along with inventive, generous dishes, and pleasant, smiling service. The room opens to the kitchen, where Raquel is seen tending happily to hzer ovens. *Below:* The owner of Caves Solignac, an excellent bistro in Montparnasse, offers a good range of vineyard-bottled wines that ideally accompany authentic regional cuisine.

there is a great deal of cheek-kissing and flitting from table to table, which continues out to the terrace that spills onto Rue Jacques-Callot (practically turning it into a pedestrian alley), then into the back room, all in a back-and-forth rush that combines ostentatious feverishness with feigned nonchalance.

From Bistro to Restaurant

A portrait of the Paris bistro: long, sinuous bars capped in gleaming pewter or zinc; round gueridon or square, iron-legged tables topped with marble or polished wood; waiters and waitresses addressed by their first name; tile floors sprinkled with sawdust; dried hams and sausages hanging from ceilings; cut-glass windows and mirrors; and a lively, barrel-chested owner able to gab proudly and endlessly about fine vintages and good produce. Unfortunately, very few authentic examples survive, because many have been remodeled, most menus have been revamped, and some have even been converted into "wine bars" (true bistros offered only two or three dishes and a choice of two wines, red or white).

Such details are important in tracing the boundary between a "good Paris bistro" and an authentic one. Too often, of course, what passes for a bistro is simply a restaurant decorated in an attractive, old-fashioned manner, with more or less haphazard service. These microenvironments of Parisian life, however, must offer traditional cuisine prepared from quality produce whose virtues are revealed more by a good chef's knack than by oversophisticated culinary feats. Every Parisian has his or her bistro, which is obviously the best in town—and a Parisian will make a point of taking friends there, but only after extracting an oath of total secrecy.

All bistros seem the same, yet every one is different. There is Le Voltaire, Chez Benoît, Chez Georges (on Rue de Mail), Chez Henri, Chez Pauline, L'Assiette, Cartet, and several others known only to the few. It would be pointless and somewhat indiscreet to sing the specific praises of each establishment. At Le Voltaire, tables are allocated according to a strict protocol. Its clientele includes the fashion crowd, antique dealers, interior decorators, publishers, and slumming society ladies (arriving by taxi rather than in their chauffeured cars). These clans comprise one big family whose behavior and manias fuel the conversation between two hearty yet subtle courses, accompanied by carefully selected wines, all under the ironic gaze of Houdon's famous statue of Voltaire. Diners arrive in couples, in groups, or alone; friends and acquaintances see and greet each other clear across the rooms; people make a show of simplicity by asking permission to have just a bite at the bar, after the theater, or else in the "compartment" affording a view of "everything."

Chez Benoît, on the other hand, is frequented by art dealers and politicians (with city hall nearby), as well as a thoroughly respectable bourgeoisie which would be right at home in a provincial restaurant. While these customers may differ in their artistic and political opinions, all agree on the need to be well fed and on the importance of mopping up gravy with a chunk of

bread. The owner generously satisfies their requirements with classic dishes to which he adds a personal little touch that inattentive diners may not notice. Chez Georges, meanwhile, occupies a long room which looks like a Viennese pastry shop, and notably displays a feature of bistros that radically distinguishes them from restaurants: the lunch crowd is not the same as the dinner crowd. Here, lunch is the affair of journalists and the fashion industry, whereas dinner is dominated by the bourgeoisie. The menu never changes—economists could abandon their clever statistics and simply keep an eye on the price of the celery-and-mayonnaise salad in order to calculate variations in the cost of living in Paris. The wine cellar holds treasures from Burgundy as well as Bordeaux, while Armagnac makes a perfect conclusion to a meal. Everything is served by attentive, bantering ladies under the watchful eye of the owner (who appears to prefer the delights of conversation with regular customers to the rigors of life in the kitchen). Of course the quality of the cuisine, like the menu itself, never changes, which is a highly civilized way of making customers feel right at home even when they dine out.

In contrast, it is better to head for Chez Pauline in the evening, if only because it is impossible to find a nearby parking spot during the day. The cuisine is almost the same as that of a restaurant, yet with the sincerity and attentiveness to fresh produce that constitute the basis of the bistro ethic. Similarly, at Chez L'Ami Louis on Rue du Vertbois, time seems to have frozen (only the smoke-darkened walls reveal the passing decades). Not only has the setting

Three establishments—restaurants rather than bistros—perfectly sum up the Parisian art of dining. *Left-hand page*: Bernard, the proprietor of Chez Georges on Rue du Mail welcomes his guests (*top*), who tend to be journalists and entrepreneurs at lunchtime, changing to a more varied clientele for dinner, always served by charming waitresses (*far left*). Meanwhile, the wood paneling of Le Voltaire (*bottom*) makes it feel like a club which, given its air of familiarity, it almost is. *Left and below*: Time seems to have come to a halt at Chez l'Ami Louis on Rue du Vertbois, attracting enthusiasts of healthy, hearty dishes. Still stenciled on the window are "ortolans" (a small bird, highly esteemed as a delicacy since antiquity), though they are no longer on the menu, since they are now considered an endangered species—as are authentic bistros, for that matter.

remained unchanged, so has the clientele. This bistro is almost like a family boarding house—patrons come to eat the same dish at the same table on the same day, served by the same artificially grumpy waiter. Staff and customers both appear to pass their entire lives here. The menu is equally timeless: *foie gras*, roast chicken, snails in a garlic sauce that has permanently perfumed the premises, thin French fries, game meats, mushrooms, scallops, and so on. In the back of the restaurant, a sideboard hosts a still life that would seem to be the work of a Flemish master—but it lacks a cat. A stove at the entrance, meanwhile, stands ready to warm patrons as well as their hearts.

The extreme antithesis of this bistro tradition is represented by Le Grand Véfour near the Palais-Royal—it incarnates the two things that French-style restaurants do best: cuisine and ambiance. A delicately decorated ceiling enlivens the room, while the painted figurines on the walls have long borne silent witness to intimate confidences, both political and literary: this is where Bonaparte seduced Joséphine; where Victor Hugo dined after the controversial performance of his play, *Hernani*; where Colette had her headquarters; where Jean Cocteau held court; where Sacha Guitry coined brilliant if gloriously misogynist aphorisms; where Jean Giraudoux poked at his food while daydreaming of diaphanous young women; and where writer and minister of culture André Malraux (when occasionally unfaithful to the restaurant Lasserre, where he always ordered pigeon) relived the Spanish civil war for guests enthralled by the scope of his dazzling, heroic exploits, which also included the art

of dining. In the 1950s, photographer Richard Avedon, when in Paris for fashion shows, would make Le Grand Véfour his cafeteria, bringing along models who epitomized that entire era—Dorian Leigh, Suzy Parker, and Dovima. Perhaps these young women had never seen anything so wonderfully exotic as a wine steward pouring champagne into crystal decanters under the watchful eye of Raymond Oliver who, just after the war, had the genius to restore the grand principles of French gastronomy in a manner as faithful as it was innovative.

Older Parisians remember when the best restaurants were grouped around the markets of Les Halles, sensitive to the rhythm of seasonal produce and fresh arrivals at that enormous, noisy, eye-opening pantry. The most famous of those restaurants, still unchanged just a few years ago, were La Grille and L'Escargot d'Or on Rue Montorgueil. People came from all over the world to sample this simple yet skillful cuisine, nourishing and authentic, served by black-jacketed waiters in long white aprons.

Paris, the political capital of France, is the gastronomic capital of the world. Without indulging in culinary imperialism, this reputation is confirmed by comments made by foreigners: "In the Western world, when a restaurant is famous for its cuisine, you can be sure that the French flag flies over the oven." Another points out that, "Signs of respect and allegiance come from all quarters—at the White House, the menus of banquets are printed in French, the international language of gastronomy."

Yet an Epicurean attitude and culinary know-how are not enough. They must be

Le Grand Véfour is a quintessential Parisian restaurant in terms of interior decoration—which is certainly the finest in Paris, with its glass-covered paintings and its neoclassical interior (*left*). Sunlight from the gardens of the Palais-Royal softly bronzes the restaurant, where each table has its own history, sheltered from the cares of life (*above*). After a period of vicissitudes following the death of legendary chef Raymond Olivier, Le Grand Véfour has once again attained culinary standards that match its interior.

accompanied by aesthetic principles and subtle sociological awareness, as the great chef Auguste Escoffier seemed to think when he wrote in his memoirs that, "I would like to see proof of France's civilization reflected in the fame of our cuisine." And when praising the merits of various provincial cuisine within France, Escoffier added, "I have often been asked why French chefs are better than those of other countries. I think the answer is simple: you need merely realize that French soil has the privilege of producing, naturally and abundantly, the finest vegetables, the finest fruit, and the finest wines in the world. France also has the most delicate fowl, the most tender meat, the most varied and tasty game. Its seacoasts provide it with fine fish and shellfish. It is therefore natural that the French simultaneously become gourmets and good chefs." Gastronomic writer La Reynière, meanwhile, declared that, "Although Paris produces nothing of its own, since not a sheaf of wheat grows there, not a lamb is born there, and not a single cauliflower is harvested there, it is a center that attracts everything from the four corners of the earth, because Paris is where the respective qualities of everything related to human nourishment are best appreciated, where they are best turned to the advantage of human sensuality."

It was in Paris that the first restaurant was founded. Caterers had a monopoly on the sale of cooked meats and dishes in the eighteenth century, until in 1765 a certain Boulanger, on Rue des Poulies near the Louvre, undertook to serve "restaurants"—a word then meaning delicacies such as broth, pigs' feet, and other stews—by the portion. Once Boulanger won the lawsuit the caterers brought against him, the door to the restaurant trade was flung open, and establishments soon proliferated in Paris, immediately acquiring both a national and international reputation. One of the main restaurants from that period, La Procope, still exists on Rue de l'Ancienne-Comédie. Le Beauvilliers is also worth mentioning, which served court cuisine at the Palais-Royal, as well as Les Trois Frères, which specialized in "exotic" cuisine from Marseilles (succulent bouillabaisse, salt cod, and so on). Since then, nothing has slowed the spread of restaurants. Today, there are

Below: Kaspia, the most Parisian of Russian restaurants, is located above a shop selling smoked fish, caviar, and other essentials of a well-ordered life. In an atmosphere almost resembling a private apartment, waiters serve simple yet perfect dishes at

any time of the day, with irreproachable courtesy, providing an elegant conclusion to an outing at the opera or theater.
Right: La Maison Prunier, not far from Place de l'Etoile, has retained its original interior, designed by René Herbst. After having been closed for several years, its mythical status is fully justified by the originality of its decor and the quality of the fish served there.

Below: Waiters at Brasserie Lipp dress in black suit, black shoes, and black bow tie, plus a long white apron. Regulars occupy their tables according to a map of puzzling complexity. The interior is the perfect archetype of a traditional brasserie, where people come to be seen as much as to eat.

Right: Diners still marvel at the heavily decorated ceiling of the vast Train Bleu. This magnificent restaurant was named for an overnight train to the Riviera which no longer runs, having been replaced by high-speed trains, yet a wonderful series of panoramas painted overhead still depict enchanted shores. Space is in such generous supply here that Parisians enjoy lounging in this traveler's rest, only to return home afterwards.

approximately one hundred restaurants for every bookstore in Paris (a few of which, for that matter, specialize in books on the art of dining). Given such choice, everyone can suit his or her palate, while at the same time satisfying aesthetic preferences—thanks to an unequaled selection of interiors.

Brasseries

A brasserie, from the French term for "brewery," was originally a place where beer was consumed, and is still associated with the Alsace region (though frequently owned by a native of Aveyron, to the south). When they spread to Paris, brasseries challenged local gastronomic codes and customs; unlike a restaurant, a brasserie serves meals all day long, from twelve noon to one in the morning, shifting from lunch to snacks to tea to dinner, right up to after-theater supper. In short, with its more flexible opening hours and its catering to various eating habits (it is perfectly possible to order a main course and a glass of beer at any time without receiving a scowl from the maitre d'), brasseries combined a new approach to dining, proposing a menu composed of simple, hearty dishes such as sauerkraut and sausages, *saveloy* (smoked pork), pickled herring, and shellfish, all of which should be accompanied by Alsatian wines or beer.

These qualities are sometimes enhanced by the elegance, beauty, and magic of the setting itself. Certain brasseries—now often listed as historical monuments—were decorated to appeal to customers' desire for a certain stateliness once reserved for the aristocracy and upper bourgeoisie. A good number of Parisian brasseries, founded in the early twentieth century, have retained their turn-of-the-century interiors where deeply carved woodwork confidently harmonizes with cut glass and tiles bearing floral and animal motifs.

Mollard, founded in 1867 on Rue Saint-Lazare, boasts a particularly magnificent interior (designed by Niermans and executed by Bichi). In the large dining room, ceramic decoration gracefully complements stone mosaics depicting flowers, stars, and butterflies. The other, smaller dining room, is decorated with ceramic panels from Sarreguemines, illustrating the cities served by the nearby Saint-Lazare train station—Trouville, Saint-Germain-en-Laye, Ville-d'Avray, and so on—interspersed with scenes of Parisian life. Below the coffered ceiling, damask-covered tables entice visitors to savor one of the impressive seafood platters for which Mollard is famous (as well as, at teatime, its creamy hot chocolate). Service is a ballet of waiters in black vests and white aprons.

Julien, a brasserie in the Faubourg Saint-Denis neighborhood, was named after the son that a pretty ballerina bore to founder Monsieur Barbarin. It bears the fruit of the combined talents of architect Fournier and decorator Trézel; the windows and mirrors in substantial stucco frames create an ideal setting for the glass panels depicting Mucha-style allegories of the four seasons. At the entrance, a bar made of Cuban mahogany by Louis Majorelle allows customers waiting for a table to observe the crowd already occupying the dining room. Another magnificent example of a

turn-of-the-century brasserie is Bofinger, in the Bastille neighborhood, which has preserved its original decor except for a few unfortunate glass tulips which now pointlessly shade the formerly bare light bulbs on the ceiling of the vast ground-floor room. The large glass skylight, the low-relief ceramic decoration in the form of butterflies, birds, and flowers, and the private salons upstairs (decorated with paintings by the Alsatian artist Hansi) combine to create a magnificent ambiance. Everything is perfectly suited to the appreciation of the opulent sauerkraut dishes which, along with the inevitable seafood, are Bofinger's specialty—a worthy conclusion to an evening at the Bastille opera house.

In the nearby Gare de Lyon station, Le Train Bleu stands as a final witness to the bygone era of train travel when stations were a whole world in themselves. Along with the delights of a voyage, the competing railroad companies once offered travelers elegant (indeed, luxurious) hotels, restaurants, and brasseries. Such a world would have disappeared completely had not the magnificent Train Bleu been spared, aloof from the surrounding bustle. Below the campanile which station architect Denis probably thought an appropriate allusion to Italy (the destination of many trains), the enormous dining room of Le Train Bleu has retained not only its interior decoration, including a ceiling painted by François Flameng, but also the arrangement of its immense tables covered with immaculate white damask tablecloths, its high benches topped with plants, its wide aisles, and above all a cuisine still influenced by Lyon, the gastronomic capital of provincial

Far left, top: Just across from the recently renovated Gare du Nord train station, Le Terminus Nord serves—even late into the evening—travelers arriving from London on the high-speed Eurostar. It is decorated with lively scenes of Parisian life in a Roaring Twenties style.
Far left, bottom: Near Place de la Bastille, the large skylight of Bofinger casts a soft light on tables. More warmth and intimacy is added by decorative details such as wood inlay in delicate floral patterns.

Left: Brasserie Lipp, in Saint-Germain-des-Prés, during the peaceful afternoon hours—one important feature of brasseries is that they serve food and drink throughout the day.
Above: Monkeys on the ceiling of Lipp.

France, which is now just two hours away by high-speed train.

Perhaps the most famous brasserie in Paris, or at any rate the most Parisian of brasseries, is Brasserie Lipp. For over a century it has fueled not only literary myths, situated in the Saint-Germain-des-Prés neighborhood, but also political gossip, given that so many governmental and parliamentary figures have made this brasserie their cafeteria. At Brasserie Lipp, choice of table counts more than choice of dish; yet it is important to feign indifference to the hierarchy instituted by the maitre d', who knows how to arrange his dining rooms into an accurate and often surprising map of current political geography.

A few yards down the Boulevard Saint-Germain is Vagenende, a former "Chartier *bouillon*" (or working-class restaurant) that now offers its holy trinity of shellfish, sausage, and veal dishes in an Art Nouveau setting of mirrors, lacy woodwork, and glass-protected landscapes by Pivain. Similarly, two restaurants from the same period, Polidor and Perraudin, also located in the Latin quarter, have equally authentic if somewhat more modest interiors, and serve family-style cooking to a stream of lunchtime regulars.

It was in 1895 that Camille Chartier founded a restaurant at 7 Rue de Faubourg-Montmartre, offering a broth-and-meat dish, or *bouillon* (simmered for seven hours!), at a reasonable, set price. Six hundred pigeonholes, each with its numbered napkin, testified to the success of his attempt to establish a regular clientele of modest office workers and artisans in this one-time working-class neighborhood. The

Right: In 1895, Camille Chartier opened his first "bouillon," or working-class restaurant, on Rue du Faubourg-Montmartre. The austere decoration has remained unchanged since that time, when it provided simple, healthy meals to students and workers with modest pocketbooks. The more diverse clientele that followed was attracted by the reasonable prices. Until recently, regulars stored their napkins in a huge set of pigeonholes lining the entrance wall.

Above: Another of these former "bouillons" has just been restored on Rue Racine in the sumptuous but austere surroundings of turn-of-the-century panelling in almond green with wrought-iron wall-lamps. Unsentimentally this restaurant has recreated a world removed from the bustle of the Latin Quarter— a world which would otherwise be lost forever.

Living in a hotel is no longer fashionable, as it once was. Generations long considered it a way to escape everyday demands without foregoing the pleasures of social life. Depending on one's means, it was possible to choose the Ritz or the Meurice, or else live in far more modest establishments in Saint-Germain-des-Prés and Montparnasse. But this waning tradition has been counterbalanced by an improvement of hotel cuisine, which was long associated with mindless conformity. In grand hotels, dining rooms are deliberately spacious, and now provide an appropriately calm and elegant setting for business lunches.

Below: A table is set at L'Espadon, the restaurant in the Hotel Ritz.

Right: Les Ambassadeurs, in the Hotel Crillon, inevitably evokes the magnificence of Versailles.

restaurant provided honest, healthy meals, and the interior decoration, considered austere at the time, is now jealously preserved by Monsieur Lemaire, the owner since 1945. The menu still features classic items such as hard-boiled egg with mayonnaise, and roast lamb—cornerstones of a French working-class lunch, even though in the evening Chartier becomes the haunt of an elegant crowd in search of the exotic.

Hotels

Even though it has long been the privilege of hotels to provide a discreet retreat for clandestine love affairs or for business conversations requiring an almost conjugal intimacy, the art of dining was not considered to be one of their attractions.

So for a long time the term "hotel cuisine" was pejorative, describing a bland compromise between dietary discipline and the need to please everyone—which of course pleased no one. In recent years, this purgatory has been transformed into a kind of secret paradise. Paris hotels, finally imitating those in the provinces, have recruited a whole generation of well-known young chefs. Interiors have been refurbished without being betrayed, for they were often the sole attraction protecting these restaurants from total desertion. Thus the Restaurant des Princes in the Hotel George V still boasts bas-reliefs of nymphs and deer, alluding to the paintings in the four alcoves, where languid beauties tremble at the sight of naked shepherds.

The Hotel Meurice, in majestic seventeenth-century decoration of gilded woodwork, marble Corinthian columns, heavy silk damask drapes, painted ceilings, and beveled-mirror screens, serves dishes cooked in the grand tradition that accords perfectly with the setting. The Espadon Restaurant in the Hotel Ritz, with its equally opulent interior, respects the same grand tradition, with a slight penchant for seafood. A similar respect is shown at Les Ambassadeurs in the Hotel Crillon and, in an more intimate way, at the Hotel Raphaël, where lunch or dinner may be concluded in one of the adjoining salons, or even at the bar.

Living in a hotel was long a fashion championed by Coco Chanel at the Ritz, Salvador Dali at the Meurice, Dirk Bogarde at the Lancaster, Roberto Rossellini at the Raphaël, and Michel Simon in more modest but certainly livelier hotels. The actress

Pauline Carton, meanwhile, who devoted much of her career portraying that eminently Parisian character of "the concierge," lived (and died) at the Hotel Brighton on Rue de Rivoli.

Living in a hotel is still synonymous with watching life go by, free from the burden of possessions. Although the vogue has passed (squeezed by the economy and by a certain conformism which insists that everyone live like everyone else of equal income), Parisian hotels survive in all their diversity, from glamorous establishments to student dives. Each has its own personality, and many tempt Parisians to "get away" for a few days without actually leaving Paris.

The name "Ritz" symbolizes luxury from Paris to London and from Lisbon to Madrid. The Paris hotel is a sprightly hundred years old, and its noble facade on Place Vendôme (the former Lauzun residence) is still flanked by the most prestigious jewelers in the capital. César Ritz wanted to found a hotel that was not only profoundly respectful of the grand traditions of hospitality but also thoroughly modern, so he installed a private bathroom in every room or suite, a unique luxury at the time. The cold water was icy in order to please Americans, while the hot water was boiling to accommodate the British. The future Edward VII, when Prince of Wales, made the Ritz his Parisian pied-à-terre. His grandson, the duke of Windsor, took refuge their after abdicating as Edward VIII. Marcel Proust arranged his rendezvous there as soon as he woke up—which was usually shortly before midnight—and ordered ice-cold beer. Ernest Hemingway, meanwhile,

liberated it in 1944 from its undesirable German occupants; the hotel would show its recognition by naming the most private of its three bars after the novelist. A list of Ritz residents would read like a high-society register crossed with the credits to a Hollywood dream film—the representatives of the last sovereign houses of Europe now follow in the footsteps of Alphonse XIII of Spain, Manuel II of Portugal, Marie of Romania, and Alexander III of Russia, not to mention a plethora of Russian grand dukes and Austro-Hungarian archdukes, while the likes of Charlie Chaplin, Marlene Dietrich, Lauren Bacall, and Humphrey Bogart are also on the register. There were great eccentrics as well—the marquise Casati (whose boa constrictor fed on live rabbits), Berry Wall (whose chow chow always dined at table dressed in black tie provided by the famous Charvet firm), and Evelyn Walsh McLean (whose hooded falcon was very fond of pigeon). Today, all untoward noise is muted by the thick carpets of the refined "French decor" in the Espadon Restaurant, as well as in the corridors.

A stone's throw away, on Rue Saint-Honoré is a newcomer who paradoxically seems to have been around since the Second Empire. The Hotel Costes, formerly the Hotel de France et de Choiseul, was founded by Jean-Louis Costes, who already startled Paris with his Café Costes in Les Halles, designed by the young Philippe Starck. Eschewing the avant-garde, Costes turned instead to past refinement, thanks to the talent of whimsical interior decorator Jacques Garcia. Classicism is leavened with extravagance, and highly diverse styles are

Far left: In the garden of the Ritz, summer light gently bathes the outdoor restaurant, an oasis of serenity.
Left: The rooms in the Hotel Montalembert combine traditional furnishings with resolutely contemporary design. Entire days can be spent reading in such rooms, going out only to buy yet more books in a neighborhood full of publishing houses.

Above and below: The Hotel Costes seems to have abolished time, thanks to the strange familiarity of an interior that seems to evoke so many memories.

Above: Some hotels seem like country houses right in the center of Paris. At the Hotel de l'Abbaye Saint-Germain, for instance, guests can lounge on a balcony, stroll in the delightfully green garden, or browse through newspapers in front of the fireplace in the salon. True luxury is not merely a question of money, it is also a way of organizing life—which requires great art in the midst of urban agitation.
Right: For those who would like to "get away" without actually leaving Paris, having breakfast in one of the capital's grand hotels is an exquisite and exotic way to begin the day. The Hotel Meurice, an establishment where the finest traditions of hospitality are maintained, offers an early morning view of the Tuileries Gardens. More stately are the crystal chandeliers at the Ritz (*page 240*).

blended with faultless taste, recreating a setting and tradition of pure invention. The Hotel Costes is more than a hotel, it is a club whose every room has a theme, displaying the spoils of a keen treasure hunt in antique shops, curio stores, and flea markets. So even though the hotel has only recently opened its doors, it appears to have always existed, demonstrating the skill with which modern facilities have been incorporated into a nostalgic setting.

Radically different is the Hotel Montalembert, surrounded by publishing houses, antique dealers, and bookstores on the Left Bank. Its proudly, yet moderately, modernist interiors are the work of Christian Liaigre, who perfectly expressed the hotel's goal to reinvigorate French interior decoration. Clean lines, light tones of gray and beige underscored by touches of black, and elegantly simple furniture generate true warmth—thanks to a few refinements such as the fireplace at the bar, where scented logs burn and pine cones crackle, flanked by shelves lined with books from Gallimard, the publishing house next door.

Another secret enclave of refined, bucolic pleasure is the artfully planted garden of the Hotel Bristol. Almost like an aviary, the garden is patrolled by high-society, gourmet sparrows who boldly alight at tables, ready to share a slice of pound cake (as long it is English). Once these guests have somewhat wistfully departed, a plunge into the pool and siesta on the teakwood deck bring dreams of the great liners of yesteryear.

In a spirit where privacy prevails, the Hotel de l'Abbaye Saint-Germain on Rue Cassette offers all the comfort of a wealthy provincial household right in the heart of the Saint-Germain-des-Prés neighborhood. Charming and sophisticated details convey a concern for attractiveness and convenience. Sophistication is understood here in the finest sense, not mere magnificence but appreciation of unique objects and noble materials. Tables are set for breakfast in the quiet of the cobbled courtyard, pervaded by luxuriant greenery, though guests can also be served on one of the charming balconies or terraces which adorn many of the rooms. Time and noise are forgotten here. It is easy to imagine spending hours at a time in the simple elegance of these rooms, or perhaps reading near the fireplace in the salon, adorned with a fine terra-cotta figure which mingles well with the surrounding paintings and objects. Here, entire days pass in delightful indolence—another authentic facet of life in Paris.

When spring comes softly to Paris, certain places convey the city's special appeal better than others. Seen from certain enchanted spots—such as the royal suite at the Hotel Meurice, overlooking the Tuileries Gardens—Paris seems to quiver all the more, its vistas becoming fluid beneath an immense, shimmering sky. Indeed, Paris has the most beautiful sky in the world—sometimes northern, sometimes Mediterranean, neither blue nor gray—constantly visited by perfectly shaped clouds floating across a wonderfully silhouetted skyline. In the time it takes to sip afternoon tea, or a cocktail, Paris reveals the perfect precision of its design, with unsuspected islands of greenery richly dotting an ocean of ardent stone.

VISITOR'S GUIDE

The best places in town:
charming hotels,
quaint traditional bistros,
Parisian cafés, antique and
second-hand shops,
unique artisans–in short
the art of living in Paris.

Paris is like a storybook which you can enjoy throughout your lifetime; one which you often consult then put aside, but which you always keep close at hand. Each neighborhood has its charm: adventure awaits you at every street corner. If splendor and opulence characterize the "beaux quartiers," other neighborhoods offer as much in their vivid authenticity. A simple taste will spur the enthusiast to seek out and discover new areas, to experience more immediately and intensely the inexpressible charm of minute detail hidden in the mundane, which in reality is often merely a question of perception. One may, for example, perceive a sense of modesty in the city, because Paris is both modest and immodest, discreet and ostentatious, alluring and severe....

In order to become more intimately acquainted with Paris, we have included the addresses (and page numbers) of all those places evoked throughout the book, both by text and photograph. You will also find a list of excellent addresses located on both the Right and Left Banks. The process of selection was difficult—how is it possible to include all the charming locations, and all the exquisite places in so little space? It seems an impossible task. We also limited our list to include only those locations most familiar to us. But in doing so we were regretfully forced to exclude all the restaurants serving delicious foreign cuisine. You will find only a few addresses in the 7th, 8th, 16th, and 17th arrondissements since they are principally residential neighborhoods.

The old bistros are concentrated around Les Halles, the Marais, and the Bastille, while the important antique shops are mostly located along the Left Bank.

In short, this guide does not aim to be a tourist manual and therefore does not list all the important museums and monuments, which can easily be found in numerous books available on Paris. We decided instead to limit our entries to a few choice small museums whose warmth reflects the *art de vivre* of the artists who lived in them before they opened to the public. Do not be impatient in your search for a hotel, a restaurant, or a bakery—instead consult the index. There you will find the addresses grouped alphabetically for each neighborhood, as they are in this guide. Paris will not bear with impatience or imprecision, or worse yet, indifference. You should love Paris passionately with a touch of blindness, by letting your dreams and desires overcome you. Paris is a storybook for everyone.

LEFT BANK

HOTELS

HÔTEL DES GRANDS-ÉCOLES
75, rue du Cardinal-Lemoine
75005
Tel.: 01 43 26 79 23
A few steps from the Panthéon at the end of a private street you will discover this old-fashioned charming hotel. Three small houses offer thirty-nine rooms overlooking a garden where, on azure mornings, you may have breakfast amidst flowers and trees (page 33).

HÔTEL DE L'ABBAYE SAINT-GERMAIN
10, rue Cassette 75006
Tel.: 01 45 44 38 11
www.hotel-abbaye.com
On a small tranquil street between the Luxembourg Gardens and Saint-Germain-des-Prés, this seventeenth-century convent has been converted into a pleasant and elegant hotel. The four balcony suites, each decorated in a different style, look out onto either the main courtyard or the garden—an emerald oasis (page 238).

L'HÔTEL
13, rue des Beaux-Arts 75006
Tel.: 01 44 41 99 00
www.l-hotel.com
Between the Seine and Saint-Germain-des-Prés, this calm hotel abounds with history: Mistinguett lived here for several years amidst her Art Deco furniture, and Oscar Wilde spent his last days here. The staircase, which leads to a balcony suite, is highly theatrical.

HÔTEL LUTÉTIA
45, boulevard Raspail 75006
Tel.: 01 49 54 46 46
www.lutetia-paris.com
The only palace on the Left Bank dates back to 1910. Built on the initiative of the department store Au Bon Marché in order to cater to its customers coming from the French provinces, the Hôtel Lutétia has always been frequented by intellectuals, artists, and politicians (General de Gaulle spent part of his honeymoon here) and continues to be their preferred hotel. Renovated in its original Art Deco style in 1983 by Sonia Rykiel and Sybille de Margerie, its bar area is considered to be one of the more pleasant meeting places in Paris—its brass decoration reflects the distinct style of the designer Slavik.

HÔTEL DES MARRONNIERS
21, rue Jacob 75006
Tel.: 01 43 25 30 60
www.paris-hotel-marronniers.com
In the heart of the Saint-Germain-des-Prés neighborhood sits this small hotel of thirty-seven rooms situated between a courtyard and a garden filled with beautiful trees, under the shade of which breakfast or tea is served.

LE RÉCAMIER
3 bis, place Saint-Sulpice 75006
Tel.: 01 43 26 04 89
A little removed from the square dominated by the church of Saint-Sulpice, this small hotel shaded by rows of plane trees offers real old-fashioned charm.

HÔTEL LE RELAIS CHRISTINE
3, rue Christine 75006
Tel.: 01 40 51 60 80
www.relais-christine.com
On a calm street and in a privileged setting near Saint-Germain-des-Prés, the cathedral of Notre Dame, and the banks the Seine, this hotel offers some fifty rooms situated between a courtyard and a terraced garden. The welcoming reception area reflects the warmth of the wood wainscoting and elegant fireplace of the lounge. The rooms are furnished in antique style and the breakfast area is in the cellar beneath the archways of the old kitchen.

LE MONTALEMBERT
3, rue de Montalembert 75007
Tel.: 01 45 49 68 68
www.montalembert.com
Between the Seine and the boulevard Saint-Germain, and a few steps from the French publishing house Gallimard (whose books line the walls of the bar) you will find, hidden behind a 1920s classical facade, a comfortable and elegantly designed hotel, conceived by the interior decorator Christian Liaigre (page 237).

HÔTEL SAINT-SIMON
14, rue de Saint-Simon 75007
Tel.: 01 44 39 20 20
www.hotelducdesaintsimon.com
Not far from the boulevard Saint-Germain and the Assemblée Nationale, you will find this charming and tranquil hotel. The bar area and the breakfast room are located in vaulted cellars, which in the seventeenth century were undoubtedly the outbuildings of the convent of the Sisters of the Visitation.

RESTAURANTS AND BRASSERIES

L'ATELIER MAÎTRE ALBERT
Guy Savoy
1, Rue Maître Albert 75005
Tel.: 01 56 81 30 01
For years now, Guy Savoy has been the toast of gastronauts. His intelligence and generosity are the driving force behind the L'Atelier Maître Albert, whose interior design is signed Jean-Michel Wilmotte. In this old Parisian district close to Notre-Dame, Savoy has created an authentic inn with a rotisserie serving dishes that are simple yet—Savoy being Savoy—highly sophisticated. The wine-cellar featuring top vintages and small regional wines is certainly one of the capital's finest, not to mention the cigar selection. For true connaisseurs.

BRASSERIE BALZAR
49, rue des Écoles 75005
Tel.: 01 43 54 13 67
www.brasseriebalzar.com
In the heart of the Latin Quarter, close to the Sorbonne, you will find the steadfast Brasserie Balzar where for lunch or dinner you can enjoy Alsacian *choucroute, gigot d'agneau, foie de veau* or *raie au beurre fondu* in a dining area often frequented by professors and academics.

ALLARD
41, rue Saint-André-des-Arts 75006
Tel.: 01 43 26 48 23
This old bistro with its ceramic and mosaic decor is a favorite meeting place for editors, in whose company you may commence with such dishes as *saucisson chaud de Lyon* or *petit salé*, and finish sumptuously with a *symphonie aux trois chocolats* or a *tarte fine aux pommes*.

LA BASTIDE ODÉON
7, rue Corneille 75006
Tel.: 01 43 26 03 65
www.bastide-odeon.com

In this pleasant restaurant filled at midday with senators, editors, and writers, and in the evening with actors and theatergoers from the Théâtre de l'Odéon, a fixed-price menu offers a rich assortment of dishes which burst with flavor when garnished with herbs and olive oil.

BOUILLON RACINE

3, rue Racine 75006
Tel.: 01 44 32 15 60
www.bouillon-racine.com
A few steps from the Théâtre de l'Odéon, this old "bouillon," no longer offers the traditional cuisine well-known in such popular restaurants. Instead, be prepared for *cuisine à la bière* and delicious pastries. The interior has retained its theatrical Art Nouveau decor with beveled mirrors, stained glass, woodwork, and calligraphy with gilded leaf trimming.

CHEZ MAÎTRE PAUL

12, rue Monsieur-le-Prince 75006
Tel.: 01 43 54 74 59
In a classical setting, Jean-François Debert continues the great Franche-Comté tradition initiated by Paul Maître twenty years ago—*cuisine à la crème* or with white wine. Senators and editors have not far to go in order to taste this genuine rural cuisine which is best when accompanied by a bottle of Arbois wine.

BRASSERIE LIPP

151, boulevard Saint-Germain
Tel.: 01 45 48 53 91
www.brasserie-lipp.fr
This famous brasserie, located in the heart of Saint-Germain-des-Prés, has for generations seen the comings and goings of political, literary, and entertainment celebrities in Paris. Established in the late nineteenth century by an Alsacian, its terra cotta tile decor, adorned with cranes and parrots, has been listed as a historical monument. Traditional brasserie cooking is accompanied by a guaranteed show, especially on the first floor (pages 228 and 231).

MARKETS

Alongside the fondness Parisians retain for their markets, there coexists a ubiquitous nostalgia for country life. These markets embody and transmit the strong personalities which constitute the various villages of the capital. There is also the beauty of the stalls and the daily specialties which foreigners discover with amazement.

There are about ninety-four markets in Paris. Some are covered—such as the Saint-Quentin market, whose elegant metallic structure oc cupies the place where once stood the old Saint-Laurent fair which drew crowds of Flemish merchants. The Saint-Germain market is itself a vestige of a fair which can be traced back to the twelfth century. Then there is the Secretan market. Numerous other markets fill the sidewalks on certain days, such as those on the avenue du Président-

Wilson, and the boulevard Raspail— now an ecological sanctuary, perhaps because it unwinds on a narrow divider strip surrounded by the incessant procession of automobiles. There are also those on the boulevard Edgar-Quinet, Rue de la Convention and the boulevard Richard-Lenoir (page 61)—where people come from far and wide since it is the most renowned—and the market on the boulevard Menilmontant, by far the most exotic with a splendid array of aromas and hues. There are others which for many years have occupied lively squares: the place Monge or the trendy place d'Aligre, where the fashionable gather to exchange inquisitive glances. Others have transformed certain streets into permanent markets, such as the Rues Montorgueil, Lepic, de Buci, Cler, Mouffetard, or Poncelet.

Curious folk, nature-loving *flâneurs*, collectors, and enthusiasts of second-hand objects adventure into the more specialized markets, such as the famous flower market on the Ile de la Cité (see page 21), the bird market on the Quai de la Mégisserie along with the plant nursery shops, the stamp market in the Champs-Elysées gardens, and the book market under the old covered market of the one-time Vaugirard slaughterhouse, which is now the Parc Georges Brassens. To browse even more, venture into the numerous city-limit flea markets at, for example, Porte de Montreuil and Porte de Vanves and the Saint-Ouen market which is composed of a conglomerate of lots skillfully arranged to cater to a hierarchy of interests which differ in quality and scope. There is everything to satisfy the most ardent browsing enthusiasts.

LA CLOSERIE DES LILAS

171, boulevard du Montparnasse 75006
Tel.: 01 40 51 34 50
Henry James and Ernest Hemingway were regulars of the Closerie and its piano bar. The intellectual tradition continues in this artists' hideout which offers the customer two possibilities: the terrace restaurant, where the traditional menu is relatively expensive, and the brasserie, where one may order a *steak tartare* or a *salade niçoise* at an affordable price. The bar is a pleasant place to have a drink while listening to the sound of an inspired pianist's improvised melodies (page 2).

LE COMPTOIR

9, Carrefour de l'Odéon 75006
Tel.: 01 44 27 07 97
Riding on a wave of success, Yves Camdeborde has sold La Régalade to open, with his wife Claudine, a hotel on the ground floor of which he has set up a

restaurant complete with a terrace. The menu, revealing essentially South-West influences, offers tuna belly served with sucrine lettuce, excellent boudin blanc (white sausage), and a whole range of pasta—pressed or marbled, such as the artichoke, foie gras, and pork cheek combination – or else, on a completely different register, iced shellfish and ginger juice or Salers tournedos... The definition of happiness: securing a table for dinner (bookings only).

LA MÉDITERRANÉE

2, Place de l'Odéon 75006
Tel.: 01 43 26 02 30
Who can remember the Balthus painting that used to welcome clients as they entered this establishment? The painting may have gone, but the Bérard and Vertès frescoes are still there, and since the young chef Denis Rippa took over the kitchen in 2001, this mythical restaurant has regained the full

splendor of its aura. Savor the crispy lobster-tail croustillant, the tuna tartare, the mille-feuille of Beefheart tomato and crabmeat, as well as the Mediterranean bouillabaisse or the roasted wild bass with carbonara risotto. Impeccable, attentive service matches a talented, simple, and inventive cuisine. Ideal for business lunches or suppers after a night at the Théâtre de l'Odéon.

PERRAUDIN

157, rue Saint-Jacques 75005
Tel.: 01 46 33 15 75
The cordial reception at this small traditional restaurant makes you feel very much at home—the regulars rush here at midday.

POLIDOR

41, rue Monsieur-le-Prince 75006
Tel.: 01 43 26 95 34
This authentic bistro, which has preserved its 1845 decor, is now considered to be one of

the cornerstones of the Latin Quarter. Its large clientele can choose from the various copious dishes offered.

LE PROCOPE

13, rue de l'Ancienne-Comédie 75006
Tel.: 01 40 46 79 00
www.procope.com
Founded in 1689, Le Procope is the oldest café in the world. A few steps from the Odéon intersection, whether in the ground-floor rooms or in the small Napoleon III chambers on the first floor, you may enjoy the decor while lunching or dining, even until quite late.

VAGENENDE

142, boulevard Saint-Germain 75006
Tel.: 01 43 26 68 18
www.vagenende.fr
This old turn-of-the-century bistro, now listed as a historical monument, has preserved its remarkable Art Nouveau decor: dark woodwork, beveled mirrors, globe-shaped lamps, and of course the marvelous organ. Come for the decor and to savor the traditional cuisine.

L'ATELIER DE JOËL ROBUCHON

Hôtel Pont-Royal
5, Rue Montalembert 75007
Tel.: 01 42 22 56 56
The trend is for great chefs to open canteens, more artistically named "ateliers." In this way, following Guy Savoy's example, Joël Robuchon has created his own atelier with an admirable sense of perfection, an ideal balance between decor, service, and cuisine. It would be vulgar, in this context, to speak of a formula, so inventive is the variety of dishes and accompanying wines, so exceptional their quality. One would have to be extremely blasé not to fall for this new concept of "fast food"—tasty, elegant, and creative.

LA CIGALE-RÉCAMIER

4, Rue Récamier 75007
Tel.: 01 45 48 86 58
A family affair. Gérard Idoux is at the helm of the kitchen, while his wife oversees the dining

room in the evening, his daughter Estelle at lunchtime, and his son Etienne looks after the administrative side of business. The sheer honesty of what is called la cuisine bourgeoise, in its most traditional, simple, and balanced guise, makes this "canteen"—which could not be better frequented, drawing as it does, editors, literary and cinematic figures, hotshot lawyers, and prominent journalists – a must-go place for lunch. In the evening, La Cigale-Récamier becomes an elegant neighborhood restaurant where regulars frown upon passing visitors. The soufflé takes pride of place here, and we are particularly fond of the salted-butter caramel variety. A fine cook herself, Caroline Heylliard, co-director of V & P Design, has succeeded in fitting out the rooms with discretion. Her delicacy is revealed in the simplicity of textiles, colors, and furniture, while particular care is taken to provide comfortable lighting. The only decorative item—a large light-wood bookshelf. We only wish that we could join this exclusive club, all the more inaccessible as no entry rules exist.

RAYA
44, rue du Bac 75007
Tel.: 01 45 44 73 73
It was at the Gaya, on rue Duphot, where the Bœuf sur le Toit (the original restaurant) was born at the turn of the century. It is therefore appropriate that the Gaya carries on the name today. More Parisian than its elder, the Gaya of the rue du Bac seems to function as a nightclub which allows only neighborhood members to enter. However, it would be senseless to compare each other's worth, since they are both alike in one essential way: the great quality of their seafood.
The other address:
17, rue Duphot 75007
Tel.: 01 42 60 43 03.

LE VOLTAIRE
27, Quai Voltaire 75007
Tel.: 01 42 61 17 49
Monsieur Picot, son of

the founder, and his wife govern this institution with all the majesty of absolute monarchs— nobody would dare venture inside without a formal invitation. In this slightly hierarchical atmosphere, the regulars greet each other only very discreetly—a simple glance will do: they see each other almost every day. The cooking and service are impeccable (page 222).

L'ASSIETTE
181, rue du Château 75014
Tel.: 01 43 22 64 86
Owner Lucette Rousseau has thoroughly respected the *fin-de-siècle* decor of this one-time butcher's shop. Today, she offers savory and imaginative cooking which is oftentimes influenced by the cuisine of her native region in Southwest France. Lulu herself prepares the fresh *foie gras* with loving care for a clientele composed of friends and regulars who enjoy gathering here on Sunday evenings (when many good restaurants are closed) even if the check is at times a bit steep.

LA CAGOUILLE
10, Place Constantin Brancusi 75014
Tel.: 01 43 22 09 01
Since the 1980s, the table of former French president François Mitterand, who came here to taste scallops and other shellfish with his friends, has become part of the myth of this excellent seafood restaurant decked out in a seaside theme. This is a meeting place for real food lovers who come to enjoy the Marenne d'Oléron from oyster-farmer David Hervé, pan-fried baby sole, haddock salad, scallops in a balsamic sauce, fillet of mullet with aioli, or else John Dory in butter and chervil... In short, a peerless choice of dishes that changes from day to day depending on the market and inspiration, served in a congenial atmosphere.

CAVES SOLIGNAC
9, rue Decrès 75014
Tel.: 01 45 45 58 59
Amidst small colonnades

and carved glass windows, which characterize its typical turn-of-the-century decor, you will encounter the very loquacious owner who runs this bistro. You must, nevertheless, find a minute to try the traditional country cooking and the excellent selection of wines (page 220).

LA COUPOLE
102, boulevard du Montparnasse 75014
Tel.: 01 43 20 14 20
www.flobrasseries.com/coupole paris
This immense and illustrious brasserie, which in the 1920s was flooded by Montparnasse celebrities, was recently renovated. Its famous centerpiece was replaced by a contemporary sculpture, and the dome—from which it takes its name—can no longer be seen reaching up above the second floor. La Coupole has nevertheless retained its original pillars—decorated by Othon Friesz and Fernand Léger—its dancing, its bar, and some of its prestige. You can purchase various articles and china emblazoned with the house emblem in the downstairs area (page 232).

LA RÉGALADE
49, avenue Jean-Moulin 75014
Tel.: 01 45 45 68 58
Though situated off-the-beaten-path of Parisian gastronomic connoisseurs, La Régalade deserves the extra effort, and all the more so because you can dine until midnight. Its jovial atmosphere is accompanied by top quality and very affordable traditional country cooking—notably that of Southwest France. Yves Camdeborde who built up the restaurant's fine reputation is no longer in the reins but his successor's menus mantain the very high standards.

WINE BARS

AU SAUVIGNON
80, rue des Saints-Pères 75007
Tel.: 01 45 48 49 02
Here is an authentic wine bar which existed before they

became trendy. In a beautiful ceramic turn-of-the-century setting—the walls adorned with enologically inspired aphorisms and drawings—you can enjoy various dishes and sandwiches, accompanied by a large selection of excellent wines. The closely arranged tables are filled daily by the eager lunchtime business crowd of the Sèvres-Babylone neighborhood.

AU VIN DES RUES
21, rue Boulard 75014
Tel.: 01 43 21 82 60
The regulars, oftentimes journalists, are willing to wait just to savor the house-prepared specialties—*pâté, pieds de mouton ravigote, pot-au-feu*, or *brandade de morue*—accompanied by the house wines, such as Brouilly or Juliénas, served in small and medium-sized carafes or in bottles, which patrons may take with them and enjoy at home.

CAFÉS

CAFÉ DE FLORE
172, boulevard Saint-Germain 75006
Tel.: 01 45 48 55 26
www.cafe-de-flore.com
A literary café which perpetuates the memory of Jean-Paul Sartre, Simone de Beauvoir, and Juliette Gréco, among others, such as Picasso, who often came here after the war. The Art Deco style has not changed at all since its construction. Breakfasts are as unique a treat here as the Welsh rarebit (a *croque-monsieur* with English cheese and beer) which you can order throughout the day (page 211).

LES DEUX MAGOTS
6, place Saint-Germain-des-Prés 75006
Tel.: 01 45 48 55 25
www.lesdeuxmagots.fr
Its large sidewalk terrace at the corner of the boulevard Saint-Germain and the rue Bonaparte, across from the church of Saint-Germain-des-Prés, is a strategic locale for

celebrity watching. In this café, which has continued to animate Parisian cultural life since 1885, notably with the creation of the Deux-Magots Award in 1993, you may enjoy tea, espresso, hot chocolate, or one of the thirty whiskies offered. It is also possible to have a light lunch or snack such as a salad, an omelette, a plate of assorted cheeses or simply a pastry (page 211).

LA PALETTE
43, rue de Seine 75006
Tel.: 01 43 26 68 15
An ideal spot for an espresso on a sunny terrace or a pause for a hot lunch before continuing your stroll through this neighborhood of art galleries, antique shops, and the École des Beaux-Arts (academy of fine arts). Its collection of paintings is also worth the trip (pages 1 and 212).

LE SÉLECT
99, boulevard du Montparnasse 75006
Tel.: 01 45 48 38 24
This café in its original 1925 setting, with its moleskin benches and wrought-iron lamps, is one of the last places which bears witness to the golden age of Montparnasse. Lawyers, doctors, and cinematographers come to dine or straighten out the world's problems around cocktails prepared by barman Philippe.

SALONS DE THÉ

LA FOURMI AILÉE
8, rue du Fouarre 75005
Tel.: 01 43 29 40 99
A few steps from the cathedral of Notre Dame, this cozy bookstore specializing in women's writing includes a tea room, where, on weekends, you can enjoy a light meal, tea, or brunch next to the fireplace.

MARIAGE FRÈRES
13, rue des Grands-Augustins 75006
Tel.: 01 40 51 82 50
www.mariagefreres.com
On this small tranquil street next to the Seine, the store

Mariage Frères has opened
a boutique and a salon de thé
(page 251).

LADURÉE

21, rue Bonaparte 75006
Tel.: 01 44 07 64 87
The decor in the Ladurée
Bonaparte carries the hallmark
of Madeleine Castaing, the
inspired decorator who used to
occupy the mythical antique
shop at the corner of Rue Jacob
and Rue Bonaparte, first opened
in 1947. A temple of
neoclassicism and all things
extravagant, the Castaing shop
was a magnet for upmarket
Parisians. These days, at
breakast or afternoon tea,
expect to see nostalgic lovers of
the Saint Germain des Prés of
old—the district is no longer
what it once was—taking refuge
here. Choose to sit on the first
floor where the blue salon is
open all hours of the day to
tempt you with delicious hot
meals, memorable hot
chocolate, or those world-
famous macaroons and pastries.
Two tea-rooms along with the
chocolate shop and pastry shop.
A must.

TEA CADDY

14, rue Saint-Julien-le-Pauvre
75005
Tel.: 01 43 54 15 56
A cozy atmosphere with tea,
scones, and muffins, as well
as some Viennese specialties—
all home-made.

LA PAGODE

57 bis, rue Babylone 75007
Tel.: 01 45 55 48 48
This cinema enthusiasts' temple
in Japanese-style decor,
dating from the end of the
nineteenth-century, includes
a salon de thé where you may
wait comfortably for showtime
while dreaming in the setting
of its exotic garden (page 149).

FOOD AND WINE

LA MAISON DES TROIS THÉS

33, Rue Gracieuse 75005
Tel.: 01 43 36 93 84
The most unusual—one may
even say mysterious—tea cellar
that could ever be conceived, is
hidden away behind the

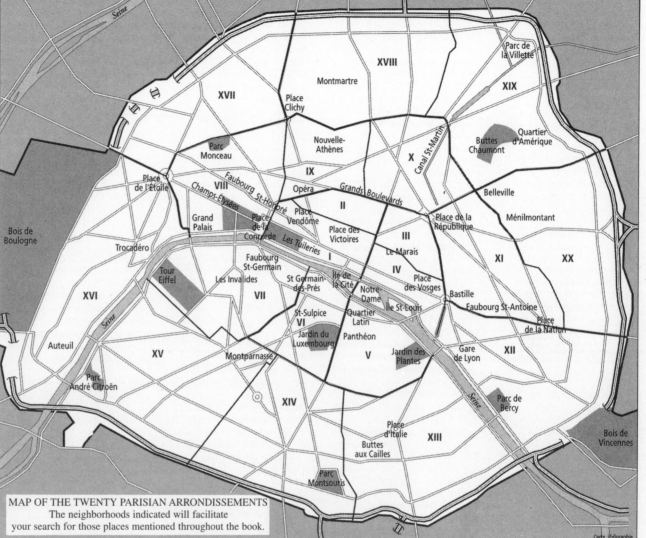

MAP OF THE TWENTY PARISIAN ARRONDISSEMENTS
The neighborhoods indicated will facilitate
your search for those places mentioned throughout the book.

Panthéon. It offers several
thousand teas from diverse
origins, essentially from Taiwan
and eastern China. The most
ancient varieties date from 1890.
The decor created by architect-
designer François Muracciole
comes straight out of the film
The Shanghai Gesture.

CHRISTIAN CONSTANT

37, rue d'Assas 75005
Tel.: 01 53 63 15 15
www.christianconstant.com
A few tables are available
for the truly famished—but
remember that Christian
Constant is an excellent
confectioner. If you are lucky

enough to secure a table we
particularly recommend the
Orfeu Negro (chocolate and
raspberries), or the *Soleil Noir*
(a dome of bittersweet
chocolate mousse topped with
cinnamon).

DEBAUVE & GALLAIS

36, rue des Saints-Pères 75006
Tel.: 01 45 48 54 67
www.debauve-et-gallais.com
At the time of its creation in
the beginning of the nineteenth-
century, this elegant emerald-
and-gold boutique—the work of
Percier and Fontaine which is
now historically listed—was a
pharmacy which specialized in

making chocolates for medical
use. The owner, Monsieur
Debauve, was Louis XVI's
pharmacist. Today, it is the
oldest chocolate-making house
in Paris, offering a fine array of
chocolates rich in cocoa, with
sumptuously antiquated names:
*les croquignoles du roi, les
pastilles de la reine, le chocolat
de santé, le chocolat des
demoiselles, le chocolat des
affligés*, and many others.

PATRICK ROGER

108, Boulevard Saint-Germain
75006
Tel.: 01 43 29 38 42
A new address in Paris, though

this chocolate-maker is already
well-known in the Parisian
suburb of Sceaux. This boutique
on Boulevard Saint-Germain,
close to the Odéon, immediately
catches the eye with its
spectacular window display –
a strikingly unusual bright
turquoise serves as a backdrop
for the house specialties.
We are particularly fond of
the "caramel ball" giftbox, the
chocolates with ginger or
jasmine flower, as well as the
chocolates with peppered mint
and lemongrass. Acclaimed by
his peers, Patrick Roger has
maintained a freshness that
comes through in his creations.

POILÂNE
8, rue du Cherche-Midi 75006
Tel.: 01 45 48 42 59
www.poilane.fr
In Poilâne's factory, millstone ground French flour, leaven, and sea salt are mixed together to make large loaves of bread, nutbread, and apple pie. This famous baking company exports these delights throughout the world.

LA GRANDE ÉPICERIE DU BON MARCHÉ
38, rue de Sèvres 75007
Tel.: 01 44 39 81 00
www.lagrandeepicerie.fr
Besides a large selection of traditional products from many different countries and an excellent wine cellar, the foreign specialties offered by the Grande Épicerie include, in particular, Italian, Chinese, and Alsacian dishes. You may also be tempted to try the fresh coffee which is ground while you wait.

MICHEL CHAUDUN
149, rue de l'Université 75007
Tel.: 01 47 53 74 40
The beautiful store windows of this master of chocolate attract many who would not even consider any other chocolate maker. The chocolate icing cracks lightly in the mouth to release an intense rich flavor. Among chocolate cakes, another Michel Chaudun specialty, we suggest the *bûche tout-chocolat*—chocolate biscuits (without flour) and chocolate mousse—or the *bûche Haïti*—a sumptuous chocolate and caramel explosion.

LE MOULIN DE LA VIERGE
105, rue Vercingétorix 75014
Tel.: 01 45 43 09 84
www.lemoulindelavierge.com
Genuine Belle Époque decor, two historically listed ovens and impeccable quality combine to make traditional bread in all forms, using organic-based flour: *pains de campagne, pains aux céréales, fougasses*.
Other addresses:
82, rue Daguerre
166, avenue de Suffren.

HAVARD PERE ET FILS
123, boulevard du Montparnasse 75006
Tel.: 01 43 22 34 87
www.havard.fr
Established in 1872, this old mirror factory is dedicated today to frame production, framing, and gilded-wood restoration. You can choose from among more than eight hundred models—in gold and silver leaf—in the highest artisan tradition. Many eminent painters—Modigliani, Matisse, Nicolas de Staël, and contemporary artists such as Botero—have come to stretch and prepare their canvases in this atelier.

LISON DE CAUNES
20, rue Mayet 75006
Tel.: 01 40 56 02 10
For almost twenty years, Lison de Caunes has been working with rye straw—which she crushes and then dyes in varying shades. Her expertise also extends to *galuchat, coquille d'œuf,* and parchment. In the serenity of her workshop, you will find this straw-marquetry specialist restoring an eighteenth-century writing case or perhaps a small piece of Art Deco furniture. She refurbishes, on order, various objects, tables, and folding screens for antique dealers, interior decorators, or even non-professionals.

LORENZI FRERES
19, rue Racine 75006
Tel.: 01 43 26 38 68
www.lorenzi.fr
Since 1871, successive generations of the Lorenzi family have been casting the most celebrated statues and bas-reliefs in their same Odéon workshop. Here, art lovers who wish to embellish an apartment or home may acquire the hand of Chopin, the bust of the child Louis XVII, or that of an unknown patron from the town of Nevers. The workshop will also reproduce your grandfather's bust for all the members of the family (page 184).

SEROD
42, rue de Varenne 75007
Tel.: 01 45 44 54 78
By following the tiny paved alleyway, you will discover—within a very beautiful courtyard accentuated by a chestnut tree, a dwarf rose, and bamboo—this top quality atelier which restores and rejuvenates antique furniture. The *compagnons* who work here are all graduates of the École Boulle and disciples of Henri Desgrippes, one of the privileged twenty artisans nominated *maître d'art* in 1994 by the French Ministry of Culture.

STUC ET STAFF
204, rue de la Croix-Nivert 75015
Tel.: 01 45 57 47 33
This company carries out all types of plastering and construction work, including—as its name reveals—stucco and staff. It can boast a brilliant record of achievement in both classical and modern architectural renovation. The company's expertise can be admired in the newly restored Château de Compiègne and Château de Fontainebleau, in the adjustments made to the Palais de l'Élysée and the Musée d'Orsay, but also in many private town houses (page 185).

ANNE-SOPHIE DUVAL
5, Quai Malaquais 75006
Tel.: 01 43 54 51 16
www.annesophieduval.free.fr
Expert authority in antiques and Art Deco specialist, Anne-Sophie Duval offers original 1920s' and 1930s' furniture by the most eminent names of the time: Jean Dunand, Eugène Printz, Pierre Chareau, Jacques-Émile Ruhlmann, Auguste Rateau. You can also find many charming objects; lamps and rugs, as well as rare twentieth-century items which may still be purchased at affordable rates.

CAMOIN-DEMACHY
9, Quai Voltaire 75007

Tel.: 01 42 61 82 06
Across from the Louvre, the Camoin-Demachy gallery occupies the first and second floors of an old town house. Devoted essentially to the seventeenth and nineteenth centuries, the gallery has opened its doors to foreign productions, as well as rare objets d'art, hard stone marquetry tables, and panoramic wallpaper. A small adjacent suite has recently been inaugurated for fine furniture and objets d'art designed by Eugène Printz, Louis Majorelle, or Misia Sert, among others.

DEYROLLE
46, rue du Bac 75007
Tel.: 01 42 22 30 07
Since its re-opening twenty years ago by M. Corbet, the house, which is more than one hundred and fifty years old and formerly owned by the famous taxidermist Émile Deyrolle, is now dedicated to interior decorating. On the second floor of this splendid eighteenth-century town house with its period wood-carved paneling, a vertiginous world of stuffed animals of all sizes awaits interior decorators, photographers, and advertising agents—seeking something exotic and different—who can rent a baby camel or elephant, a lion, a polar bear, a deer or a horse, and all types of feathered creatures. You can immortalize your favorite animal or the spoils of the hunt. The educational illustrations in this illustrious house, which were once used in classroom studies, now deck the kitchen walls of country houses (page 28).

DOWN TOWN
33, rue de Seine 75006
Tel.: 01 46 33 82 41
www.galerie-downtown.com
In this small gallery, Jean Prouvé and the 1950s are the center of attraction, with original period pieces and works by Charlotte Perriand, Le Corbusier, Carlo Molino, and George Nelson.

GALERIE DORIA
16, rue de Seine 75006

Tel.: 01 43 51 73 19 or
01 43 15 43 25
Following the example of several neighboring galleries, Denis Doria's gallery has specialized in furniture and modern objets d'art, with a penchant for artists such as Pierre Chareau, René Herbst, Francis Jourdain, Le Corbusier, Fernand Léger, Robert Mallet-Stevens, and Jean Puiforcat (page 125).

GALERIE DUTKO
13, rue Bonaparte 75006
Tel.: 01 43 26 96 13
www.dutko.com
In a surprising and explosive blend, Jean-Jacques Dutko presents, in background decor designed by Jean-Michel Wilmotte, furniture created by Pierre Chareau, Eugène Printz, and Eileen Gray, as well as African statues and masks. The gallery walls are covered with modern paintings by Degottex, Poliakoff, and Pincemin.

GALERIE VALLOIS
41, rue de Seine 75006
Tel.: 01 43 29 50 84
www.vallois.com
Bob and Chesca Vallois were taking a risk in the 1970s when they decided to devote their gallery to Art Deco. However, now considered an essential period in art history, their gallery can speak with authority on the subject. You will find furniture and objects by eminent designers—Pierre Chareau, Jean Dunand, Jean-Michel Frank, Eileen Gray, André Groult, Eugène Printz, Auguste Rateau, and Jacques-Émile Ruhlmann (page 122).

CATHERINE MEMMI
11, rue Saint-Sulpice 75006
Tel.: 01 44 07 02 02
www.catherinememmi.com
In this delightful boutique, Catherine Memmi offers striped or solid household linen in shades of white, golden yellow, and beige, decorated with motifs such as

beehives, caviar, or soft sponges, all fabricated with linen cloth, cotton, or both. You will also find original designs and pillowcases which fasten with large buttons. She also provides an embroidery service.

LA MAISON DE FAMILLE
29, rue Saint-Sulpice 75006
Tel.: 01 40 46 97 47
Just behind the church of Saint-Sulpice sits a tiny department store. The blue storefront hides three floors where, on the first, you will find china and kitchen accessories, on the second, bathroom and table linens in mixed fabrics or simply linen cloth and Venetian-embroidered bedsheets and pillowcases, and on the third, clothing, furniture, and garden utensils.

NUIT BLANCHE
41, rue de Bourgogne 75007
Tel.: 01 45 50 39 29
In this old dairy shop whose *fin-de-siècle* decor has been historically listed, Sabine Marchal opened a boutique in 1993 devoted to household linens and decorations in eighteenth-century and English country style. She will also embroider linens in your favorite colors as well as prepare your personalized lampshades or gaming table

cloths so as to color harmonize them with your home's interior.

MUSEUMS

MUSÉE HÉBERT
85, rue du Cherche-Midi 75006
Tel.: 0142 22 23 82
Along the elegant rue du Cherche-Midi, the old hôtel Montmorency, bequeathed by the heir of the nineteenth-century painter Ernest Hébert to make a museum, exhibits several of the artist's works in lavish frames in Belle Époque-style salons. (Museum closed until 2008/2009).

MUSÉE ZADKINE
100 bis, rue d'Assas 75006
Tel.: 01 55 42 77 20
www.paris.fr/musees/Zadkine
At the end of a closed alleyway away from curious glances, between Montparnasse and the Luxembourg Gardens, Zadkine's home-cum-atelier and garden today constitute a pleasant museum harboring three hundred of the artist's works in bronze, terra cotta and lacquered wood—as well as his plans to build monuments to Alfred Jarry, Apollinaire, Rimbaud, and Van Gogh.

FONDATION DINA VIERNY—MUSÉE MAILLOL
59, rue de Grenelle 75007
Tel.: 01 42 22 59 58
www.museemaillol.com
The Musée Maillol sits next to the Fontaine des Quatre-Saisons in the sumptuous hôtel Bouchardon where Alfred de Musset lived until he was twenty-three years old, and where he wrote several of his works. Dina Vierny, Aristide Maillol's inspiration in the early 1940s, devoted a part of her life to the creation of this museum in order to publicly exhibit the artist's works. Its twenty-seven renovated rooms present pastels, pencil sketches, oils, and sanguine drawings by the artist. You will also find works by the sculptor's friends, notably Matisse, Bonnard, and Dufy, but also sketches and aquarelles by Gauguin, Renoir, Picasso, Degas, Cézanne, Duchamp, and of course Maillol's own statues.

MUSÉE RODIN
77, rue de Varenne 75007
Tel.: 01 44 18 61 10
www.musee-rodin.fr
It is in the beautiful eighteenth-century hôtel Biron, a stone's throw from the Invalides, that you can admire the works of sculptors Auguste Rodin and Camille Claudel. The exhibit continues in the park where you

will find the famous *Bourgeois de Calais*, the *Portes de l'Enfer*, the *Trois Ombres* and the *Penseur*. The outdoor café provides a pleasant break during this artistic stroll—weather permitting.

MANUFACTURE DES GOBELINS
1, rue Berbier des Mets 75013
Tel.: 01 44 08 52 00
Henry IV introduced Flemish loom setters into the Gobelin dyeing industry. Colbert initially turned the industry into the Crown's furniture manufacturer. Then, at the behest of Charles Le Brun, preeminent painter to the Sun King Louis XIV, the company played a significant role in spreading French taste and as a result, Gobelin tapestries suddenly became world renowned. A 14.420-tonne dyeing machine with seventy-two colors is still used to dye wool woven on vertical looms for tapestry projects commissioned by the government. The somber factory buildings, whose workshops are open to the public, give onto a very pleasant walled garden (page 148).

MUSÉE BOURDELLE
16, rue Antoine-Bourdelle 75015
Tel.: 01 49 54 73 73
www.paris.fr/musees/bourdelle
The red-brick garden/museum, a few steps from the Montparnasse Tower, was expanded in 1992 by the architect Christian de Portzamparc to accommodate practically all the works of this sculptor who was Rodin's assistant. In the home-cum-atelier and the garden, you can view the original plaster casts of his monumental statues (the *Vierge à l'offrande* and equestrian statues), a series of Beethoven busts, and many more (page 148).

MUSÉE EUGENE-DELACROIX
6, rue de Furstenberg 75006
Tel.: 01 44 41 86 50
www.musee-delacroix.fr
Among the least-known places in the capital—though easily accessible—the Musée Delacroix occupies the artist's old atelier in the very provincial rue de Furstenberg, where he passed the last years of his life. In what was once the living-room, the bedroom, and the study are exhibited gouaches, aquarelles, and sanguine drawings, along with parts of his correspondence, notably with his friend George Sand.

RIGHT BANK

HOTELS

HÔTEL COSTES
239, rue Saint-Honoré 75001
Tel.: 01 42 44 50 00
Though one of the most recent hotels to open in Paris, it seems to be the oldest. Jean-Louis Costes, creator of the now defunct Café Costes, chose to abandon momentarily his taste for young designers by entrusting the decoration of his hotel to Jacques Garcia—who knew how to recreate the atmosphere of an old-time hotel in minute detail. Each living area and each room reflect

his fruitful pursuit of rare objects from flea markets, second-hand stores, and antique shops, bestowing upon this establishment an aura of undeniable authenticity. Perhaps only the undaunted are able to escape its charms and wander into the tumult of Paris (page 237).

HÔTEL MEURICE
228, rue de Rivoli 75001
Tel.: 01 44 58 10 10
www.meuricehotel.com
Situated in front of the Tuileries Gardens and a few steps from the place de la Concorde, this luxurious hotel once

provided asylum to foreign exiled sovereigns, and sponsored Florence Gould's *salon littéraire* whose participants included François Mauriac, André Gide, and Jean Cocteau. Salvador Dali had a room reserved here all year round. This relatively discreet palace hotel remains one of the city's most pleasant, with beautiful living areas and a historically listed period elevator.

LE RITZ
15, place Vendôme 75001
Tel.: 01 43 16 30 30
www.ritzparis.com

Probably the most famous hotel in the world—luxury, period furniture, august fireplaces, majestic chandeliers, silken fabrics, attention to minute detail—all combine in the splendor of this establishment reserved for the world's elite. Lunch and dinner are served at the Espadon restaurant (pages 234 and 236).

HÔTEL FAVART
5, rue Marivaux 75002
Tel.: 01 42 97 59 83
www.hotel-paris-favart.com
This former inn, where the Spanish painter Francisco de Goya spent the summer of

1824, was also the American military headquarters following the Second World War. Today, a serene hotel situated in front of the Opéra-Comique, it is a historically listed monument and caters to a regular business and tourist clientele.

HÔTEL DE NICE
42 bis, rue de Rivoli 75004
Tel.: 01 42 78 55 29
A tiny bit old and a tiny bit noisy—nevertheless, comfortable. A cordial and friendly reception awaits you.

HÔTEL SAINT-MERRY
78, rue de la Verrerie 75004

Tel.: 01 42 78 14 15
www.saintmerrymarais.com
Wood furniture and stone walls—everything is Gothic in this small charming hotel of eleven rooms which was once the rectory to the church of Saint-Merri, situated a few steps from the Georges-Pompidou Center.

HÔTEL BRISTOL
112, rue du Faubourg-Saint-Honoré 75008
Tel.: 01 53 43 43 00
www.lebristolparis.com
Located on one of the most elegant of Parisian streets near the Palais de l'Élysée, this old convent—transformed into a palace—with marble bathrooms and a covered swimming pool on the roof—is the privileged meeting place for diplomats. The winter-season restaurant occupies the small, old theater of the hôtel de Castellane. Stained-glass windows, frescoes and sculpted-oak paneling—this Regency decor shows pure sophistication.

HÔTEL DE CRILLON
10, place de la Concorde 75008
Tel.: 01 44 71 15 00
www.crillon.com
Marvelously situated on the world's most beautiful square, this old eighteenth-century town house, which was converted into a hotel in 1907, has preserved its antique furniture, Aubusson tapestries, and wainscoted gallery. Its name known throughout the entire world, the Hôtel Crillon welcomes government dignitaries on official business as well as the most eccentric celebrities. Its restaurant, the Ambassadeurs, is one of the best and most beautiful in Paris, though the Obélisque offers a much more reasonable menu (page 235).

HÔTEL BALZAC
6, rue Balzac 75008
Tel.: 01 44 35 18 00
www.hotelbalzac.com
One street away from the avenue des Champs-Élysées, behind a *fin-de-siècle* facade, the Hôtel Balzac offers serenity to stressed business people and fatigued tourists in a luxurious atmosphere—oriental rugs, thick wall-to-wall carpeting, and period furniture for its small parlors. The rooms and bathrooms are spacious and very bright.

HÔTEL DE VIGNY
9, rue Balzac 75008
Tel.: 01 42 99 80 80
www.hoteldevigny.com
Completely restored in 1990 by the English interior decorator Nina Campbell, this very comfortable hotel has thirty-seven rooms which offer all the charm of old England. Woodwork, wainscoting, and wooden fireplaces combine to create a cozy atmosphere in the living areas, while the leather and burr ash wood create a warm ambiance in the bar where drinks and light meals are served. The reception and service are discreet and courteous.

HÔTEL CHOPIN
46, Passage Jouffroy 75009
Tel.: 01 47 70 58 10
A haven of peace amidst the tumult of the boulevards, this small hotel of thirty-eight rooms is located behind the Musée Grevin, on one of the three covered passageways that make this a charming neighborhood. The rooms open either onto the roofs of Paris, the glass awnings of the passageway, or the workshops of the Musée Grevin. You can sleep peacefully with the window open and only birdsong to disturb you.

HÔTEL DE LA TOUR D'AUVERGNE
10, rue de la Tour-d'Auvergne 75009
Tel.: 01 48 78 61 60
Not far from the Nouvelle Athènes neighborhood, between Montmartre and the boulevards, you will find this small commodious hotel where each room is decorated in a different style, including Louis XV, Louis XVI, 1900, and Art Deco.

HÔTEL RAPHAEL
7, avenue Kléber 75016
Tel.: 01 53 64 32 00
www.raphael-hotel.com
On one of the avenues leading to the place de l'Étoile, this luxurious hotel dating back to the "roaring '20s" offers spacious rooms to a clientele composed mainly of film producers and celebrities. Antique furniture, hanging tapestries, thick rugs, and an original painting by Turner create a unique atmosphere of tranquillity and refinement—surpassed only by the elegance of the bar area.

TERRASS HÔTEL
12-14, rue Joseph-de-Maistre 75018
Tel.: 01 46 06 72 85
www.terrass-hotel.com
On the slope of the Butte Montmartre—next to the cemetery where the trees tower above—this hotel is known for its terrace view of Paris, where in the summertime you can dine in one of the city's most wonderful restaurants. Ask for a balcony room so you can relish the spectacular panorama above the rooftops of Paris.

RESTAURANTS AND BRASSERIES

CAFÉ VERY
Jardin des Tuileries 75001
(across from the entrance on rue de Castiglione)
Tel.: 01 47 03 94 84
The only way to take advantage of the Tuileries Gardens until midnight is to enjoy a light meal in this wood-paneled locale, whose name is inspired by the sumptuous restaurant which once stood in the gardens in Stendhal's time.

LE GRAND VÉFOUR
17, rue de Beaujolais 75001
Tel.: 01 42 96 56 27
Its highly sophisticated, historically listed eighteenth-century decor, one of the capital's most impressive, provides an appropriate backdrop for the celebration of a big occasion or simply to succumb to the serene charm of the Palais-Royal Gardens. Beneath the inspirational shadow of one-time regulars—notably Colette and Cocteau, to whom certain dishes are dedicated—you can savor the *raviolis de foie gras truffé* or the *pigeon prince Rainier III* in this gastronomic Mecca. Ask for the champagne served in carafes (pages 224-225).

PIERRE TRAITEUR
10, rue de Richelieu 75001
Tel.: 01 42 96 27 17
Not far from the Palais-Royal Gardens, this fine restaurant, which is a little noisy, nevertheless offers quality Auvergnate cuisine or more sophisticated dishes to a crowd of regulars. You can enter either from the rue de Montpensier or the rue de Richelieu.

AUX LYONNAIS
32, rue Saint-Marc 75002
Tel.: 01 42 96 65 04
After passing the crimson facade of this authentic turn-of-the-century bistro, you can savor—amid its historically listed ornate faïence tiling (listed as an historic work of art)—several Lyonnaise specialties such as *saucisson chaud, quenelles, gras double,* and other less typical dishes, all topped with vintage Lyonnaise regional wines. The house also offers quite a rarity—you can choose from a large menu of still or sparkling mineral waters.

CHEZ GEORGES
1, rue du Mail 75002
Tel.: 01 42 60 07 11
A genuine Parisian bistro with its row benches, mirrors, and charming waitresses. Patrons come from all around to savor this traditional cuisine: *filet de hareng* or *terrine de foies de volaille, sole, turbot, rognon,* or *foie de veau* (page 222).

LE GRAND COLBERT
4, Rue Vivienne 75002
Tel.: 01 42 86 87 88
Built in 1835 during the creation of the Galerie Colbert, Le Grand Colbert, owned by the National Library, was restored in 1985 at the same time as the gallery of the same name, before being taken over by the affable and talented Monsieur Fleury in 1992. Here, one can dine on all the great brasserie classics, served by a perfectly choreographed ballet of waiters in the traditional uniform of the long apron. Not to be missed in this magnificent district between the Place des Victoires and the Palais Royal.

CHEZ L'AMI LOUIS
32, rue du Vertbois 75003
Tel.: 01 48 87 77 48
This Parisian bistro in characteristic decor—smoke-darkened by the years—was for half a century the dominion of the illustrious Antoine Magnin. It continues to attract a very eclectic clientele comprised of genuine connoisseurs, epicures, and gourmands whose pockets are never empty. It is essential to come with a robust appetite so as to savor this bountiful cooking composed of regal *escargots,* supreme *volaille,* and impeccable *foie gras* (page 223).

L'AMBROISIE
9, place des Vosges 75004
Tel.: 01 42 78 51 45
Undoubtedly the most discreet and intimate of the three-star Parisian restaurants listed in the Michelin guide. L'Ambroisie is situated beneath the archways of the place des Vosges in an elegant decor conceived by François-Joseph Graff, each table trimmed with a splendid bouquet of flowers. A very attentive service blends well with an exquisite cuisine in this establishment whose tables are set *à la française* (if you wish), and not in the English style to which restaurants traditionally abide. In spite of the hefty check, it is wise to reserve a month in advance.

BENOÎT
20, rue Saint-Martin 75004
Tel.: 01 42 72 25 76
The only Parisian bistro to be awarded one star in the Michelin guide. This venerable establishment masterfully run by the Petit family for 93 years

was sold to the Alain Ducasse group which, in September 2005, opened a Benoît in Tokyo. In this charming setting featuring a Napoleon III interior with red velvet bench-seats and a wooden counter, delightful bourgeois cuisine awaits you – beef mode à l'ancienne, homemade cassoulet stew or cod gratin. Their service is amongst the most gracious around.

BOFINGER

3, rue de la Bastille 75004
Tel.: 01 42 72 87 82
www.bofingerparis.com
The second-floor dining area decorated by the Alsacian painter Hansi and its rare ceramic turn-of-the-century rotunda make the Bofinger the most genuine and sought-after Parisian brasserie. The menu proposes seafood, *choucroute* (the house specialty), and grilled steaks—a perfect address for supper after an evening at the Opéra de la Bastille (pages 188-189).

GEORGES

Centre Georges Pompidou,
19, Rue Beaubourg 75004
Tel.: 01 44 78 47 99
Two young architects, Dominique Jakob and Brendan MacFarlane, have created a metallic decor featuring brightly colored tubes – a perfect match for the architecture of the Centre Georges Pompidou. The view of Parisian rooftops is one of the most beautiful available in the capital. Quality "Coste" cuisine is ideal fare for this sophisticated venue. What more can be said? Just turn down the music a little so we can more intensely savor this exquisite meeting of heaven and earth.

MA BOURGOGNE

19, place des Vosges 75004
Tel.: 01 42 78 44 64
In the purest Parisian bistro tradition, Ma Bourgogne is an ideal place to savor the specialties of the Burgundy, Tarn, and Aveyron regions, as well as an excellent steak tartare, in the magnificent place des Vosges setting. The heated terrace, situated underneath

the square's archways, is empty in neither summer nor winter.

LE FOUQUET'S

99, avenue des Champs-Élysées 75008
Tel.: 01 47 23 50 00
www.lucienbarriere.com/localiz ed/en/rest/fouq
Recently listed in the register of historical monuments. Le Fouquet's is undeniably the most fashionable meeting place for journalists and celebrities. Its wine cellar and daily specials almost surpass its scrumptious *mille feuilles* (page 38).

KASPIA

17, place de la Madeleine 75008
Tel.: 01 42 65 33 32
www.kaspia.fr
Situated on the second floor of a Baltic specialty store, with an unobstructed view of the church of La Madeleine, you will find the most Parisian of Russian bistros. Here, in a dusky ambiance, you can savor excellent caviar, smoked salmon, and iced vodka. Friendly and rapid service guarantees agreeable afternoon and after-theater meals— regulars are discreetly tolerant of tourists (page 226).

LA MAISON BLANCHE

15, avenue Montaigne 75008
Tel.: 01 47 23 55 99
Built on the rooftop of the Théâtre des Champs-Élysées in 1990, this elegant restaurant – a favorite amongst the Arab princes residing in the neighboring palaces – is the chic melting pot for those in the worlds of fashion, politics, journalism, and the arts. In a decor conceived by Imaad Rahmouni, where a spectrum of pastel, white, and purple shades freely mingle, dominating the sparkling waters of the Seine, the golden dome of the Invalides, and the majestic Eiffel Tower, you can relax and appreciate the bold contrasts in the cuisine of the Pourcel brothers whose innovative menu juxtaposes sugar and salt, sweet and bitter, hot and cold, creamy and crispy.

AU PETIT RICHE

25, rue Le Peletier 75009
Tel.: 01 47 70 68 68
www.aupetitriche.com
This restaurant was for a long time the lunchroom for the directors of the newspaper *Le Monde*, which at the time was located nearby. This old Parisian bistro, set in a decor of beautiful dark wood and carved glass, offers a very reputable bourgeois cuisine: *bœuf gros sel* and *foie de veau* accompanied by carafes of Vouvray or Bourgueil wines.

CASA OLYMPE

48, rue Saint-Georges 75009
Tel.: 01 42 85 26 01
Situated near the place Saint-Georges, one of the city's most lovely squares, the famous Olympe offers a savory southern cuisine in its small ochre and saffron-colored *mas provençal* restaurant—inundated with the lovely smell of thyme and olive oil—where you can enjoy *thon au lard et aux oignons, poivrons aux anchois*, and *épaule d'agneau Sisteron*, topped with a bottle of Gigondas. A hot spot for intellectual and trendy Paris, a fixed-price menu makes this wonderful cuisine accessible to all epicures.

CHARTIER

7, rue du Faubourg-Montmartre 75009
Tel.: 01 47 70 86 29
www.restaurant-chartier.com
At the far end of a courtyard, next to the Passage Jouffroy, Chartier offers family-style cuisine—*œuf mayonnaise, roastbeef, rôti de veau*—all at affordable prices. A courteous reception and competent service—in spite of the hoards of patrons served each day— allow this restaurant and its awesome turn-of-the-century decor to boast a strong clientele of Parisians, students, and tourists (page 232).

MOLLARD

115, rue Saint-Lazare 75009
Tel.: 01 43 87 50 22
www.mollard.fr
Across from the Gare Saint-Lazare, this one-time coal

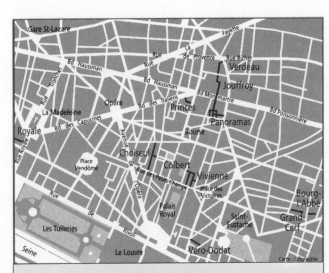

ARCADES

These passageways and galleries are mainly situated between the boulevards and the place de la Madeleine. Here is where you can find those places mentioned throughout the book:

Galerie Colbert: 6, rue des Petits-Champs, 4, rue Vivienne (page 193).
Galerie Véro-Dodat: 8, rue du Boulot, 19, rue Jean-Jacques Rousseau (page 198).
Galerie Vivienne: 4, rue des Petits-Champs, 6, rue Vivienne (page 195).
Passage Bourg-l'Abbé: 120, rue Saint-Denis, 3, rue de Palestro (page 190).
Passage Choiseul: 42, rue des Petits-Champs, 25, rue Saint-Augustin.
Passage Jouffroy: 10, boulevard Montmartre, 9, rue Grange-Batelière (page 194).
Passage du Grand-Cerf: place Goldoni, 145, rue Saint-Denis (page 199).
Passage des Panoramas: 11, boulevard Montmartre, 10, rue Saint-Marc (pages 192 and 197).
Passage Verdeau: 6, rue Grange-Batelière, 31 bis, rue du Faubourg-Montmartre (pages 191, 196, 197).

To this list we add two recently restored or created arcades: the Passage de Retz in the Marais district between the rue Charlot and the rue Pasturelle, and the Galerie Royale, between 9 rue Royale and the rue Boissy d'Anglas—where all the big names in culinary art are located, along with the extremely pleasant salon de thé, Bernardaud, and the boutique, Eli-Bleu, whose precious wooden boxes are striking.

market from 1867 became, in 1895, a sumptuous Art Nouveau brasserie, decorated in Sarreguemines ceramic tiles depicting allegorical figures or daily life at the time. You can savor all the different types of seafood possible, and for dessert, the *omelette surprise*,

a recipe which is almost fifty years old.

JULIEN

16, rue du Faubourg-Saint-Denis 75010
Tel.: 01 47 70 12 06
www.julienparis.com
Renowned for its very beautiful

Art Nouveau decor, its famous molten glass Trézel paneling, its mahogany bar by Cuba de Lajorelle, and its windows by Buffet (the elder), this restaurant serves traditional brasserie cuisine with specialties such as *sole cuite "à la plancha" sauce béarnaise, cassoulet d'oie maison, escalope de foie de canard chaud aux lentilles,* and *profiteroles.*

TERMINUS NORD

23, rue de Dunkerque 75010
Tel.: 01 42 85 05 15
www.terminusnord.com
Located in front of the Gare du Nord, this brasserie offers a traditional yet diverse menu served in an immense hall decorated in 1920s decor, garnished with paintings depicting jovial scenes of Parisian life during the "roaring '20s." The service and reception are impeccable.

ASTIER

44, rue Jean-Pierre-Timbaud 75011
Tel.: 01 43 57 16 35
www.restaurant-astier.com
Pleasant reception, a menu à la carte at reasonable prices, cooking just as you like it, a generous cheeseboard, and finally a choice of more than 200 wines have, for several years now, given this bistro the fine reputation it deserves. It offers one of the most enticing menus: *filet de saumon rôti au beurre de poivrons,* or *lapin à la moutarde aux pâtes fraîches.* The dessert menu too contains scrumptious surprises.

AU CAMELOT

50, rue Amelot 75011
Tel.: 01 43 55 54 04
A few steps from the Cirque d'Hiver, in typical Parisian decor, this bistro offers a unique menu assembling all catering qualities: an imaginative menu, excellence, a simplicity in the wines and dishes served, and efficiency.

CHEZ PAUL

13, rue de Charonne 75011
Tel.: 01 47 00 34 57
A genuine landmark of the Bastille neighbourhood. Patrons stampede to its low-ceiling dining area to savor its traditional bistro cooking. The waitresses are particularly jovial and enhance an already pleasant atmosphere for brunch on Sundays—when many restaurants are closed (page 60).

LE VILLARET

13, rue Ternaux 75011
Tel.: 01 43 57 89 76
A restaurant so discreet that it has no insignia to draw attention to it outside and is located in an out-of-the-way neighborhood. But, set in a pleasant decor, it offers creative and excellent cuisine at very good prices. You can dine until two in the morning. The desserts are mouth-watering and the wine list quite satisfactory.

LE SQUARE TROUSSEAU

1, rue Antoine-Vollon 75012
Tel.: 01 43 43 06 00
In a perfectly designed early twentieth-century setting with glass ceilings and walls, woodwork, columns, and benches, this bistro situated a few steps from the Bastille counts among its amiable patrons theater-goers and fashion celebrities. The terrace which faces the square is packed in the summer. Accompanying its traditional and creative cuisine, inspired by market specialties, is a particularly interesting wine list (pages 45 and 218).

LE TRAIN BLEU

Gare de Lyon, 20, boulevard Diderot 75012
Tel.: 01 43 43 09 06
www.le-train-bleu.com
This restaurant, which overlooks both the street and the TGV platforms, is renowned for its historically listed Belle Époque decor. The sculpted and painted ceilings of its luxurious dining area are alone worth the trip. Traditional brasserie cuisine and Lyonnaise and Forezien specialties add up to a hefty check. You can however still admire the decor simply by ordering a drink at the bar, which—with its comfortable Chesterfield leather armchairs—is a magical place to take a break for a glass of whisky, a cocktail or simply tea (page 229).

CRYSTAL ROOM DE BACCARAT

11, Place des Etats-Unis 75016
Tel.: 01 40 22 11 10
Just think of the astonishing Maharajah palaces with salons covered in mirrors that served as backdrops for Baccarat crystalwares in the 1920s and the 1930s… Such are the dreamlike, cinematographic decors that seem to have inspired Philippe Starck, who has added his touch of humor and modernity to invent the Crystal Room, the only such restaurant in Paris in a district that is sadly lacking in fantasy.

MAISON PRUNIER

16, avenue Victor-Hugo 75016
Tel.: 01 44 17 35 85
www.prunier.com
Though closed for a number of years, the Maison Prunier once more offers its nostalgic seafood specialties. The first-floor dining area has preserved the historically listed decor by René Herbst. The second floor was renovated by Pierre-Yves Rochon in a 1925 style. The choice is difficult between a *plateau de dégustation, saumon cru à la crème de caviar,* a *marmite dieppoise* or a *bar flambé.* For dessert, patrons hesitate between a delicious *fondant au chocolat à la crème de pistache* or the traditional *petits pots de crème Émile Prunier.* An excellent selection of wines (page 226).

AU BŒUF COURONNÉ

188, avenue Jean-Jaurès 75019
Tel.: 01 42 39 44 44 or 01 42 39 54 54
Dark oak and marble at the counter, red velvet on the benches "le Bœuf" has retained its Belle Époque setting and its traditional cuisine, where meats, steaks, and sweetmeats take center stage. This restaurant, where you will no longer encounter the cattlemen of the old Villette slaughterhouses, today caters to *côte de bœuf, tête de veau,* or *pieds de porc-* loving business people, as well as to performers from the neighboring Cité de la Musique. The "Petit Bœuf" offers lighter and quicker meals in a bistro atmosphere.

DAGORNO

190, avenue Jean-Jaurès 75019
Tel.: 01 40 40 09 39
Across from the Grande Halle of the Villette sits a more than one hundred-year-old brasserie which, though completely redecorated in 1989, has preserved its Belle Époque paintings by Jules Chéret. Entrepreneurs on weekdays and families on Saturdays and Sundays come to feast on a *salade de haricots verts frais aux copeaux de foie gras,* a *pavé du boucher* or a *pot-au-feu de canard à la moelle* before ending with a *soufflé glacé aux oranges confites* or a *fondant au chocolat.* The cellar stocks mainly Bordeaux. In the evening, you may dine to the accompaniment of piano-bar music.

LE BARATIN

3, Rue Jouye-Rouve 75020
Tel.: 01 43 49 39 70
Raquel is to the stove what Raquel Mayer was to the bel canto: vision, imagination, and freedom that set off a faultless technique. A union of authenticity and market-based cooking, of remarkable freshness and generous portions. A daily risotto, semi-cooked calamari, saffron swordfish, black-bean and pork-cheek ragout, stewed rhubarb... these are accompanied by a selection of wines by small winemakers who have, without a doubt, produced enormous results. The charming simplicity of the setting, with mismatched tables and a wooden counter, is a marvelous match for the dishes on the menu. In other words, a rare bistro, well worth visiting.

WINE BARS

LA CLOCHE DES HALLES

28, rue Coquillière 75001
Tel.: 01 42 36 93 89
This locale has preserved the hustle and bustle of the old Les Halles neighborhood. Today regulars include those in the meat trading industry as well as local office workers who come to taste the delights of a Morgon, Brouilly, Côtes-du-Rhône, or Saumur, accompanied with *quiches lorraines* or *charcuteries.*

LE RUBIS

10, rue du Marché-Saint-Honoré 75001
Tel.: 01 42 61 03 34
Situated next to the recently renovated Saint-Honoré market, redesigned by the Catalonian architect Ricardo Bofill, an eclectic crowd rushes—especially at lunchtime—to this old Parisian bistro. Here, you will find a fine selection of wines from each French region which you can enjoy with a *tartine de rillettes,* an *omelette au jambon,* or assorted cheeses.

WILLI'S WINE BAR

13, rue des Petits-Champs 75001
Tel.: 01 42 61 05 09
www.williswinebar.com
A few steps from the Palais-Royal sits one of the capital's best wine bars, founded fifteen-years ago by the Englishman Mark Williamson. An eminent connoisseur, his wine menu lists no fewer than three hundred vintage bottles, and demonstrates a penchant for the Rhône Valley. You can savor them either by the glass or half-liter carafes. It is the perfect locale to indulge in a Saint-Joseph, a Côtes-Rôtie or a Hermitage, or even discover, at less risk, an exceptional Bordeaux or Burgundy vintage. Italian and Australian wines also have their place here, without forgetting the Xérès and Porto wines. The cooking is delicious and the desserts—*terrine de chocolat amer* or *crème brûlée*—top off this majestic feast wonderfully.

LA TARTINE

24, rue de Rivoli 75004
Tel.: 01 42 72 76 85

With its large zinc *avant-guerre* bar counter, its marble, its chandeliers, and its old-fashioned advertisements, La Tartine is the prototype of Parisian bistros. Wine is served by the glass or bottle and may accompany delicious assorted cheeses or *charcuterie*. Of the sixty vintage wines offered, some are bottled on the premises by the owner.

LE CLOWN BAR
114, rue Amelot 75011
Tel.: 01 43 55 87 35
Right next to the Cirque d'Hiver sits a pleasant bistro with a magnificent early twentieth-century ceramic decor in a clown theme. A large menu offers an abundant selection of French wines and traditional dishes: various salads, *terrine*, and *andouillettes* (page 219).

JACQUES MELAC
42, rue Léon-Frot 75011
Tel.: 01 43 70 59 27
www.melac.fr
Not far from the Faubourg Saint-Antoine, an up-and-coming trendy working-class neighborhood, sits a boisterous wine bar where you may have to jostle a bit, but which is worth the trip. You can savor the *tripes aveyronnaises, pot-au-feu, petit salé*, or assorted cheeses while tasting a fine regional wine, which you can purchase by the bottle and take away.

LE PASSAGE DES CARMAGNOLES
18, Passage de la Bonne-Graine 75011
Tel.: 01 47 00 73 30
Andouillette-lovers will find in this pleasant restaurant eight or nine varieties of this pork delicacy delivered fresh each morning from all over France. Accompanying this specialty is an impressive wine list of some three hundred vintage wines, which you can order by the glass or bottle. Specialists in Rhône Valley wines, and notably the renowned Côte-Rôtie, the house organizes wine-sampling sessions with the help of wine-growers on

---

MUSEUM CAFÉS

Nothing is more relaxing than a coffee break while visiting a museum—especially when the location is charming. Among those cafés and restaurants which are also open on Sundays, here are some of our favorites.

JARDIN DES PLANTES
In the Museum of Natural History, the **Café de la Grande Galerie** provides a spectacular view of the zoological landscape comprising hundreds of stuffed animals set in an African wilderness atmosphere (Tel.: 01 40 79 39 41).

MUSÉE JACQUEMART-ANDRÉ
Light lunches and tea are served in one of the most beautiful recently renovated rooms or on the terrace in nice weather. The **Café du Musée**, in period decor, provides an ideal break in a neighborhood where tearooms and light lunches are hard to find (Tel.: 01 45 62 04 44).

MUSÉE DU LOUVRE
Among the various places from which to choose, we recommend the **Café Marly** (Tel.: 01 49 26 06 60) and the **Café Richelieu** (Tel.: 01 49 27 99 01).

MUSÉE DES MONUMENTS FRANÇAIS
Enjoy the panorama of the Trocadéro Gardens from morning till evening in the **Café des Monuments**, which, in pleasant weather, remains open until midnight (Tel.: 01 44 05 39 10).

MUSÉE D'ORSAY
One of the two huge clocks of the facade takes up an entire side of the **Café des Hauteurs** situated behind the room harboring Degas's pastels. Though salads and pies are served, most come to view the panorama of the old state roof trussing and zinc-decked building. The **Restaurant du Musée d'Orsay** occupies the space where once stood the former train station's old hotel dining room. Modern armchairs contrast well with the ceiling's turn-of-the-century decor, covered with voluptuous frescoes depicting the spring season. The menu includes both a buffet and prepared dishes (Tel.: 01 45 49 47 03).

MUSÉE RODIN
Spend an enchanting moment in the **Cafeteria** amidst Rodin's garden (Tel.: 01 45 50 42 34).

MUSÉE DE LA VIE ROMANTIQUE
A splendid salon de thé, whether in the winter garden or beneath the foliage (Tel.: 01 40 16 16 28).

---

selected dates. Also try their annex: the Café du Passage, 12, rue de Charonne 75011 Tél: 01 49 29 37 64

CAFÉS

CAFÉ MARLY
93, rue de Rivoli 75001
Tel.: 01 49 26 06 60
The Café Marly is privileged to be located inside the Louvre between the Marly and Napoleon courtyards. Its warm-tone decor designed by Olivier Gagnère elegantly extends in pleasant weather beneath the archways looking onto the Pyramid. Light and savory meals are served for breakfast, lunch and dinner in an atmosphere invigorated by a young trendy crowd, as well as by others who are less young but still trendy (pages 216-217).

CAFÉ RICHELIEU
Place du Carrousel 75001
Tel.: 01 49 27 99 01
Situated in the Louvre's Richelieu Wing, in what used to be the Ministry of Finance's offices, this café opened its doors in 1993 at the same time as the rest of this part of the museum. The furniture and decor reveal the distinct style of Jean-Michel Wilmotte, Jean-Pierre Raynaud, and Daniel Buren. The photography is by Francis Giacobetti and the "Compressions" are by César. The walls, restored to their original Tollens blue, surround the Napoleon III hardwood floors and create an ideal place for a break during your museum visit where after lunch you can enjoy a remarkably exquisite old-fashioned hot chocolate. Museum tickets are required for entry.

LE COCHON À L'OREILLE
15, rue Montmartre 75001
Tel.: 01 42 36 07 56
The zinc bar counter, the varnished-wood benches aligned in booths, and the splendid painted ceramic conjure up once-upon-a-time images of this old Les Halles neighborhood. Le Cochon à l'Oreille is a very charming spot where you can savor the daily specials together with a Brouilly or a Loire Valley wine while perusing the counter pamphlets left by local patrons. A cordial reception and a genial exuberant atmosphere await you (pages 207-208).

LE CAFÉ
62, rue Tiquetonne 75002
Tel.: 01 40 39 08 00
This unique café situated in an ever-changing neighborhood is set in a wayfaring decor which Ernest Hemingway would have appreciated. Whether it is lunch or an after-theater meal, the house prepares the best *croque-monsieur* in Paris, with roquefort or goat's cheese, honey or cinnamon, as well as salads and daily specials which reflect the owner's creative and generous character.

CAFÉ BEAUBOURG
43, rue St Memi 75004
Tel.: 01 48 87 63 96
In a location large enough to accommodate three cafés, Christian de Portzamparc designed the Café Beaubourg which opened its doors in 1987. In this immense café decked with contemporary art, such as groundfloor tables portraying works by young painters set beneath glass coverings, you can sit back and have a drink while reading the paper or enjoy a light meal. The terrace, where you can lounge comfortably in black or burgundy woven armchairs, is a vantage point to watch the permanent and improvised street show which unfolds daily on the place du Centre Georges-Pompidou. The Genitron (digital clock) which once stood on the square, ticking away the seconds separating us from the year 2000, has been moved to the Villette Science Center.

BAR DES THÉÂTRES
6, avenue Montaigne 75008
Tel.: 01 47 23 34 63
The television and fashion worlds have made this one of their favorite spots. They come throughout the day to enjoy breakfast or tea, or a drink after an evening at the Théâtre du Champs-Élysées. You can also enjoy *foie de veau, choucroute*, or a *steak tartare* for lunch or a post-theater dinner.

CAFÉ CHARBON
109, rue Oberkampf 75011
Tel.: 01 43 57 55 13
A very old bistro in late nineteenth-century decor with an array of perfectly integrated incongruous objects, such as the Greek fishing lamps which hang above and illuminate the café, and one of the longest bar counters in all of Paris. You can enjoy breakfast, a light lunch at noon, or brunch on Saturdays and Sundays in this establishment which is open every day all year round. A young evening crowd hastens to have a drink and take part in the uproar of conversation and the latest underground music (pages 214-215).

CAFÉ DE L'INDUSTRIE
16, rue Saint-Sabin 75011
Tel.: 01 47 00 13 53
Once past the bar where owner Gérard Le Flemin is busy concocting mixed drinks, you step into two rooms furnished with wooden tables and moleskin benches, and walls decked with black-and-white photos of celebrities or paintings. The soft light penetrating this café invites you to stop for lunch or dinner and savor the kitchen specialties which change daily. Young waitresses provide a very cordial service.

SALONS DE THÉ

ANGÉLINA
226, rue de Rivoli 75001
Tel.: 01 42 60 82 00
www.angelina.fr
Beneath the archways of the rue de Rivoli, across from the Tuileries Gardens, sits the old Rumpelmayer house which at one time was a favorite stop for Marcel Proust and Coco Chanel. The beautiful decor with its fresco-covered ivory wainscoting, which was renovated at the beginning of the century, now harbors an eclectic mix of senior citizens and a young crowd of sophisticated idlers. House dessert specialties include the tasty *chocolat africain*, prepared in old-fashioned style, and the delectable *mont-blanc*, a meringue pastry with chestnut cream. If you are watching your waist, you might prefer a salad or a club sandwich.

CADOR
2, rue de l'Amiral-de-Coligny 75001
Tel.: 01 45 08 19 18
Across from the Louvre's *Grande Colonnade*, the chimes resonating from the church of Saint-Germain-Auxerrois can be heard in this 1880s' pastry shop and salon de thé. Its Louis XVI interior wainscoting with white-and-gold relief and period furniture create a majestic atmosphere to savor a *petit cador* (a bittersweet chocolate orange cake) or the daily special at lunchtime.

À PRIORI THÉ
35-37, Galerie Vivienne 75002
Tel.: 01 42 97 48 75
Once you have gotten past the humorous play-on-words of the house insignia, you can take a seat at one of the tables set in the center of the gallery. Here, while watching the pedestrians, you can enjoy a hot meal or salad in a tranquil setting. You can also choose from a variety of twenty-five teas while savoring a *tarte au fromage blanc*, a *charlotte*, or a *reine-de-saba*, a marvelous chocolate-almond cake (page 195).

MARIAGE FRÈRES
30, rue du Bourg-Tibourg 75004
Tel.: 01 42 72 28 11
www.mariagefreres.com
Hundreds of teas from various origins are served in this colonial-style tea room, where you can relax in a cane armchair beneath the glass canopy. The employees in white linen will serve the intoxicating aroma of your choice, which you can savor with pastries or tea-flavored light dishes. The house also proposes several brunches. Try their other location as well: see page 224.

LADURÉE
75, avenue des Champs-Élysées 75008
Tel.: 01 40 75 08 75
Situated on Europe's most beautiful avenue, Ladurée has a fine reputation for its exquisite patisseries, and in particular its macaroons. An unequalled team of 90 chefs including 45 pastry chefs create the sweet and savory delights to carry the food lover through from breakfast to diner. All this in a elegant setting with period furniture.

L'ARBRE À CANNELLE
57, Passage des Panoramas 75002
Tel.: 01 45 08 55 87
Within the calm and comfort of these passageways which, for the writer Jules Romain, "harbor and protect the promenader in an almost homelike warmth," sits the Arbre à Cannelle. This salon de thé has retained decorated

ceilings and its amazing wood-carved storefront where you can still decipher the advertisement "thés de caravane, cafés, vanille". Hot meals and grilled steak are served, but you may prefer a cup of tea with a scrumptious piece of *crumble aux pommes* or a delectable *tarte au citron* (page 197).

CARETTE
4, place du Trocadéro 75016
Tel.: 01 47 27 88 56
Carette's terrace on the place du Trocadéro is a popular meeting place for the wealthiest neighborhood's young and trendy. The only pastryshop in Paris which makes delicious giant macaroons is also open to all epicures. A light menu makes it a perfect place to take a break at any time of the day.

FOOD AND WINE

JEAN-PAUL HÉVIN
231, Rue Saint-Honoré 75001
Tel.: 01 55 35 35 96
A rigorous knowledge of cocoa beans, an innate sense of how to harmonize blends, and a subtle balance between primary ingredients, are the secrets behind the exceedingly high quality of chocolates signed JPH. Over forty different varieties to choose from, not to mention the delectable chocolate bars in flavors including Java, Trinity, Ecuador. A master pâtissier, his cakes are also astounding: the Pyramide, the Caracas, the Safi, the Marquise... Situated on the first floor of the Rue Saint Honoré boutique, the salon de thé is recommended for a quick light lunch or a teatime snack over a hot chocolate.
Other addresses:
3, Rue Vavin 75006
Tel.: 01 43 54 09 85
23 bis, Avenue de la Motte-Piquet 75007
Tel.: 01 45 51 77 48

AU PANETIER
10, place des Petits-Pères 75002
Tel.: 01 42 60 90 23
A few steps from the place des Victoires sits Au Panetier

which, founded at the end of the nineteenth-century, has preserved its period decor. Everyday, two hundred and fifty warm crispy baguettes, along with many other types and forms of delicious bread, are prepared in the old oakwood-burning brick oven. The chocolate—and coffee—flavored eclairs alone are certainly well worth the trip.

LEGRAND FILLES ET FILS
1, rue de la Banque 75002
Tel.: 01 42 60 07 12
This lovely store—one-time grocery-candy shop from 1890 whose storefront Belle Époque decor remains intact—offers a fine selection (perhaps the best in the capital) of French wines and spirits, as well as other delights such as the *fondants à la menthe* and the *guimauve* which are stocked in glass jars in the store window. Discover a wine enthusiast's paradise, by passing through the back entrance from the Galerie Vivienne, to find a wonderful array of cellar articles, such as glasses, carafes, bottle-openers, filters, and various corks.

BERTHILLON
31, rue Saint-Louis-en-l'Île 74004
Tel.: 01 43 54 31 61
www.berthillon-glacier.fr
The most renowned ice-cream parlor in all of Paris offers indisputable quality and a unique selection of flavors. Ice-creams and sorbets are served in cones or cups in the new salon de thé, but you can purchase your own by the liter, three-quarters of a liter, or half-liter. Be patient if you simply want a cone—you may have to wait!

IZRAËL
30, rue François-Miron 75004
Tel.: 01 42 72 66 23
This wonderful grocery shop sells just about everything: alcohol and wines, condiments, appetizers, bulgur wheat, milled wheat, rice in bulk, barrels of seasoned olives in all colors and sizes, mustard, cooking oils,

and hundreds of spices. Sweets are not lacking either with its nuts and dried or candied fruit, its lukums (Turkish delights), or its crisp oranges—all of exceptional quality. Once you have gotten past this modern Ali Baba cavern, your journey continues into an enchanted world of colors, aromas, and fragrances.

ALBERT MENÈS BOUTIQUE
41, boulevard Malesherbes 75008
Tel.: 01 42 66 95 63
Spices, rare condiments such as pickled cherries or artichokes, caramelized onion sauce and strawberry preserves with whole fruits—here you can find all these old-time favorites. The Albert Menès boutique carefully chooses and presents more than four hundred and fifty hand-made products. The shop will also help you create your own personalized gift basket.

FOUQUET
22, Rue François-Ier 75008
Tel.: 01 47 23 30 36
Founded in 1852, Fouquet is now a highly sought-after chocolate-maker. Its convenient location in the heart of the Fashion and Luxury Goods district may well be one reason for this, but surely not the sole reason, for its chocolates and fine foods maintain an extremely high standard. Excellent are the pralines, ganaches, fruit-flavored varieties, as well as traditional chocolates such as truffles, liqueur cherries, and nougats. And let's not forget the caramel-coated dried fruits and toffees, the fruit pastes, and acidulated candies... All in all, not to be missed!

LA MAISON DU CHOCOLAT
225, rue du Faubourg-Saint-Honoré 75008
Tel.: 01 42 27 39 44
52, rue François-Ier 75008
Tel.: 01 47 23 38 25
8, boulevard de la Madeleine 75009
Tel.: 01 47 42 86 52
89, avenue Raymond-Poincaré 75016
Tel.: 01 40 67 77 83

19, rue de Sèvres 75006
Tel.: 01 45 44 20 40
www.lamaisonduchocolat.com
The illustrious chocolate creator Robert Linxe reigns in this chocolate enthusiasts' Eden, where you can tempt yourself with exquisitely palatable regal vintage chocolates, regular or flavored (lemon, mint, fennel), packaged in beautiful boxes. Alongside the cakes, the chocolate eclairs are undoubtedly the capital's best.

À LA MÈRE DE FAMILLE
35, rue du Faubourg-Montmartre 75009
Tel.: 01 47 70 83 69
Founded in 1761, converted into a candy shop and redecorated in 1900 in period style, this gourmet shop is most likely the oldest in France. Behind its historically listed storefront, you will discover wood-carved furniture with enameled cast-iron handles, the house insignia engraved in white and blue on the floor tiles, and above the Napoleon III cash register, the original gas fittings. Chocolate is owner Serge Neveu's life and craft, and he has been preserving the house tradition for ten years now. He continues to serve the shop's claim-to-fame regional specialties to a loyal clientele— *caramels à l'ancienne, negus de Nevers*, and other marshmallow delights, to which he has now added home-made fruit preserves and chocolates, such as the famous *délices de la Mère* (page 194).

À LA PETITE FABRIQUE
12, rue Saint-Sabin 75011
Tel.: 01 48 05 82 02
Jean Rambaud has, for more than thirty years, been perfecting his craft in this genuine chocolate factory next to the Bastille. Among the forty-two different types of chocolates, you will discover delicious Calvados truffles and fifteen different kinds of chocolate bars, including a bitter chocolate with a mouth-watering seventy-two percent cocoa.

TRAVEL AND TOURISM

North America

The following travel companies put together tour packages for Europe, and will customize an itinerary that includes reserving your seat on the plane and finding the perfect hotel for you in Paris.

THE FRENCH EXPERIENCE
370 Lexington Avenue, New York, NY 10017
Tel.: (212) 986-3800
www.frenchexperience.com

AMERICAN DREAM VACATIONS
412 East Shore Trail, Sparta, NI 07871
Tel.: (973) 729-9195
www.american-dreamvacation.com
American Dream Vacation offers the Paris As You Please, package which allows you to coordinate your own travel itinerary in advance instead of leaving your plans for the last moment.

DISCOVER FRANCE
8360E Via De Ventura, Scottsdale, AZ 85258-3326
Tel.: 1800 960-2221 or (480) 905-1235
www.discoverfrance.com

FRENCH LINKS TOURS
5 Chestnut Street
Medford, MA 02155
Tel.: (781) 391 6183
www.frenchlinks.com

BUTTERFIELD AND ROBINSON
70 Bond Street, Toronto, Ontario, M5B 1X3 Canada.
Tel.: (416) 864-1354
www.butterfield.com

Great Britain

FERRY SERVICES
The ferry services suggested below can be boarded at several locations in Great Britain and will take you to different points along the northern French coast.

HOVERSPEED
International Hoverport
Dover CT17 9TG
Tel.: 0870 240 8070
Fax: 0870 460 7102
www.hoverspeed.co.uk

P & O EUROPEAN FERRIES
Channel House
Channel View Road
Dover CT17 9TJ
Tel.: 08705 980 333
www.poferries.com
This ferry company offers the option of a night crossing. You may wish to contact P & O European Ferries to ask for the exact season dates and times of the crossings.

AIRLINES

The advantage of taking the plane to Paris is the number of points of departure in Great Britain. Once at the airport, Air France's shuttle bus and the Roissybus or Orlybus are only a fraction of the cost of a taxi ride and reduce the stress of arrival.

AIR FRANCE
10 Warwick Street
1st floor
London WR1 5RA
Tel.: 0870 142 4343
Fax: 020 7734 7879
www.airfrance.com

BMI
Donington Hall
Castle Donington
Derby DE74 2SB
Tel.: 0870 607 0555
www.flybmi.com
BMI offers flights to Paris from a number of British airports including London Heathrow. Reduced-cost flights departing from Cardiff or Durham can also be booked on www.bmibaby.com.

BRITISH AIRWAYS
213 Piccadilly
London W1J 9HQ
Tel.: 0870 8509 850
Fax: 020 8759 4314
www.britishairways.com

EASYJET
EasyLand
London Luton Airport
Bedfordshire LU2 9LS
Tel.: 0871 244 2366
www.easyjet.com
Easyjet flights leave Newcastle, Liverpool and London Luton for Paris Roissy airport.

RYANAIR
Customer Service Department
Ryanair Corporate Head Office
Dublin Airport
Co. Dublin
Ireland
Tel.: 0871 246 0000
www.ryanair.com
Ryanair offers flights from Glasgow, Dublin, and Shannon to Paris Beauvais airport, one hour from central Paris. A shuttle bus operates between the airport and Paris Porte Maillot. Bus tickets can be pre-purchased on internet (www.ticket.airportbeauvais.com).

RAILSERVICES

EUROSTAR
Tel.: 0870 518 6186
www.eurostar.com
With Eurostar, the highspeed train through the Channel Tunnel, you can be in Paris in under three hours.

RAIL EUROPE
www.raileurope.com
Tel.: 0870 830 2008
www.raileurope.co.uk
Eurodomino Rover Tickets are actually two remarkable deals (Eurodomino and point to point) whereby you can travel to France and have unlimited use of the rail network in France for periods of time that last 3, 5, or 10 days consecutively in a month.

LE SHUTTLE
Customer Relations Department
PO. Box 300
Folkestone
Kent CT18 8XY
Tel.: 0870 535 3535
www.eurotunnel.com
For those who wish to take their car to France, Le Shuttle is the ideal service. In less than an hour, your car can be in Calais ready for you to take away.

Paris

PARIS TOURIST OFFICE
25, rue des Pyramides 75001
Tel.: 08 92 68 30 00
www.parisinfo.com
You will find everything you want to know about Paris by consulting the countless pamphlets available to you which simply improve the quality of your trip at each turn. This main office can also be used to purchase tickets for any show in Paris as well as the different Metro passes offered to tourists.

BOULANGERIE KAYSER
85, Boulevard Malesherbes 75017
Tel.: 01 45 22 70 30
There's no doubt about it – this is the boulangerie that one absolutely has to visit. Eric Kayser offers 60 bread varieties, including a first-class bread with a crispy crust and a crumb that is spongy to perfection. Following the tradition of fashion parades, each season brings in a new range. Today, the pastries rival with the breads on offer. Among these are the fruit tarts, as well as the specialties such as the Périgourdin, the Tarte Monge, the Rabelais, or the Noir Désir... Since 2003, Eric Kayser has opened a restaurant at 85, Boulevard Malesherbes, where one can taste simple and varied dishes that change with the season: scallop carpaccio, shrimp and coriander soup, lamb skewers... Or else wonderfully garnished sandwiches.
Other addresses:
8, Rue Monge 75005
Tel.: 01 44 07 01 42
14, Rue Monge 75005
Tel.: 01 44 07 17 81
10, Rue de l'Ancienne Comédie
Tel.: 01 43 25 71 60
80, Rue d'Assas 75006
Tel.: 01 43 54 92 31
Lafayette Gourmet: 40, Boulevard Haussmann 75009
Tel.: 01 42 82 34 56
87, Rue Didot 75014
Tel.: 01 45 42 59 19
79, Rue du Commerce 75015
Tel.: 01 44 19 88 54

OLIVIERS & CO
8, Rue de Lévis 75017
Tel.: 01 53 42 18 04
Olivier Baussan has given a touch of nobility to olive oil, an ingredient of modest origins synonymous with popular Mediterranean cuisine. The incredible variety of oils and the quality of bottling offered in the Oliviers & Co boutiques conjure up the image of traditional wine-cellars. Tasting the wares at the house restaurant on Rue de Lévis is a supreme moment where the strength of flavors vies with the beauty of the landscapes they evoke.

Other addresses:
90, Rue Montorgueil 75002
Tel.: 01 44 82 62 28
81, Rue Saint Louis en l'Isle 75004
Tel.: 01 40 46 89 37
41, Rue Vieille du Temple 75004
Tel.: 01 42 74 38 40
28, Rue de Buci 75006
Tel.: 01 44 07 15 43
BercyVillage Cour Saint Emilion Chai N°20 75012
Tel.: 01 43 42 07 83
85, Rue du Commerce 75015
Tel.: 01 55 76 42 26

GANACHAUD
226, rue des Pyrénées 75020
Tel.: 01 43 58 42 62
www.gana.fr
Any true bread lover would happily cross Paris simply to visit Ganachaud's bakery. Following in his predecessor's footsteps, master baker M. Jeudon continues to make more than thirty different types and sizes of bread daily, including the renowned *flûte Gana*. Millstone-ground flour, home-made leaven and hand-kneaded dough, all baked in wood-fired ovens, combine to create bread of the highest quality. A fresh batch every hour guarantees warm loaves for breakfast, lunch, and dinner.

FASHION

MASSARO
2, rue de la Paix 75002
Tel.: 01 42 61 00 29
www.massaro.fr
A prestigious address for this high-class artisan nominated *maître d'art* in 1994, who for the last fifty years has been the unofficial shoemaker for the world's rich and famous. Established at the end of the nineteenth-century by his father, Lazzaro Massaro, the house created the famous beige and black sandals for Chanel. Today, though Raymond Massaro continues to collaborate with the world of high fashion, he still caters to those who can afford the luxury of a pair of tailor-made shoes worth about a week's salary (pages 174-175).

CHRISTIAN LOUBOUTIN
38, rue de Grenelle 75007
Tel.: 01 42 22 33 07
Original designs inspired by figurative patterns combine with unusual subject matter, such as eels, guinea fowl, or mackerel, to create an imaginative line of clothing by this young designer.
His boutique is a favorite spot for the Parisian fashion and entertainment worlds.

SHISEIDO SERGE LUTENS— SALONS DU PALAIS ROYAL
142, Galerie de Valois
25, Rue de Valois 75001
Tel.: 01 49 27 09 09
Rahät Loukoum, Tubéreuse Criminelle, Fumerie Turque, Ambre Sultan, Santal de Mysore ... just some of the elements of the aromatic universe of Serge Lutens. Each perfume is an adventure in itself, exuding traces of its creator's personality. Occupying a unique place in the perfume universe, the Salons du Palais Royal of Shiseido extend to visitors an invitation to take part in a journey, to engage in fiction. A stroll through the gardens of the Palais Royal is a must.

LOGNON "L'INDÉPLISSABLE"
43, rue Boissy d'Anglas 75008
Tel.: 01 42 65 25 33
www.lognon.fr
The fourth in the Lognon family to carry on the tradition, Gérard Lognon is devoted to pleating pure or synthetic fabrics for the *haute couture* and ready-to-wear fashion worlds. Whether chevron, sun, or exotic motifs, you will discover a remarkable collection of patterns and sketches— genuine works of art. The atelier also prepares hand-decorated and upholstered leather belts and belt buckles, as well as hand-made buttons. You can purchase all these items at the boutique listed here.

ATELIER HOGUET
2, boulevard de Strasbourg 75010
Tel.: 01 42 08 90 20
www.annehoguet.com
One of the last fan-makers in Paris, the Hoguet workshop

both restores these antique "frivolities" and invents new models for important designers such as Karl Lagerfeld and Christian Lacroix. A museum devoted to this luxurious collection since 1993 is walled with glossy wooden drawers where seven hundred and seventy objects made from mother-of-pearl, ivory, bone, and wood are exhibited (page 170).

LEMARIÉ
103, rue du Faubourg-Saint-Denis 75010
Tel.: 01 47 70 02 45
Once you pass the heavy wooden door with antique hinges, follow the stone staircase directly to this kingdom of feathers and artificial flowers. Founded in 1880 and established in its current spot in 1901, this family business caters to the opulent *haute couture* and ready-to-wear fashion worlds. The twenty-five workshop employees fashion ostrich, rooster, guinea fowl, egret, or bird-of-paradise feathers for Dior, Balmain, Nina Ricci, and many others. They also meticulously reproduce all varieties of flowers, including the famous Chanel camellias. Owner André Lemarié was nominated *maître d'art* in November 1994 (page 168).

RIECHERS MARESCOT
3, rue Saint Fiacre 75002
Tel.: 01 40 26 05 07
Established in 1880, the house of Riechers (later known as Riechers Marescot) became fashion designers' preferred supplier—a position it has never relinquished. Known for its gauzy fabric, lavished with gold, silver, pearls, spangles, or sequins and worked into different patterns and colors, Marescot lace is chosen for the wedding gowns, evening dresses, and bustiers of Paris, Milan, Tokyo, and New York *haute couture* and ready-to-wear designers. Young designers such as Christian Lacroix will boldly mix several patterns at once. While fashion trends come and go, lace is eternal.

JOHN LOBB
51, rue François-Ier 75008
Tel.: 01 45 61 02 55
www.johnlobb.com
If the shoe is truly the decisive touch and sign of pure elegance, it is essential to pay John Lobb a visit. This London shoemaker opened his boutique near the Tuileries Gardens around 1840 and immediately began tailor-making Parisian footwear. You can still enjoy the supreme luxury of tailor-made boots or Oxford shoes, as well as its line of ready-made shoes, in grainy calfskin or soft crocodileskin, found in both the Right and Left Bank shops. John Lobb is also at:
226, boulevard Saint-Germain 75007
Tel.: 01 45 44 94 12.

LESAGE
13, rue Grange-Batelière 75009
Tel.: 01 48 24 14 20
www.lesage-paris.com
This embroidery house was established in 1858 by Michonnet (later becoming Lesage) and immediately began collaborating with the big names in fashion at the time—Worth, Paquin, Poiret—as well as with royalty, notably the Empress Eugénie and the Countess Greffulhe.Throughout the years, numerous lines of clothing were garnished with Lesage embroideries, such as Vionnet, Schiaparelli, Dior, Balmain, while Yves Saint Laurent and Lacroix scintillated with success donning Lesage strass, sequins, and pearls. Lesage will embroider just about anything, including mussel shells and plastic. An international school for the art of Lesage embroidery (l'École de broderie d'art Lesage) opened in 1992 in order to pass on its unique *savoir-faire* to future generations (pages 1721-73).

SEGAS
34, Passage Jouffroy 75009
Tel.: 01 47 70 89 65
www.canesegas.com
One-time actor Gilbert Segas has, for twenty-five years, been so enamored of canes that he renounced his original vocation for a life devoted exclusively to their production. A cane

expert primarily, Segas opened a store in 1982, set in complete theatrical decor with heavy crimson velvet curtains, and has in its impressive collection, walking sticks ranging from simple to multi-use canes. Every material imaginable was used, whether for the shaft or the handle, including wood, glass, ivory, antler, leather, wrought iron, braided silver, porcelain, or precious stones—and bears witness to the unlimited imagination of inventors, especially from the nineteenth-century. The house also takes on repairs.

TEINTURERIE LOUCHE
84, rue des Entrepreneurs 75015
Tel.: 01 45 79 14 32
What would become of the *haute couture* and ready-to-wear fashion worlds without this dry-cleaner? It is the only one in Paris which guarantees fabrics (generally silk) in the color requested by the creator. Located in a small alleyway in the 15th arrondissement, the atelier now run by M. Perrochon uses the same materials it used at the time of its creation—a vapor boiler still heats the baths and the spin-dryer will soon be a hundred-years old.

FLOWERS

OLIVIER PITOU
23, Rue des Saints-Pères 75006
Tel.: 01 49 27 97 49 and
01 42 60 11 45
The face of Rue des Saints-Pères has changed ever since Olivier Pitou settled there. Wade through the shrubs and bouquets that cover the sidewalk and once you're inside the shop which doubles as a hothouse, find your way through to the owner who blends right into the decor as he welcomes you with an armful of flowers. A passion for flowers carried out to this extreme can only be remarkable.

GARANCE
46, Rue de Dunkerque 75009
Tel.: 01 48 78 35 95
Following her art studies at the renowned École des Beaux Arts, this gifted young woman turned

to graphic design. Yet it is through flowers that she has chosen to express herself. Her professional activities have taken two different directions. Plant styling for photography allows her to discover extraordinary plants or rare flowers in mossy hues. At the same time, she sells flowers and creates floral displays for receptions. In her shop, she offers, all year round, a surprising selection of roses. In winter, they come from Ecuador or Colombia, in spring and summer, they are fragrant and seem to have been gathered the same morning from a neighboring garden. Pure poetry.

ARTISANS

STERN
47, Passage des Panoramas
75002

Tel.: 01 45 08 86 45
Founded in 1830 by an Alsacian metal engraver, this family business supplied all the royal courts of Europe, in particular Napoleon III, with hand-painted coats-of-arms, personalized monogram stamps, headed writing paper, visiting cards, invitations, and announcements. The store's magnificent insignia depicting a lion resting his paw on a coat-of-arms is historically listed. The stucco interior, with Cordova-leather-inspired wallpaper, sculpted wood, and "barley-sugar" columns—perhaps the remnants of a canopy bed—are most attractive. The Passage des Panoramas, which has lost some of its old-fashioned charm, is in itself worth a visit and a pleasant stroll.

À BRU ET PERRIN
4, rue Elzévir 75003
Tel.: 01 42 77 68 42

www.abru-et-perrin.fr
In the heart of the Marais district, in a seventeenth-century vaulted cellar, Jean-Paul Bru and François Perrin provide loving care to damaged violins, cellos, and bows. But they also create these precious instruments and take part in all the details of the woodwork—whether it be spruce, maple, or ebony—including the final touches of varnish. Serious students as well as concert musicians know they can trust the work of Jean-Paul Bru, himself a violinist, and François Perrin, a guitarist, who know how to achieve the precise sound each musician desires.

ATELIER GUY MONDINEU
36, rue Pastourelle 75003
Tel.: 01 48 87 84 89
Guy Mondineu has been working out of his Marais atelier for some twenty-five years, where he prepares canvases—oftentimes using natural wood—for several contemporary painters. His patrons consist of artists, galleries, and modern art museums, as well as the general public.

ATELIER RENOUVEL
3, rue Elzévir 75003
Tel.: 01 42 72 15 28
Former assistant at Jansen's and considered the country's best artisan, Jean Renouvel was finally nominated *maître d'art* in 1994. He has been sculpting oak, beech, and lime in the form of cornices, chairs, and tables for fifty years. He has not only the restoration of Marie-Antoinette's boudoir, the hôtel Beaufremont, and the château Vaux-le-Vicomte to his credit, but this artisan maestro has also won an export award for having participated in the decoration of the French Chateau—Taillevent and Rebuchon's restaurant in Tokyo. Though today Jean Renouvel is planning to retire, he will be able to enjoy his new life knowing that his assistant of many years, Anne Nicolle, will continue in his footsteps (pages 178-179).

ATELIER GLASER
9, rue Beautreillis 75004

Tel.: 01 42 72 68 04
Georges Glaser has been practicing the copperware trade for many years in this workshop in the Marais. Every day, he fashions vases, mugs, trays, and numerous storefront signs out of metal for neighboring shopkeepers, while his wife Anne produces jewelry, brooches and ornaments in copper, gold, and silver.

GERMOND
78, Quai de l'Hôtel-de-Ville
75004
Tel.: 01 42 78 04 78
Across from the Île Saint-Louis, Michel Germond and his assistants have set up their workshop, where they specialize in the restoration of chairs and seventeenth- and eighteenth-century furniture. He has also patented all the house's marquetry work, about which he is particularly enthusiastic. Though he often works for museums, châteaux (Champs-sur-Marne, Compiègne, Maisons-Lafitte, etc.), ministries, and the Bibliothèque Nationale, he also welcomes individual clients hoping to restore their valuable furniture and is always full of good advice.

VENDEL-SHAKESPEARE
109, boulevard Haussmann
75008
Tel.: 01 42 65 28 92
The opulent marble and mahogany facade has not changed since its creation in 1860. The Vendel family, which already had Marcel Proust as a client at the time, continues to engrave wedding and birth announcements, business cards and monograms for a high-class clientele, including the Palais de l'Élysée, the Greek royal family, as well as the Parisian fashion and celebrity worlds.

BATAILLARD
10, rue Rochambeau 75009
Tel.: 01 42 82 02 84
www.ateliersbataillard.com
In one of the last blacksmith workshops in Paris, the Bataillard family continues, in eighteenth-century tradition, to forge andirons, lamps,

staircases, and gates (notably those on the place Stanislas in Nancy) for châteaux and mansions.

MAHIEU
15, Impasse des Primevères 75011
Tel.: 01 43 55 88 25
It was not long ago that Claude Kern, nominated *maître d'art*, began to manage this already hundred-year-old company which is one of the last to specialize in the practice of mercury gilding as it was exercised in the sixteenth and seventeenth centuries. Even if for a good twenty years the house collaborated with the Shah of Iran, it still caters to numerous individual patrons, antique shops, museums, châteaux, and ministries. Whether bronzes, lamps, clocks, or stylish objects, the craft is enormous and it also fashions luxurious domestic appliances, as well as kitchen and bathroom fitments.

MAISON RIOT
24, rue de la Folie-Méricourt 75011
Tel.: 01 47 00 34 47
In 1986, Jeanne Privat reassumed her position as manager of this house which has for five generations been passing on the craft of silvering and gilding from father to daughter. The Riot house specializes in bronze and goldsmithing (cutlery, candlesticks) or religious objects (ciboriums, monstrances) and works mostly for individual clients and professionals, especially for the Mobilier National, eminent jewelers, and distinguished hotels.

VIADUC DES ARTS
1–129, avenue Daumesnil 75012
www.viaduc.des.arts.com
A stone's throw from the place de la Bastille, harbored beneath the red-brick archways of this recently restored nineteenth-century viaduct, is the home of a union of some sixty skilled artisans: framers, cabinetmakers, blacksmiths,

and ceramists. The Ripamonti society specializes in stone sculpture and the Le Tallec atelier hand-paints porcelain as they did in the eighteenth century. The Copper and Silver Workshop will resilver household cutlery, reproduce old silver tea and coffee pots, and even construct sumptuous all-copper baths. Ardustyl gilds mirror frames in old-fashioned style. The viaduct itself has been transformed into a public walkway.

MARIE LAVANDE
83, avenue Daumesnil 75012
Tel.: 01 44 67 78 78
www.marie.lavande.com
Her love for beautiful objects and passion for old and embroidered linen inspired Jöelle Serre to open her atelier in 1988. Her three linen experts maintain and refurbish old family lace and tablecloths, while two embroiderers fashion monograms and other personalized insignias. You will also rediscover the famous eighteenth-century accordion pleats, which give any tablecloth an elegance worthy of royalty.

LAVERDURE ET FILS
58, rue Traversière 75012
Tel.: 01 43 43 38 85
www.laverdure.fr
In these three old boutiques next to the rue du Faubourg-Saint-Antoine, you will find all the materials necessary to maintain or refurbish furniture, frames, leather, floors, etc.. Experienced suppliers of cabinetmakers and museums, the staff's practical advice and patience will help you find the exact varnish needed for an old piece of furniture or will allow you to create your own colors using the numerous pigments available.

BRAZET TAPISSIER
22, rue des Belles-Feuilles 75016
Tel.: 01 47 27 20 89
Discreetly situated in a 16th arrondissement courtyard next to the Palais de Chaillot, Brazet Tapissier continues to refurbish chairs and manufacture drapes,

curtains and even bedspreads using traditional methods—animal hair stuffing, down-filled pillows, hand-sewn braids. This tapestry-maker can be proud of its work not only for museums and châteaux (the Emperor's bedroom at Malmaison and the Empress's room at the Château de Fontainebleau), but also for individual clients seeking quality handicraft.

MAISON MEILLEUR
24, rue des Amandiers 75020
Tel.: 01 43 66 45 13
This blacksmith and ornamental bronze workshop creates only the most unique objects. It models lamps and decorative ironwork using only old-fashioned methods—each generation carries on this unique *savoir-faire*. Many of the country's national heritage treasures, such as the Palais-Royal lanterns and the impressive lamps of Comédie-Française, rediscovered their original brilliance in this old atelier.

ATELIER NECTOUX
112, rue de la République 92800 Puteaux
Tel.: 01 46 98 03 11
www.atelier-nectoux.fr
The Atelier Nectoux manufactures zinc bar counters in bistro style. It is precisely because of its unique handicraft—embodying the very essence of Parisian life—that this workshop, which for a longtime was situated on the rue du Faubourg-Saint-Antoine, deserves a place among our entries, in spite of its new location outside the capital.

HOUSEHOLD GOODS

DEHILLERIN
18, rue Coquillère 75001
Tel.: 01 42 36 53 13
www.e.dehillerin.fr
This culinary shop in the heart of the Les Halles neighborhood is well-known to the most distinguished restaurants in France and throughout the world. In its 300-meter

shopping area, founded in 1820, the Dehillerin family offers perhaps the most impressive array of culinary utensils for gastronomic magicians, professionals, and simple enthusiasts. The store has no fewer than four thousand items in stock and eight thousand on order, from 100 liter stewpots to individual casseroles. Copper and cast iron are house favorites (page 72).

MURIEL GRATEAU
37, rue Beaune 75007
Tel.: 01 40 20 42 82
Inside you will discover a marvelous array of household linen in sophisticated tones, ranging from the lightest pastels to the deepest hues (no fewer than sixty colors), which magnificently blend with Murano glass and high-temperature porcelain designed by Muriel Grateau herself.

ANTIQUES AND SECOND-HAND SHOPS

ÉRIC PHILIPPE
25, Galerie Véro-Dodat 75001
Tel.: 01 42 33 28 26
www.ericphilippe.com
As soon as Éric Philippe created his shop twenty years ago in the very elegant Galerie Vérot-Dodat, he was immediately appreciated for the quality and immense broadmindedness of his decision to exhibit essential, though at that time unknown, twentieth-century designers, such as Jean-Michel Frank, André Arbus, Ernest Boiceau, Emilio Terry, René Prou, Jacques Adnet, Gilbert Poillerat, and Jacques Quinet. The precision and care central to his presentation are the signs of a genuine connoisseur.

JACQUES KUGEL
25, quai Anatole-France 75007
Tel.: 01 42 60 86 23
www.kugel.artsolution.net
Until recently located on the right bank, Nicolas and Alexis Kugel have brilliantly continued in the tradition of their forebears and lead one of the capital's antiques dynasties into its fifth generation. Renowned

DESIGN IN THE MÉTRO

On the way to the Conservation des Arts et Métiers (60, rue Réaumur 75003; Tel.: 01 53 01 82 00; www.arts-et-metiers.net)—one of the capital's most fascinating museums—it is worth taking the time to explore the metro station Arts et Métiers. Inside you will discover Belgian illustrator François Schuiten's astounding decor. He redecorated the station's interior in copper and wood, giving it a submarine look, with portholes containing the miniatures of machines exhibited in the museum. This artist, inspired by Jules Vernes, also illustrated the author's recently recovered manuscript entitled *Paris au XXe siècle*, published by Hachette in 1995.

among art collectors for its rare silver and gold treasures, Jacques Kugel offers a large collection of "museum" furniture and objets d'art, which often come directly from eminent collectors without first passing through auctions or other antiques houses. Situated on two floors in an interior designed by François-Joseph Graf in conjunction with the Kugel brothers.

AVELINE
94, rue du Faubourg Saint-Honoré 75008
Tel.: 01 42 66 60 29
www.aveline.com
Jean-Marie Rossi has assembled the most beautiful furniture and objets d'art from the seventeenth and eighteenth centuries, though he is also interested in certain nineteenth-century rarities—providing they are unique (pages 100, 101, and 103).

GISMONDI
20, rue Royale 75008
Tel.: 01 42 60 73 89

DESIGN IN PARIS

Since the end of the 1970s, French interior design has undergone a renaissance after years in the shadow of Scandinavian, and especially Italian, designers. Mainly associated with the field of new architecture in which Paris provides numerous contrasting examples, French design appeared in boutiques and galleries where you would least expect it—thereby perpetuating another particularly Parisian tradition—a taste for the new.

MATALI CRASSET
Lieu Commun, 5, Rue des Filles-du-Calvaire 75003
Tel.: 01 44 54 08 30
Blue sky invades the walls, the ground, and ceiling, while treelike forms support the structure, and furniture is scattered on the floor and on platforms. These are the work of the designer Matali Crasset herself, but also her friends, Ron Orb, and the founders of the F. Communication label, Eric Morand and Laurent Garonier. In a word, the most creative in what today's design has to offer.

LIBRAIRIE-BOUTIQUE DU CENTRE GEORGES-POMPIDOU
Place Georges-Pompidou 75004
Tel.: 01 94 78 12 33
www.cnac.gp.fr

This bookshop also exhibits numerous works, some of which are the most famous creations by contemporary interior designers, especially those by Philippe Starck for Alessi.

AVANT-SCÈNE
4, place de l'Odéon 75006
Tel.: 01 46 33 12 40
Across from the Théâtre de l'Odéon-Théâtre de l'Europe. Élisabeth Delacarte promotes young and little-known interior designers who are inspired by poetry, movement, the baroque, and the imagination. Working outside traditionally defined areas, Mark Brazier Jones, Thierry Peltrault, Pierre Deltombe. Frank Evennou, and Hervé Van Der Straeten—to name a few—design furniture, lamps and objets d'art for professionals or contemporary interior design enthusiasts.

ÉDIFICE
27 bis, boulevard Raspail 75007
Tel.: 01 45 48 53 60
This gallery is devoted to furniture and contemporary objets d'art: the famous Starck chair from the now defunct. Café Costes, the bookworm bookshelf by Ron Arad as well as other imaginative works by Antonio Citterio, Enzo Mari, Vico Magistretti, and Michele De Lucchi. It also stocks Alessi's creative culinary utensils.

CONRAN SHOP
117, rue du Bac 75007
Tel.: 01 42 84 10 01
www.conran.com
Interior design is the reason for the Conran Shop's existence. This is not in the least surprising since its founder, Terence Conran, himself designed several pieces of high-class furniture, along with his most famous creation—the chain of Habitat stores. This small store situated across from the big department store, Le Bon Marché, offers creative works by young designers for interiors and gardens. But big names in interior design are hardly lacking — you will find the famous armchair designed by Charles Eames for the film producer Billy Wilder, the white-tiled bathroom with the metal sink by Andrée Putman, and lamps and ornaments by Philippe Starck, Alessi, and others.

SENTOU
26, boulevard Raspail 75007
Tel.: 01 45 49 00 05
18-24, rue du Pont-Louis-Philippe 75004
Tel.: 01 42 71 00 01
www.sentou.fr
Sentou's two galleries exhibit contemporary creative works for interior design. Inside you will find the results of an intense search for classically simple forms: tables, armchairs and rockingchairs by Charlotte Perriand, Huberty and Chanvel, and Alvar Aalto. The famous helix staircase was conceived by Roger Tallon, the beds designed by either Robert Sentou or Alain Tave, the lamps created by Isamu Noguchi, the ornaments fashioned by either Tsé-Tsé or Migeon & Migeon, and the chairs by either Ron Arad, James Irvin, or Mathieu Hilton, Robert Le Héros designed the collection of fabrics and dishes.

VIA
29-37, avenue Daumesnil 75012
Tel.: 01 46 28 11 11
www.via.fr
This association which was founded in 1979 is currently located beneath the archways of the old Bastille railroad. At that time, the city had the idea of rounding up a group of artisans to create the association VIA (*Valorisation de l'innovation dans l'ameublement*).Its purpose is to promote the creation of contemporary French furniture in France and throughout the world. VIA's plan is to encourage architectural designers to collaborate with manufacturers,and manufacturers with publishers. The association has thereby undoubtedly become the unofficial representative of the latest trends in architectural design—whether eternal or ephemeral.

JEAN-MICHEL WILMOTTE
68, rue du Faubourg-Saint-Antoine 75012
Tel.: 01 53 02 22 22
www.wilmotte.fr
Wilmotte is one of those designers who captures the era's *zeitgeist*. His urban design enhances the capital in many places, while his other creative works find their place in our daily lives—gray flannel sofas, public park chairs, and even the Champs-Élysées lampposts. You can admire all of his innovative works in his architecture firm's showroom not far from the place de la Bastille.

KREO
22, Rue Duchefdelaville 75013
Tel.: 01 53 60 18 42
Design and contemporary art whizz, Didier Krzentowski has created the capital's most spectacular design meeting spot. Rub shoulders with Bonetti, the Bouroullec brothers, Newson, Sottsass, Szekely, and numerous other talents. Located in the heart of the gallery district of the 13th arrondissement, this address is a must for lovers of quality furniture and art objects, as well as books, for the Kreo gallery has recently expanded its activities to publishing by joining forces with Images Modernes editors.

www.franceantiq.fr/sna/gismondi
This shop located next to the church of La Madeleine offers the elite artistry of eminent eighteenth-century woodworkers and carpenters. However, you will also find nineteenth-century paintings, interesting furniture such as Flemish and Italian cabinets, and Renaissance retables—and certain items from the beginning of the twentieth century, all in the long tradition of French excellence.

YVES MIKAELOFF
10-14, rue Royale 75008
Tel.: 01 42 61 64 42
www.yves-mikaeloff.fr
Known above all by French and foreign collectors as one of the most distinguished dealers of rugs and tapestries, Yves Mikaeloff also provides an abundance of paintings, sketches, furniture, and objets d'art ranging from the sixteenth to nineteenth centuries, and even the beginning of our own century. He is also undoubtedly

the only art dealer to possess a most important and coherent collection of German furniture.

GALERIE DU PASSAGE PIERRE PASSEBON
5, Passage Charles Dallery 75011
Tel.: 01 48 06 00 22
www.galeriedupassage.com
Pierre Passebon recreates a certain period "ambiance" by offering a curious array of furniture and other articles in his shop. His eclectic choice of

pieces attracts private clients seeking a personal esthetic, as well as his interior decorator friends. Furniture by Jean Royère, a set of Syrian ornaments composed of eighteenth-century wood-stretched canvases, sits in elegant harmony next to an eighteenth-century heart-shaped Venetian chesstable made of *bois d'amourette*.

AUX SALLES DE BAINS RÉTRO
29, rue des Dames 75017

Tel.: 01 43 87 88 00
www.sbrparis.com
During his fifteen years of work in the world of plumbing, where he developed a strong taste for beautiful bathroom fixtures, Nicolas Beboutoff became a serious collector of anything dealing with bathrooms. In his amazing boutique on the rue des Dames, you will find an impressive array of baths, decorated bidets, and Victorian-style washstands. But the owner's pride and joy are his

bathroom fixtures: period faucets and replicas—all equipped with an old-fashioned system of parts.

BERC ANTOINE
22, rue Parmentier
94210 Saint Maur
Tel.: 01 48 85 14 85
www.berc-antoine.com
This immense warehouse harbors all the furniture and equipment needed to open or run a café, tobacco shop, or restaurant. New or second-hand moleskin and velvet benches, classic marble pedestal tables, and bar stools await professional caterers as well as others seeking a change of decor.

MUSEUMS

PALAIS DU LOUVRE
Richelieu Wing: Pyramid entrance in the Cour Napoléon
Tel.: 01 40 20 50 50
www.louvre.fr
Musée des Arts Décoratifs
107, rue de Rivoli 75001
Tel.: 01 44 55 57 50
www.lesartsdecoratifs.fr
It is not our aim here to guide the reader through the world's biggest museum. The Louvre does however contain some of the interiors presented in this book. For example, you may visit the Duc de Morny's rooms on the second floor of the Richelieu Wing—its luxurious salons bring to life the splendor of the Second Empire (pages 118-119). The Grand Louvre also collaborates with the Musée des Arts Décoratifs, which has its own separate entrance. Renovated in 1996, its rooms offer period interiors from each century, including a remarkable Art Nouveau–Art Deco retrospective as well as Jeanne Lanvin's rooms decorated by Arnaud Rateau in 1920s' style (pages 206-207).

MUSÉE CARNAVALET
23, rue de Sévigné 75003
Tel.: 01 44 59 58 58
www.paris.fr/musees/musee_carnavalet
This museum located in the heart of the Marais district is a hybrid of the hôtel

ANGLO-AMERICAN BOOKSTORES

There are many stores in Paris where you can find anglophone reading material—the following are among the best-known and best-loved.

THE ABBEY BOOKSHOP
29, rue de la Parcheminerie 75005
Tel.: 01 46 33 16 24
The official Canadian bookshop in Paris, situated in an old townhouse-mansion in the Latin Quarter, just steps away from the Seine and the Sorbonne, offers many services to its clients such as mail/phone orders and subscriptions to Canadian newspapers. The Canadian Club in Paris was recently founded here through the efforts of the owner Brian Spence who organizes many events such as book readings and signings where one can meet some of Canada's and America's best contemporary writers.

BRENTANO'S
37, avenue de l'Opéra 75002
Tel.: 01 42 61 52 50
www.brentanos.fr
Brentano's is actually two bookstores in one in which the English language books section is located in the spacious shop seen from the avenue de l'Opéra window and where the back of the store leads to a small area that has an authentic newspaper/bookstore feel of the early twentieth century. This annex to Brentano's can be accessed from the side-street entrance as well.

GALIGNANI
224, rue de Rivoli 75001
Tel.: 01 42 60 76 07
Being the first such bookstore in Paris and the oldest one in Europe as well, Galignani is the original messenger of English language literature to the French public. The bookstore was immortalized in J. K. Huysmans's *Against the Grain* by the principal character who replaced his trip to England with a visit to Galignani where he preferred to purchase a Baedeker tourist guide of England rather than see the real thing. In this elegant store, you will find an array of book sections to choose from and, among these, a very impressive tourist guide section for the armchair or mobile traveler.

SHAKESPEARE & COMPANY
37, rue de la Bûcherie 75005
Tel.: 01 43 26 96 50
www.shakespeareco.org
Shakespeare & Company is as unique a concept for a bookstore as one can dream up. A writer, poet, philosopher, wanderer, or any bibliophile may request room and board for a night or two in exchange for lending a hand in the shop, classing books or some useful task. One thing to note is Monday nights when poets read from their unpublished manuscripts. It is possible that you may listen to the verses of the future W.H. Auden or T.S. Eliot.

TEA AND TATTERED PAGES
24, rue Mayet 75006
Tel.: 01 40 65 94 35
Not only is this bookstore of inexpensive and used books open every day, it also has Sunday brunches and homemade lunches during the week so that one can take time out to eat in between browsing through the wide selection of paperbacks.

VILLAGE VOICE
6, rue Princesse 75006
Tel.: 01 46 33 36 47
www.villagevoicebookshop.com
This internationally known bookstore has an extensive range of literature from the US and the UK and devotes a section to translations, and socio-political as well as philosophy books. It also carries the major newspapers from around the world.

W.H. SMITH
248, rue de Rivoli 75001
Tel.: 01 44 77 88 99
www.whsmith.fr
The British bookchain W.H. Smith opened this Parisian store to cater to French anglophiles and to offer to those interested all the Anglo-American literature and culture possible. The staff are so well informed and the selection of books so varied that it is almost impossible to walk out of the store empty-handed or dissatisfied.

distinguished artisans, and precious objets d'art in a suite of very impressive salons.

MUSÉE PICASSO
Hôtel Salé
5, rue de Thorigny 75003
Tel.: 01 42 71 25 21
www.musee.picasso.fr
The splendid hôtel Salé, built in the Marais in the seventeenth-century, contains the Pablo Picasso collection. The painter's works were bequeathed to the state in order to settle inheritance taxes at the time of his death. The museum's rooms which were rebuilt in 1986 hardly modified the old hotel's interior layout. You can follow the painter and sculptor's entire evolution from the blue and pink periods, to Cubism and on through his final years.

MAISON DE VICTOR HUGO
6, place des Vosges 75004
Tel.: 01 42 72 10 16
www.paris.fr/musees/maison_de_victor_hugo
It was in the old hôtel de Rohan-Guéménée on the marvelous place des Vosges where Victor Hugo and his family lived for 16 years. Today, in this very place that was once his three-story home, you can admire sketches, paintings, and engravings depicting the poet and his family as well as the characters in his novels. You can also discover works in the writer's own hand, who at certain times had a certain penchant for decoration, drawing, and painting. Certain items taken from his different residences, such as the Chinese living room, a dining room and his bedroom, were reconstructed here with their furniture and drapes. The house was converted into a museum in 1902 (page 204).

PAVILLON DE L'ARSENAL
21, boulevard Morland 75004
Tel.: 01 42 76 33 97
www.pavillon.arsenal.com
Behind its imposing glass-and-iron nineteenth-century facade, the Pavillon de l'Arsenal regularly sponsors exhibits, organized by Paris's city hall, on subjects such as the

Carnavalet and the hôtel Le Peletier de Saint-Fargeau. Hidden within its walls are the memories of another Paris. The ground floor is devoted to the capital's origins and history up until the sixteenth-century. On the second floor, you will discover its magnificent seventeenth- and eighteenth-century interiors. It is also possible to admire nineteenth-

and twentieth-century works, such as Marcel Proust's room, Mucha's decor for Fouquet's jewelry, and the breathtaking ballroom of the hôtel Wendel (page 207).

MUSÉE COGNACQ-JAY
8, rue Elzévir 75003
Tel.: 01 40 27 07 21
www.paris.fr/musees/cognacq_jay

In the Marais near the Musée Carnavalet, the beautiful hôtel de Donon exhibits the collection of Ernest Cognacq—founder of the Samaritaine department stores, and distinguished collector of eighteenth-century art: watercolors and oil paintings by Watteau, Ingres, Boucher, Chardin, Greuze, and Fragonard. The museum also holds Dresden china and furniture by

capital's architectural history, development, urban planning, and old or new projects, and produces interesting publications on the city's architecture.

MUSÉE JACQUEMART-ANDRÉ

158, boulevard Haussmann 75008
Tel.: 01 45 62 11 59
www.musee-jacquemart-andre.com
The Jacquemart-André Museum finally revived its glorious past after years of closure and temporary openings. The imposing facade of this magnificent town house built in 1875, overlooking a public garden, contrasts with the uniformity of the boulevard Haussmann and bears witness to the bold taste of one of the era's most renowned art collectors. Édouard André knew how to harmonize an abundance of splendid works of art capturing the beauty of the Age of Enlightenment, in which paintings by Rembrandt, Van Dyck, Frans Hals, Reynolds, and Gainsborough are gracefully interspersed. The collection seems endless, as you will discover with astonishment when visiting the "Italian Museum" on the first floor, containing paintings by Botticelli, Bellini, Carpaccio, and Tiepolo—all in a sumptuous setting evoking the esthetic of one of the last great art collectors (page 79). You can also take a break during your visit in the pleasant salon de thé or dine in the terrace restaurant. Call for information on how to organize receptions.

MUSÉE NISSIM-DE-CAMONDO

63, rue de Monceau 75008
Tel.: 01 53 89 06 40
www.lesartsdecoratifs.fr
This recently refurbished town house set between a courtyard and a French garden is close to the Parc Monceau. Sixteenth-century specialist Moïse de Camondo bequeathed his collection to the state, hoping to name this museum after his son Nissim who perished during the First World War. Among

the treasures in its salons, you can admire tapestries, precious wooden furniture by famous artisans, Savonnerie, Gobelin, and Aubusson rugs, and Sèvres and Dresden china (pages 90, 91, and 93).

MUSÉE DE LA VIE ROMANTIQUE

16, rue Chaptal 75009
Tel.: 01 55 31 95 67
The museum has preserved the charm of a private mansion in the New Athens quarter, once owned by the painter Ary Scheffer and his nephew writer Ernest Renan. The main pavilion, revamped by Jacques Garcia, presents the life and work of George Sand, and the Romantics in general. Opposite is the workshop where Ary Scheffer worked from 1830 to 1858. It is in this workshop-salon containing a book collection and works by the painter and his contemporaries, that Scheffer received Chopin, Liszt, Lamartine, and Delacroix. The high quality of exhibitions organized by Daniel Marchesseau since 1999 has given a new lease of life to this museum, placing it on the circuit of places to visit for an understanding of Parisian artistic life. The English garden dominated by roses and hollyhocks is enchanting.

MUSÉE GUSTAVE-MOREAU

14, rue La Rochefoucauld 75009
Tel.: 01 48 74 38 50
www.musee-moreau.fr
A symbolist painter in the second half of the nineteenth century, Gustave Moreau was one of the first artists to exhibit his work while still alive. The second floor of his family home has been transformed into a sort of sentimental museum, and the painter's six thousand works (paintings, sketches, and watercolors) are exhibited in an extraordinary two-story studio connected by a marvelous wrought-iron stairwell (page 203).

MUSÉE NATIONAL DES ARTS D'AFRIQUE ET D'OCÉANIE

293, avenue Daumesnil 75012
Tel.: 01 44 74 84 80

www.musee-afriqueoceanie.fr
Built for the 1931 Colonial Art Exhibit in Art Deco style, the museum holds a particularly interesting collection of primitive art, as well as a huge tropical aquarium, and the facade's bas-reliefs celebrate a triumphant colonialism. A ground-floor room has been specially renovated in order to reconstruct Marshall Lyautey's office, the exhibit's superintendent from 1927 to 1931. Beyond the red ropes, you can admire the exquisite forms and refined materials of the beautiful furniture created by Jacques-Émile Ruhlmann (page 206).

MUSÉE MARMOTTAN

2, rue Louis-Boilly 75016
Tel.: 01 44 96 50 33
www.marmottan.com
This museum's Empire-style furniture and fabulous collection of Impressionist paintings were brought together by the Marmottan family. Claude Monet, the family favorite, is accompanied by certain other masters: Renoir, Gauguin, Sisley, Pissarro, Caillebotte, and Berthe Morisot.

MAISON DE BALZAC

47, rue Raynouard 75016
Tel.: 01 55 74 41 80
www.paris.fr/musees/balzac
Though this little house and charming garden in the Passy neighborhood were only inhabited by Balzac from 1840 to 1847, the illustrious writer's presence can still be felt in this personable museum. Inside, along with his other belongings, you will be moved by the sight of the study and desk where he revised the final draft of *La Comédie Humaine* and wrote other masterpieces. The library contains both the author's complete works as well as a collection of studies devoted to him.

MUSÉE DE MONTMARTRE

12, rue Cortot 75018
Tel.: 01 46 06 61 11
www.musee-de-montmartre.net
Once the atelier of Suzanne Valadon, Maurice Utrillo, and finally Auguste Renoir, this splendid house (and garden)

on the rue Cortot seek to perpetuate the history of Montmartre and those who brought it fame. You will also discover a remarkable china collection fashioned by the now defunct Clignancourt porcelain manufacturer (pages 202-203).

GUIDED TOURS

GARDENS
Mairie de Paris
Service des Visites
3, avenue de la Porte-d'Auteuil 75016
Tel.: 01 40 71 75 60
If you enjoy visiting neighborhood and historic gardens or taking strolls in the city, visits are available all year round led by informative guides through the capital's main gardens and on chosen routes. It is nevertheless wise to call in advance for information and reservations, especially as the tours become more popular.

CYCLING THROUGH

ROUE LIBRE
1, Passage Mondétour 75001
37, boulevard Bourdon 75004
Tel.: 08 10 44 15 34
www.rouelibre.fr
RATP, the Parisian public transport authority, has set up bicycle rental services at several central locations. Cycle through the capital at your own pace or with a guide. Organized tours follow themed itineraries such as musical Paris, gourmet Paris, or waterside Paris…

PARIS VÉLO
2, rue du Fer-à-Moulin 75005
Tel.: 01 43 37 59 22
www.paris-velo-rent-a-bike.fr
In this meeting place near the Jardin des Plantes, be prepared for an unusual guided tour across Paris. You can also rent bicycles for your own journey through the capital.

PARIS À VELO C'EST SYMPA
22, rue Alphonse Baudin 75011
Tel.: 01 48 87 60 01
www.parisvelosympa.com
Looking for the hidden and

melancholic Paris? Take a ride with former Belgian librarian turned cross-country biking fanatic Michel Noé who organizes cycling sprees through a very different Paris. For night folks, two itineraries beginning after nine in the evening are possible: one from the Louvre to the place Charles de Gaulle-Étoile and the other around Montmartre.

WALKING TOURS

VISITES-CONFÉRENCES DES MONUMENTS HISTORIQUES

7, boulevard Morland 75004
www.monum.fr
By dialing 01 44 54 19 30, you will receive information on how to participate in *visites-conférences* organized by this governmental organization. These lecture-tours allow you to discover private historically listed monuments and interiors, such as the marvelous decors within the major embassies.

PARIS WALKABOUT

137, rue de Ménilmontant 75020
www.pariswalkabout.com
Discover cultural and historic aspects of Paris with your personal English-speaking guide.

PARIS WALKS

12, Passage Meunier 93200
St Denis
Tel.: 01 48 09 21 40
ourworld.compuserve.com/homepages/ParisWalking
English-speaking guides will lead you through a history-laden corner of Paris, such as Montmartre or the Marais, or help you explore the city through themes including fashion, Art Nouveau, and Hemingway.

PARIS BY ROLLERSKATE

PARI ROLLER

55, avenue d'Italie 75013
www.pari-roller.com
At 9.30 pm every Friday evening, some 15 000 roller-skaters gather at the foot of the Tour Montparnasse (place Raoul Dautry 75014) for a unique and exhilarating tour of Paris. The itinerary changes every week.

BIBLIOGRAPHY

GUIDES

Americans in Paris, Brian Morton, Ann Arbor, Olivia and Hill, 1986.
France Today, John Ardagh, 1988.
Charming Small Hotel Guides France, edited by Andrew Duncan, Hunter, 2001.
Exploring the Flea Markets of Paris, Sandy Price, Three Rivers Press, 1999.
Fodor's France 2005, New York, Fodor's, 2005.
Gayot's The Best of Paris, New York, Gault Millau, 1997.
Guide to Modern Architecture in Paris 1900-1990, Hervé Martin, Syros-Alternatives, 1996.
Guide to the Architecture of Monuments in Paris, André Gabriel, Syros-Alternatives, 1991.
Guide littéraire des monuments de Paris, Christine Ausseur, Hermé, 1994.
Guide littéraire des passages de Paris, Patrice de Moncan, Hermé, 1996.
Guide des maisons d'hommes célèbres, Georges Poisson, Horay, 2000.
Le Guide des passages couverts de Paris, Patrice de Moncan, Éditions du Mécène, 1996.
Le Guide des passages de Paris, Patrice de Moncan and Christian Mahout, Seesam, 1991.
Guide du chineur parisien, Catherine Vialle, Parigramme, 1994.
Guide des 400 jardins de Paris, Jacques Barozzi, Rustica, 2001.
Guide du routard Paris 2005–2006, French & European Publications, 2005.
Guide des statues de Paris, Georges Poisson, Hazan, 1990.
Michelin Green Guide Paris, Michelin Travel Publications, 2001.
Le Nouveau guide des statues de Paris, Pierre Kjellberg, Bibliothèque des arts, 1995.
Le Marais, guide historique et architectural, Alexandre Gady, Le Passage, 2002.
Paris, Steve Fallon, Lonely Planet Guide, 2004.
Paris, Guide Gallimard, 2000.
Paris Access, Richard Saul Wurman, Harper Resource, 2004.
Paris Anglophone: Essential Contacts in Paris for English-Speakers, ed. D. Applefield, Midpoint Trade Press, 2000.
Paris: Birthplace of the USA, Daniel Jouve, Gründ, 1995.
Paris Eyewitness Travel Guide, New York/London, Dorling Kindersley, 2003.
Paris au fil de la Seine, Jean-Marc Léri, Hervas, 1991.
Paris, le guide du patrimoine, Jean-Marie Pérouse de Montclos, Hachette, 1994.
Paris inattendu, Michel Dansel, Hachette Tourisme, 1997.
Paris Inside Out: The Insider's Handbook to Life in Paris, David Applefield, Globe Pequot, 2002.
Paris pas cher 2005, French and European Publications, 2004.
Paris secret et insolite, Rodolphe Trouilleux, Parigramme, 1996.
Pauper's Paris, Miles Turner, London, Pan Books, 1997.
The Rough Guide to Paris, Rough Guides, 2003.
Time Out Guide to Paris, London, Time Out Books, 2003.

HISTORY

Almanach de Paris, des origines à nos jours, Michel Fleury and Jean Tulard, Encyclopædia Universalis, 1990.
Archives de Paris, Jacques Borgé and Nicolas Viasnoff, Michèle Trinckvel, 1996.
Les Canaux parisiens, Marc Gayda and Bruno Lapeyre, Éditions de l'Ormet, 1995.
Connaissance du vieux Paris, Jacques Hillairet, Rivages, 2003.
Le Cœur de Paris, Albin Michel, 1991.
Le Front de Seine Paris XVᵉ, Hervas, 1994.
Histoire et dictionnaire de Paris, Alfred Fierro, Robert Laffont, coll. Bouquins, 1996.
Panorama des Grands Boulevards, Honoré de Balzac, Hervas, 1970.
Paris: The Biography of a City, Colin Jones, Viking Adult, 2005.
Paris-Haussmann, exhibition at the Pavillon de l'Arsenal, Picard, 1991.
Paris: An Illustrated History, Elaine Mokhtefi, Hippocrene, 2002.
Paris, histoire d'une ville, edited by Jean-Robert Piette, Hachette, 1993.
Paris's Fountains, Thomas Renaut, Asa, 2000.
Quais et ponts de Paris, Marc Gaillard, Martelle, 1993.
Seven Ages of Paris, Alistair Horne, Vintage, 2004.

ARCHITECTURE AND SCULPTURE

An Architect's Paris, Thomas Carlson-Reddig, 1993.
The Architecture of Paris, Andrew Ayers, Axel Menges, 2004.
Le Bestiaire de Paris, Jacques Barozzi, Hervas, 1995.
La Brique à Paris, Bernard Marrey, Pavillon de l'Arsenal-Picard, 1991.
Les Cariatides de Paris, Jacques Nebout, Hervas, 1992.
Les Cimetières artistiques, Josette Jacquin-Philippe, L. Laget, 1993.
Demeures parisiennes, sous Henri IV et Louis XIII, Jean-Pierre Babelon, Hazan, 1991.
Le Fer à Paris, Bernard Marrey, Pavillon de l'Arsenal-Picard, 2000.
Les Fontaines de Paris: de la Renaissance à nos jours (collectif), Délégation à l'action artistique de la Ville de Paris, 1995.
Hector Guimard: Architect, Designer (1867–1942), Georges Vigne, Delano Greenridge, 2003.
Paris XIXᵉ siècle, François Loyer, Hazan, 1994.
Paris: An Architectural History, Anthony Sutcliffe, Tale Art, 1996.
Paris Architecture 1900–2000, Jean-Louis Cohen et al., Norma, 2001.
Paris Architecture and Design, Chris van Uffelen, Teneues, 2004.
Paris façade, Françoise Goy-Truffaut, Hazan, 1989.
Planning Paris before Haussmann, Nicholas Papayanis, John Hopkins University Press, 2004.
La République et ses grands hommes, Catherine Chevillot, Guides Paris-Musée d'Orsay, Hachette-Musées nationaux, 1990.
Les Statues de Paris, June Hargrove, Albin Michel, 1991.
Les Toits de Paris, François and Philippe Simon, Pavillon de l'Arsenal-Hazan, 1994.

CAFÉS AND RESTAURANTS

La Belle Époque des cafés et des restaurants, Bruno Girveau, Hachette-Musées nationaux, 1990.
Les Deux Magots, Arnaud Hofmarcher, Cherche-Midi, 1994.
Café de Flore: mémoire d'un siècle, Christophe Durand-Boubal, Indigo Côté Femmes, 1993.
La Coupole: 60 ans de Montparnasse, Françoise Planiol, Denoël, 1986.
The French Café, Marie-France Boyer, Thames and Hudson, 1994.

PARKS AND GARDENS

Jardins d'hier et d'aujourd'hui, Sylvie Patin, Guides Paris-Musée d'Orsay, Hachette-Musées nationaux, 1991.
Le Guide du jardin du Luxembourg, Carlos Zito, La Manufacture, 1994.
Le Jardin des Tuileries, Anne Pingeot, Du May-Musées nationaux, 1993.
Paris des jardins, Henri Queffélec, Éditions Ouest-France, 1988.
Private Gardens of Paris, Madison Cox, Harmony, 1989.

THE MÉTRO

The Paris Metro : A Ticket to French History, Susan L. Plotkin, Xlibris, 2001.
Petite Histoire des stations de métro, Pierre Miquel, Albin Michel, 1993.
Les Stations de métro, Gérard Roland, Éditions Christine Bonneton, 1980.

LITERATURE

Aragon, Louis, *Paris Peasant*, trans. Simon Taylor, Exact Change, 1995.
Baltard, Victor, *Les Halles de Paris*, Éditions de l'Observatoire, 1994.
Balzac, Honoré de, *La Comédie Humaine* esp. *Wild Ass's Skin, Scenes of Paris Life, Père Goriot*, Penguin Classics.
Bard, Patrick, *Paris Chansons, Les Cent Plus Belles Chansons de Paris*, Spengler, 1996.
Beaune, Colette, *Journal d'un bourgeois de Paris : 1405 à 1449*, LGF, coll. Lettres Gothiques, 1990.
Bessand-Massenet, *Air et manières de Paris*, Grasset, 1951.
Bonardi, Pierre, *De quoi se compose Paris*, Albin Michel, 1927.
Breton, André, *La Clé des Champs*, LGF, 1991.
— *Nadja*, Gallimard, coll. Folio, 1972.
— *Poisson soluble*, Gallimard, coll. Poésie, 1972.
Cendrars, Blaise and Fernand Léger, *Paris ma ville*, Bibliothèque des Arts, 1987.
Dabit, Eugène, *Faubourgs de Paris*, Gallimard, 1993.
Fargue, Léon-Paul, *Le Piéton de Paris*, Gallimard, coll. Poésie, 1993.
— *English Translation of Léon-Paul Fargue's Poèmes*, trans. Peter Thompson, Edwin Mellen Press, 2003.
Follain, Jean, *Paris*, Phébus, coll. Verso, 1989.
Les Haut Lieux de la littérature à Paris, Jean-Paul Clébert, Bordas, 1992.
Ganay, Valentine de, and Jérôme Godeau, *Les Mots de Paris*, Actes Sud RMN, 1996.
Goncourt, Edmond and Jules, *The Goncourt Journals, 1851–1870*, Greenwood Press, 1969.
Green Julien, *Paris*, trans. J A Underwood, London: Marion Boyars, 1991.
Hemingway, Ernest, *A Moveable Feast*, Cape, 1964.
Hugo, Victor, *Les Misérables*, trans. N Denny, Penguin Classics, 1982.
— *The Hunchback of Notre Dame*, trans. John Sturrock, Penguin Classics, 1978.
Huysmans, Joris-Karl, *The Bièvre River*, trans. D Halpern and E Moerman, Langtry, 1986.
Léautaud, Paul, *Le Paris d'un Parisien, Le Petit Ami*, in *œuvres*, Mercure de France, 1988.
Leroux, Gaston, *The Phantom of the Opera*, Armada, 1988.
Malet, Léo, *Œuvres complètes*, 5 vol., Laffont, coll. Bouquins, 1985-1989.
Maupassant, Guy de, *Bel-ami*, trans. D Parmee, Penguin Classics, 1975.
Mercier, Louis-Sébastien, *Tableau de Paris* in *Paris le jour, Paris la nuit*, Laffont, 1990.
Miller, Henry, *Quiet Days in Clichy*, Allison and Busby, 1988.
Modiano, Patrick, *Place de l'Étoile*, Gallimard, 1968.
— *Quartier perdu*, Gallimard, 1988.
Morand, Paul, *Lettres de Paris*, Paul Salvy, 1996.
— *Paris*, Bibliothèque des Arts, 1980.
Nerval, Gérard de, *Promenades et souvenirs, Les Nuits d'octobre*, in *œuvres complètes*, 3 vol., Gallimard, coll. Bibliothèque de la Pléiade, 1993.
Paris dans la littérature de 1780 à 1914, Association internationale des études françaises, 1990.
Paris, rive noire, Autrement, 1996.
Perec, Georges, *Species of Spaces*, trans. John Sturrock, Penguin, 1998.
— *Les Lieux d'une fugue*, Éditions du Seuil, 1990.
— "Tentative d'épuisement d'un lieu parisien", in *Cause commune* n° 1, 1975.
— *Life: a User's Manual* trans. D Bellos, London: Collins Harvill, 1987.
Proust, Marcel, *Remembrance of Things Past*. 2 vols. trans. C K S Moncrieff and T Kilmartin, Penguin Classics, 1989.
Queneau, Raymond, *Zazie in the Metro* trans. B Wright, Calder, 1981.
Réda, Jacques, *Les Ruines de Paris*, Gallimard, coll. Poésie, 1993.

Réau, Louis, *Histoire du vandalisme*, Laffont, coll. Bouquins, 1994.

Restif de la Bretonne, Nicolas, *Les Nuits de Paris or The Nocturnal Spectator*, trans. Linda Asher and Ellen Fertig, Random House, 1964.

Sontag, Susan (foreword), *A Place in the World Called Paris (Paris, as seen by the twentieth century's greatest writers)*, Chronicle Books, 1994.

Soupault, Philippe, *Last Nights of Paris*, trans. William Carlos Williams, Exact Change, 1993.

Sue, Eugène, *Mysteries of Paris*, Dedalus, Sawtry, 1988.

Villon, François, *The Legacy and the Testament*, trans. Louis Simpson, Story Line Press, 2000.

Verne, Jules, *Paris in the Twentieth Century*, trans. Richard Howard, Balla, 1997.

Zola, Émile, The Rougon-Macquart Novels esp. *The Kill, The Belly of Paris, L'Assommoir*, Penguin Classics.

PHOTOGRAPHY

Belleville-Ménilmontant, Willy Ronis, Arthaud, 1999.

The First Time I Saw Paris, Peter Miller, Crown, 1999.

Mémoires de Paris, une anthologie littéraire et photographique, Jacques-Louis Delpal, Éditions de la Martinière, 1994.

Metropolitain: A Portrait of Paris, Fiona Biddulph with photos by M. Weinreb, Phaidon, 1994.

Paris 360°, Antoine Blondin, photographies d'Attilio Bocazzi-Varotto, Olizane, 1996.

Paris années 30, Hazan, 1996.

Paris in 500 photos, Maurice Subervie, Flammarion, 2003.

Paris from Above, Anne et Yann Arthus-Bertrand, Hachette, 2003.

Paris imprévu, Joe Friedman and Jérôme Darbley, Flammarion, 1989.

Paris, photographies et poèmes, Marie de They, Stock, 1995.

Paris: Photographs of a Time That Was, David Travis, Yale University Press, 2005.

Paris After Dark: Brassaï, Thames and Hudson, 1987.

Paris tendresse, Brassaï, Patrick Modiano, Hoëbeke, 1990.

Paris vu du Louvre, Frédéric Vitoux and Alfred Wolf, Adam Biro, 1993.

Paris, visages et paysages, Françoise Marquet, Paris-Musées, 1998 (bilingual French-English edition).

Photographer's Paris, Jean-Claude Gautrand, Dorset, 1990.

Sundays by the River, Willy Ronis, Smithsonian, 1999.

Le Tour du monde de Paris, Nicolas de Bélizal, Hervas, 1993.

WALKS

Architectural Walks in Paris, Bert McClure and Bruno Régnier, Paris, La Découverte/Le Monde, 1989.

City Walks: Paris, Christina Henry de Tessan, Chronicle, 2004.

Découvrir Paris est un jeu d'enfant, Isabelle Bourdial and Valérie Guidoux, Parigramme, 2000.

Frommer's Memorable Walks in Paris, Haas Mroue, Frommers, 2001.

Paris à pied, Fédération française de la randonnée pédestre, 2001.

Paris, plan piéton, edited by Pascal Chevalier, Média-Cartes, 1996.

Paris et petite couronne, Guide Franck, Glénat, 2002.

Walking Paris: Thirty Original Walks in and around Paris, Gilles Desmons, McGraw Hill, 1999.

FRANCOPHILE MAGAZINES PUBLISHED IN ENGLISH

United States and Great Britain

FRANCE MAGAZINE
Circulation Department
4101 Reservoir Road NW
Washington, DC 20007
(202) 944-6069
www.francemagazine.org
A magazine allowing American readers to keep in touch with French society, business, culture and travel.

FRANCE TODAY
P.O. Box 15758
North Hollywood, CA 9165-5758
Tel.: (800) 232-1549
www.francetoday.com
French food, wine, travel, and culture for armchair or real-life traveling.

PARIS NOTES
P.O. Box 3668
Manhattan Beach, CA 90266
Tel.: (310) 545-2735
www.parisnotes.com
Restaurant reviews, articles of cultural or historic interest, and travel tips make this a useful guide for visitors to the French capital.

TANDEM
A Franco-British arts review which appears in January, May, and September, published by the Institut Français in London. It covers cultural events of interest to a French and British audience. For details contact:
Institut Français
17 Queensbury Place
London SW7 2DT
Tel.: 020 7 073 1350
Fax: 020 7 838 2145

Paris

FUSAC
(France-USA Contacts)
26 rue Benard 75014
Tel.: 01 56 53 54 54
www.fusac.org

This fortnightly magazine is widely consulted by English speakers for its employment and housing ads.

GOGO
15, rue Martel 75009
Tel.: 01 47 70 45 05
www.gogoparis.com
A guide to alternative happenings in Paris.

IRISH EYES: THE IRISH-EUROPEAN CULTURAL MAGAZINE
2 rue des Laitières 94300 Vincennes
01 41 74 93 03
www.irisheyes.fr
While featuring issues of Irish interest, this magazine carries articles on a wide range of cultural topics.

PARIS VOICE
7 rue Papillon 75009
01 47 70 45 05
www.parisvoice.com
Different aspects of English-speaking Paris are covered by this magazine: cultural events, fashion, food, books...

THIS CITY PARIS
83 bis, avenue Carnot 93360 Neuilly Plaisance
01 42 28 67 60
www.thiscityparis.com
A magazine with a focus on Paris fashion, gastronomy, art, and style.

INDEX

PICTURE CREDITS

Photos by Christian Sarramon: Front jacket; pages 8 (top); 9; 10; 11; 12–13; 20 (bottom, right); 22 (right); 23; 24 (bottom); 26; 28 (bottom left, bottom right); 29 (top left and right; bottom right); 31 (right); 32 (bottom); 34; 35; 37; 38 (bottom); 39; 42 (right); 43; 48 (top); 49; 50; 51; 52 (top; top middle; right; bottom right); 53 (left); 54 (bottom); 57; 58; 60; 62; 63; 66; 67 (right); 70; 71 (bottom left, right); 72; 74; 76; 79; 83; 84; 85; 88; 89; 90; 91; 92; 93; 94; 95; 96; 96; 97; 98; 100; 101; 102; 103; 104; 105; 110; 111; 112; 113; 114; 115; 116; 117; 120; 121; 122; 124; 125; 126 (bottom left); 127; 128; 129; 130; 131; 132; 133; 134; 135; 138; 139; 140 (top); 141; 142 (bottom); 143; 144; 146 (top left, bottom); 147; 148; 149; 150; 151; 151; 154 (left); 156; 159; 161 (top); 166; 172; 173; 174; 176 (top); 178 (bottom); 179; 181 (left); 182; 183; 184 (bottom); 187; 188–189; 190; 192; 193; 194 (bottom); 195; 196 (left); 197 (left: top); 198; 199; 205; 206; 207; 208; 209; 210; 214; 215; 216 (top); 218; 219; 223; 224; 226; 227; 230; 231 (right); 232; 233; 235; 237; 238; 239.

Photos by Nicolas Bruant: pages 1; 2; 6; 7; 8 (bottom); 14; 15; 16; 17; 18; 19; 20 (left); 21 (left); 22 (top left; bottom left); 24 (top); 25; 27; 28 (top); 29 (top middle; bottom left); 30; 31 (top); 32 (top); 33; 36; 38 (top); 40; 41; 42 (top left, bottom left); 44; 45; 46; 47; 48 (bottom); 52 (top left; bottom middle; bottom left); 53 (right); 54 (top); 55; 56; 59; 61; 64; 65; 67 (left); 68; 68–69; 71 (top); 73; 74; 75; 77; 78; 80–81; 82; 86; 87; 106; 107; 108; 109; 118; 123; 126 (top left, top right; bottom right); 136–137; 140 (bottom); 142 (top); 145; 146 (right); 152; 153; 154; 155; 155; 157; 158; 160; 161 (bottom); 162; 163; 164–165; 167; 168; 169; 170; 171; 175; 176 (bottom); 177; 178 (top); 180; 181 (right); 184 (top); 185; 186; 191; 194 (top); 196 (right); 197 (bottom left; right); 200; 201; 202; 203; 204; 211; 212; 213; 216 (bottom left, bottom right); 217; 220; 221; 222; 225; 228; 229; 231 (left); 234; 236; 240.

ACKNOWLEDGMENTS

The author would like to express his warmest thanks to Annie Lecat, Isabelle d'Hauteville, and Gérard-Julien Salvy for their help and friendly support. He is also grateful to Jean-Pierre Biron, Josy and Michel Broutin, Manuel Canovas, Sophie and Denis Doria, Didier Grumbach, Barbara Hottinger, Marin Karmitz, Dominique Kieffer, Françoise and Pierre Lafage, Hubert Le Gall, Barthélémy de Lesseps, Jean-Marie Rossi, Chesca and Bob Vallois.

Christian Sarramon would like to thank Safia Bendali, designer and organizer of all the photography, for her aesthetic choices and unfailing kindness; also the entire editorial team at Flammarion, especially Ghislaine Bavoillot for her perfectionism and her high standards that lend this collection its quality.

He would also like to offer thanks, from the bottom of his heart to his wife, Inès, a "special partner" at every stage of the development of this book, and to his two sons, Diego and Kim for their impatience.

A special mention should be made of his father, Henri Sarramon, who died before the completion of this book, as well as of his mother, an attentive and critical observer of his work.

The Editor would like to express sincere thanks to all who shared their knowledge of the neighborhoods of Paris, or those who were frequent and helpful partners in the search for locations—especially Pablo Goldschmidt, Béatrice and Laurent Laroche, Joe Fitchett, Anne Iselin, and Frédéric Iselin. In particular thanks are due to M. Alain de Roquemaurel, general secretary of the Traveller's Club.

Warmest thanks to all who participated in the preparation of this book and most especially to Marc Walter for the design, Olivier Canaveso and Barbara Kekus (Octavo) for their patient efficency, Margherita Mariano, Jimmy Tsao, Fiona Ng, and Soo Ha (Colorscan France and Singapore) who attended to the quality of the images. Murielle Vaux who took charge of the production, and finally Anne-Laure Mojaïsky, Christophe Boulat, Vincent Guillemard, Pascaline Sala, Laetitia Darmon, and Véronique Manssy.